Theory of Problem Solving

An Approach to Artificial Intelligence

MODERN ANALYTIC AND COMPUTATIONAL
METHODS IN SCIENCE AND MATHEMATICS
A Group of Monographs and Advanced Textbooks

Editor: Richard Bellman, University of Southern California

Already Published:

In Preparation:

MODERN ANALYTIC AND COMPUTATIONAL METHODS IN SCIENCE AND MATHEMATICS

MÉTHODES MODERNES D'ANALYSE ET DE COMPUTATION EN SCIENCE ET MATHÉMATIQUE

NEUE ANALYTISCHE UND NUMERISCHE METHODEN IN DER WISSENSCHAFT UND DER MATHEMATIK

НОВЫЕ АНАЛИТИЧЕСКИЕ И ВЫЧИСЛИТЕЛЬНЫЕ МЕТОДЫ В НАУКЕ И МАТЕМАТИКЕ

Editor

RICHARD BELLMAN, UNIVERSITY OF SOUTHERN CALIFORNIA

Theory of Problem Solving

An Approach to Artificial Intelligence

by

Ranan B. Banerji

Case Western Reserve University, Cleveland, Ohio

American Elsevier Publishing Company, Inc.
New York   1969

AMERICAN ELSEVIER PUBLISHING COMPANY, INC.
52 Vanderbilt Avenue
New York, N.Y. 10017

ELSEVIER PUBLISHING COMPANY
Barking, Essex, England

ELSEVIER PUBLISHING COMPANY
335 Jan Van Galenstraat, P.O. Box 211
Amsterdam, The Netherlands

Standard Book Number 444–00053–4

Library of Congress Card Number 69-13067

PRINTED IN THE UNITED STATES OF AMERICA

To
Dr. Bijan Behari Banerji, Ph.D.
in
affectionate gratitude

CONTENTS

CHAPTER 4

Describing Patterns

CHAPTER 5

Learning and Generalization

PREFACE

This book is intended to set forth in an orderly manner the motivations and viewpoint that my colleagues and I and our students at the Case Western Reserve University maintain in our researches in the field commonly known as artificial intelligence. The school of thought that we represent cherishes the belief that the field of artificial intelligence, like many fields of science, can and should be discussed with mathematical precision. As a cursory perusal of the book will show, we do not mean "numerical precision" when we say "mathematical precision." The latter term is used here to stand for the clarity of statement and rigor of discussion that characterizes mathematics. Very often, this precision is not attempted in artificial intelligence research. This book attempts to deal with some aspects of the field axiomatically.

Any axiomatic discussion of this nature has to use some undefined terms. The undefined ideas in this book are those associated with sets and non-negative integers. Since discussions that lead into the classical paradoxes have been avoided in this book, it was considered best not to delve any deeper into definitions than these. Also, we felt that most of our readers would be acquainted with the concepts.

Thus, it has been assumed that the readers of this book have some passing acquaintance with nonnumerical mathematics. That is, it has been assumed that they are acquainted with terms like "set," "element of a set," "ordered pair," and "ordered n-tuple." It has also been assumed that they are conversant with such elementary set-theoretical operations as union, intersection, and Cartesian products, as well as with the set-theoretical meanings of terms like "function" and "relation." Interested readers not acquainted with these will find them discussed in the first few pages of any recently written book on modern algebra; he will probably get more out of such a book than we could possibly give him in a brief set of definitions of terms. We might recommend the first 25 pages of MacLane and Birkhoff's *Algebra* (Macmillan, New York, 1967). In some places I have used notations from symbolic logic for facility of expression; these notations are well explained in Schoenfield's *Mathematical Logic* (Addison-Wesley, Reading, Mass., 1967).

This book is thus directed toward people who have taken interest in the past in research in artificial intelligence (by reading, say, Feigenbaum and Feldman's *Computers and Thought*, McGraw-Hill, New York, 1963) and who have an elementary acquaintance with modern algebra and its axiomatic methods. It is also directed at professional mathematicians who may want to know what the field of artificial intelligence is all about. Also, since very few deep mathematical results are used in the text, this may offer a tempting area for the professional mathematician to develop.

Because the initial mathematical model used in this book turns out to be an abstraction from the usual model used by control theorists, we believe that control theorists will find food for thought in this book and will often discover parallels between their techniques and those suggested in this book. This may eventually lead to stronger interaction between the fields of control theory and artificial intelligence and perhaps the transfer of techniques and points of view across the boundaries (with suitable abstraction).

This book also intends to describe the more successful parts of artificial intelligence research at the Case Western Reserve University. It is not intended as a treatise on the field; neither is it intended to be a critique of the work of other schools, nor a comparative evaluation of the success and failures of different approaches to the subject. However, at this time I acknowledge, both in the interests of truth and in gratitude for many past discussions, that the school of thought represented by this book is not restricted to the Case Western Reserve University. Dr. Saul Amarel of the Radio Corporation of America has, for the past few years, been working with a unified approach to what he calls "deduction-type problems." Our model and Dr. Amarel's model are quite different; each has its own characteristic advantages and disadvantages. Yet, some of the techniques used by one may well be transferred into techniques used by the other. That such transferences have not yet been made does not in any way preclude the desirability of such endeavors. Some of Dr. Amarel's work has been referred to in the text. Other work has not been mentioned, merely because the relationship between it and our work has not been investigated yet. A few works are, however, included in the Bibliography as useful supplements for the interested reader.

For the past few years, Dr. Richard Bellman of the University of Southern California has been taking interest in this field also. In the case of special games he has used much more sophisticated techniques than those used in this book. In the general model (which is quite similar to ours), his work has thrown light on many aspects of the structure of problems in artificial intelligence. A short list of some of his work in the field is included in the Bibliography. Concepts developed by him in the past have influenced much of our thought. There are numerous acknowledgments of his work in this book and the publications of our group.

The pioneering work of Newell, Simon, and Shaw on the General Problem Solver is, naturally, discussed in this book in some detail. However, the extensive research that, in recent years, they and other workers in the field have conducted on the computer models of human cognitive activity is not mentioned. The reason, of course, is that we have been basically interested in the mathematical interpretation of their work.

In the course of the book, there has been occasion to refer to the work of other workers in the field, when it has been found possible to interpret their work with reference to our model. These references are scattered throughout the book with appropriate citations where they occur.

Problems and games are modeled in this book in terms of a set (of situations) and a set of partial functions (moves) defined on it. The major finding of the book deals with the fact that any solution method depends, for its efficiency, on the ease with which certain "strategic" situations can be described and recognized. This establishes in a formal way the relationship between heuristic programming on the one hand and pattern recognition on the other. Full justification of this relationship, however, depends on set-theoretical definitions of terms and techniques in pattern recognition, uncluttered by the special assumptions necessitated by special pattern recognition techniques. These have also been discussed in this book. These discussions, divested of any *ad hoc* imposition of structure, bring out very clearly the importance of the basic language in which sets ("patterns") are described. This, in turn, gives a formal justification of the well-known dictum in the field that the ease with which a problem can be solved depends heavily on the representation of the problem, that is, the language in which the sets associated with the problem and solution methods can be described.

Chapter 1 introduces the overall aim of the book in somewhat greater detail. Chapters 2 and 3 consist of the formal models of problems and games, respectively, together with solution methods. Chapters 4 and 5 discuss the theories and techniques of pattern description and recognition.

My effort throughout the book has been to state definitions and assumptions with mathematical precision and to derive all results with an adequate standard of rigor. However, this statement should not be construed as a claim to what the professional mathematician would call "depth." At the present stage of development of the formalism, the basic structures are quite weak. Generally, deeper results are easier to come by in stronger structures. This in itself, however, does not provide justification for introducing extra structure into the model (as we might easily be tempted to do). Any strengthening of the structure can only be effected with very careful consideration of the faithfulness with which the structure reflects reality. This could be done only occasionally in the body of this book. Many parts of the book, therefore, may appear to "belabor the obvious." However, this continuous effort at precision, I believe, has led to several insights that could not have been obtained otherwise. Much deeper results regarding extremely general, and therefore weak, structures are available in the literature on model theory and universal algebra. Unfortunately, those results of which we were aware had no immediate applicability to our purposes. It is my belief that if any major breakthrough in artificial intelligence occurs, it will be through the development and application of theorems in model theory that discuss the relationship between languages and the structures represented by sentences in the language. At present, this is merely a statement of faith.

This book owes its existence to a large measure to Dr. Richard Bellman, who convinced me that whatever work has been done by us in this field should be published in the form of an unified presentation. The contributions of my colleagues and our students to the development of the results scarcely need mention here: the body of the book is built up by their ideas and labor. The work reported was jointly supported by the National Science Foundation (present grant GK-1386) and the Air Force Office of Scientific Research (present grant AF-OSR-125-67) with grants dating back over five years. A part of the manuscript was developed while I was at the RCA Laboratories in Princeton, where I was partially supported by the Air Force Office of Scientific Research under contract no. AF 49(638)-1184 to RCA.

Dr. Saul Amarel of RCA and Dr. George Ernst, as well as Mr. Ronald Citrenbaum of Case Western Reserve, have helped me considerably in modifying the original manuscript and improving its readability. If parts of the book still seem obscurely written, it is in spite of their efforts.

Mrs. Brenda Vernon, Mrs. Marilyn Johnson, and Mrs. Joyce Schneider have typed the various drafts of the manuscript. To them, my thanks for their diligence and patience.

My father, to whom this book is dedicated, deserves a large part of the credit for it: not only for bringing the author into the world, but for setting an example in precise thinking, which it has been my lifelong ambition to emulate. One of the major assets of a scientist is the ability to abstract the essential elements of ideas. If I can do this at all, it is because my father taught me how.

I owe a debt of gratitude also to the three young ladies (of various ages) in my home. They have had to live with an "author at work" for an extended period of time. It is remarkable that they never voiced more than an occasional minimal complaint about the physical and psychological discomforts this entailed.

RANAN B. BANERJI

Cleveland, Ohio
Spring, 1969

Chapter I

INTRODUCTION

1.1. THE FIELD OF ENDEAVOR

The field commonly called *artificial intelligence* may, perhaps, be described as *the totality of attempts to make and understand machines that are able to perform tasks that, until recently, only human beings could perform and to perform them with effectiveness and speed comparable to a human.* There has been much controversy about the aptness of the name "artificial intelligence." This kind of discussion is probably of some use, in view of the general impression the name makes on the mind of the lay public. For the purposes of technical discussion, however, we can decide not to attach any significance to the name apart from what is implied by the definition. This kind of special technical use of well-known words is not without precedence; recall, for example, the word "energy" as used in physics, or "group" as used in modern algebra.

The definition of the field given in the preceding paragraph is certainly not very precise. It has always been extremely difficult to define areas of technical endeavors with precision. It may be worthwhile, however, to try to make some clarifying remarks.

The reference in the definition to an activity performed by a human being does not make clear what aspects of the activity are considered important. If a machine is designed to play checkers, for instance, we can demand that: (1) it win often against human players; (2) it produce electroencephalograms similar to those of humans engaged in playing checkers; (3) it hold and move pieces on a checkerboard with the same grace as some human beings; (4) it make a move in less than ten minutes. The practitioners in the field seem to have agreed that the first and fourth demands should be made, whereas the second and third should not. There is indeed some rationale for such a consensus; discussion of the rationale will, however, carry this book far from its purpose as stated in the preface. Therefore, any task under discussion will be considered to be as described by the consensus. No effort will be made to justify the consensus.

To avoid a certain unfortunate implication of the definition, another of its aspects—the interpretation of the phrase "until recently"—also bears

I

clarification. If this phrase is interpreted to refer to the recent past at any future time of discussion (within the period of relevance of this book), then the field of artificial intelligence takes on an aspect of ephemerality and becomes a clearinghouse for ill-understood techniques. This is not intended, and the phrase "until recently" should be interpreted to refer, within the period of relevance of this book, to the time of writing of the book. Hence, when a machine is made to perform a human activity for the first time, the definition should not be taken to assert that later attempts to make better versions of the machine should be considered as outside the field of artificial intelligence. Even after a machine that meets the specification of the definition is constructed, any attempts to make machines that perform the same task by a different method would still be in the field, as would theoretical attempts to shed light on the performance of such machines, since these efforts might facilitate the construction of machines that perform other similar tasks.

However, once the method of construction of machines for the performance of a certain class of human tasks is well understood, the construction of such machines would also be considered an activity in some other field, depending on the nature of the machine as well as the purpose for building it.

The last point needs discussion. A cursory glance at activities in the field of artificial intelligence reveals a number of different techniques and purposes. There have been some attempts at using digital computer programs for finding satisfactory solutions to industrial or engineering design problems whose optimal solution was either hard to define or too time consuming to obtain. If techniques for writing such programs for specific purposes become well-understood and perfected, these activities would probably be considered parts of the appropriate branches of management or engineering, or would disappear altogether, being replaced by subroutine libraries.

There have been many digital computer programs designed to simulate certain activities of the human mind [1]. There have been simulations of groups of humans, as in sociological phenomena (including economic phenomena). There have also been simulations of individual humans finding solutions to complex combinatorial problems, making deductions from a corpus of given facts, or recalling facts by association. Once the method of design of such programs and their use for psychological or sociological investigation is well understood, it may again be reasonable to classify such activities in psychology or sociology. As before, economics has been included in sociology for the purposes of this discussion.

The state of formalization of the field, however, is such that it is difficult to say, with respect to a specific attempt, whether it is an effort to simulate human processes or an effort to solve a certain problem. If the problem is one whose solution is of immediate applicability in technology or management, we can even ignore any purposes the attempt serves for the psychologist or sociologist and classify the attempt as potentially belonging to technology or management. If, however, the problem is of no immediate applicability, it would be unfair to classify the attempt as belonging to psychology or sociology unless the motivation for writing the program arose from a psychological or sociological interest. Often such programs are claimed to have been designed to simulate the way the programmer believes he would attempt to solve the problem himself; however, the motivation is these cases may come from a desire to solve the problem rather than to understand human phenomena.

There has been considerable discussion as to whether such attempts need be classified as activities in a recognized field of science. Many feel that it may be easier to classify them as recreational activities of some clever computer programmers. There have, however, been many occasions in the history of science where the recreational activities of some people have led to insights that have enriched science, or even technology or business: these computer activities may well lead to such enrichment. Study of the literature in the field indicates that the various attempts made at writing efficient programs for finding solutions to large combinatorial problems show some basic communality of approach and technique. Semiformal attempts have also been made to codify these similarities into a theory. Such study of empirical attempts and results, together with attempts to unify them, is becoming an important branch of artificial intelligence, which we can call *theory of problem solving*. It appears that the time is not too far distant when this kind of activity—a study of problems and their solutions independent of any psychological connotations—will denote a well-defined area of endeavor. Apart from the appropriateness of this field as an important subfield of artificial intelligence, it may also be considered a branch of computer science or perhaps mathematics. In a less formal way, it has also been pursued in the past by students of methodology in philosophy.

By its very nature, theory of problem solving is an applications-oriented discipline. Even at this early stage of its development, techniques and ideas that originated in the field of artificial intelligence have found and promise to find fruitful applications in science and technology [2].

Pattern recognition is often considered a separate branch of artificial intelligence, although there has been a growing recognition over the years of the close relationship between this field and what has just been delineated as theory of problem solving. However, this relationship is very ill understood.

One of the reasons for this is the lack of a clear set of definitions of terms used in the field of pattern recognition. There has been enough activity in the field to indicate that the basic idea deals with the recognition of a given object as belonging to a given set of objects. This recognition is only possible when there is a statement (in some language) that is true for all objects in the given set and is false for all objects not in the given set. For reasons associated with the history of the work at Case, the set of objects will be called the "pattern" or "concept." This procedure is at slight variance with the intuitive use of the term "pattern." The term is often used to denote the description of the set or those statements about the recognizable object that imply the description. Often the word is used to denote what has been called an "object" in this paragraph. For the purposes of this book, the words "pattern" and "concept" will stand for a set of objects.

A perusal of the usages in the field indicates that a *pattern recognizer* is a machine that can form the description of a pattern when presented with a small number of objects in it. The term "pattern learning" will be used in this book for this activity; "*recognition*" will be reserved for the much simpler activity of recognizing whether an object belongs to a pattern with a given description.

While most activities in the other fields of artificial intelligence have been carried out with the aid of digital computers, a considerable amount of the work in pattern recognition has been done with the aid of other devices. The use of adaptive-threshold logic elements was one of the first steps taken in this field of endeavor. By now the original uproar regarding the neuro-physiological significance of such devices has subsided. However, threshold logic (adaptive or otherwise) remains an interesting area of study in the field of switching theory. It is possible that a theory of "neural networks" based on such devices will have a strong influence on the theory of pattern recognition; however, such a possibility seems remote at present.

In the preceding paragraphs we have made an attempt to subdivide the field of artificial intelligence. Almost the entire content of this book deals with the area designated "theory of problem solving." Since pattern recognition (studied as a computer algorithm) is very closely related to this area, it, too, is discussed at length.

The approach that will be used may be described as systems theoretic. A model for problem situations will be set up, using certain abstract and quite elementary set-theoretic concepts. In its abstract form, such a model can be looked upon as a generalized definition only; the model does not appear to contain indications of what might be considered methods of solving the problem. To obtain such indications, certain further structures would have to be assumed. Stating the matter another way, we can say that the minimal structure needed for defining a problem is not sufficient to define methods of solution. Various forms of extra structures can be introduced as tools for the discussion of methods of solution. In this book only one such structure has been chosen. The reason for this choice is historical, in that this was the first structure that occurred to the school of investigators whose work is presented here.

The resulting model, embodying the model of problems with certain extra structures, is almost identical with the model of problems envisaged in the general problem solver (GPS) developed by Newell, Simon, and Shaw [19]. However, although the model as it stands is sufficient for the beginnings of a discussion of solution methods, this advantage was not used by the originators of the general problem solver. Instead, a specific method of solution was developed and studied, but never described with adequate precision.

It has been argued that the mere existence of an abstract model for solution methods is of no value. What is crucial is an adequate description of the problem that makes it amenable to the solution method. The argument is perfectly valid insofar as it says that abstract sets do not have sufficient structures for the study of any specific solution method. However, the argument does not imply (as it is often made to imply) that we therefore should not use a precise theoretical approach to describe solution methods. This false implication has led to the use of intuitive and imprecise descriptions of solution methods. It is hard to make any judgment whether this has been advantageous or detrimental to the field. At the present state of the art, however, an effort at making discussions precise and mathematically correct promises immediate returns: in ease of communication and documentation of ideas and results; in quick evaluation of basically erroneous ideas; and perhaps also in aiding innovations by interaction with related fields.

If we consider the major part of the argument against precise models of solution methods, we are forced to agree that a problem formulation, to be meaningful, must have with it an adequate representation of the problem in some language. This is in no way at variance with the basic tenets of systems theory. It is clear that no specific problem can be formulated unless the sets associated with it are adequately described in some language. Indeed, the effectiveness of this language of description turns out to be easy to discuss in terms of its efficiency in describing certain sets associated with the solution methods. But this needs precise definitions of the associated sets.

The foregoing discussion indicates another important belief on which this book is based. A meaningful theory of problems and their solution should include or have close relationships with a theory of descriptions and description languages. Such a theory will be discussed in this book, together with a model for problems and some models for problem solution.

It is not claimed here that either the models of problems and solutions or the theory of descriptions as they stand at present are adequate for the purposes of artificial intelligence. However, a belief is inherent that any meaningful theory of problem solving must include such precise models and theories.

1.2. OUTLINE OF THE BASIC MODELS

This book deals with models of problems and two-person games. Both of these are specializations of a general model discussed by Marino [3]. This model can be looked upon as a general model of control systems as well as of problems and games.

Basically, we are given a set of objects, which are called "states" in control theory and may be called "situations" in the theory of problems and games. In addition, there are two other sets, whose elements are called "controls" and "disturbances." Given a control paired with a disturbance, certain situations are changed to other situations. The modes of such changes are prespecified. A certain set of situations have their elements labeled as desirable or "winning situations." Given a situation, the control problem is generally stated as the problem of finding a control such that no matter what disturbance it is paired with, the resulting situation is a desirable one.

When a real control problem is posed in such abstract terms, it often happens that the set of controls and the set of disturbances are so intractable that it is practically impossible to choose an appropriate control from among the host of possibilities. Fortunately, most real problems impose certain extra properties on the situations, controls, and disturbances. Many have the property that the control and the disturbance sets are "generated" by a more tractable set of elements. This will be made precise later. For the present we can say roughly that each control is a sequence of "elementary" controls and each disturbance is a sequence of "elementary" disturbances. The problem then reduces to that of finding a sequence of elementary controls such that no matter what elementary disturbance is paired with each elementary control, the final result of the sequence of pairs is a winning situation. This problem can be called the problem of finding an "open-loop controller."

With such a specification of the problem, a difficulty often arises that is frequently ignored in control problems but is of supreme importance in games. The difficulty arises because all elementary controls may not be applicable to all situations. As a result, it is not possible to choose a sequence of elementary controls that will be applicable irrespective of what elementary disturbance they get paired with.

We can get around this difficulty by asking not for a control sequence, but for a control *strategy*, that is, an initial decision on the control to be used at each situation any time the situation arises. Given a certain situation, one decides on the control dictated for the situation by the strategy. Depending on the disturbance that is paired with this control, a new situation arises. A new control is then dictated for the new situation by the strategy and the process is repeated. If such a sequence ultimately results in a winning situation irrespective of the disturbance, the strategy is called a "winning strategy." The finding of a winning strategy is analogous to finding a "closed-loop controller."

The idea of a strategy essentially envisages a Bellman-type embedding of a problem in a larger problem [4]. It is of advantage even in cases where it is inessential; that is, when the applicability of controls is independent of the situation. Moreover, it is well known that in some control problems an open-loop controller cannot be built, whereas a closed-loop controller can.

The general model of control situations can be specialized to yield some special classes of the so-called problem situations. Mesarovic has classified problems into various types, one of which is: "Given a set S, subsets T and H of S, and a set of functions F such that each element of F maps S into S, to find a member of F which maps each element of H into some element of T" [5]. The set T may be called the set of winning situations and H the set of starting situations.

When we define a real problem in this framework, we face the same kind of difficulty as in the case of the control problems. Mesarovic had pointed out in his paper that the set F, to be tractable, should be "constructively defined." Windeknecht assumed a specific constructive structure of F by assuming that elements are obtained by composing functions from a finite set F_0 of functions [6]. He also stipulated that the elements of F_0 were partially defined over S, so that the composition operator defined a partial semigroup rather than a semigroup. H was considered a unit set. This model is followed in this book except that F_0 is not assumed to be a finite set.

If a problem is defined in the manner given in the preceding paragraph, a clear relationship can be seen between this model of a problem and the model formulated by Marino. If in the model of Marino the set of elementary disturbances be a unit set (whose element may be called "inaction"), then each elementary control defines a map from situations to situations and can be taken to be members of F_0. This analogy is pursued rigorously in the next chapter.

The model of problems discussed here is also very closely related to the model used in the general problem solver. In this model a set of situations and a set of transformations are given, each of which changes some situations to some other situations. We are supposed to change a given situation into another given situation (the "goal") by applying a sequence of transformations. The model of the general problem solver differs from the model envisaged in this book in that T is not a single situation but a set of situations or goals. This difference is not merely a matter of generalization. It is shown in the next chapter that in some of the specific cases handled by the general problem solver, we are actually interested in a set of goals rather than a single goal. This has become evident especially in view of some recent extensions of the original GPS [7].

At this point we will not discuss the major part of the general problem solver, which deals with methods for finding solutions to problems. This will be done later. For the purpose of the present section, it is more important to point out how the model proposed by Marino can be reduced to the model of a two-person game.

If the extended form of a zero-sum two-person game of the von Neumann–Morgenstern type be restricted to have payoff functions whose values are only 1, 0, and -1, then such games can readily be shown to be representable by a special class of Marino-type models [8]. In these, we fix a specific elementary control and a specific disturbance, each called "inaction." It may then be specified that in each situation either the control inaction or the disturbance inaction is applicable, but not both. This introduces the concept of the player's move and the opponent's move. Also, a further axiom can be introduced, if necessary, forcing the player and the opponent to move alternately.

The foregoing model can be made to represent an N-person game in that the disturbances may be considered to be the result of the joint action of $N - 1$ players. However, since such an assertion sheds no light on the behaviors of the separate $N - 1$ players (with respect to coalitions and related phenomena), this assertion will not be made seriously here.

However, the model here is not so specific as not to include games with incomplete information. We need not construe the elements of S as embodying the entire information regarding the past of the game. As a matter of fact, it will be noticed that in the present model the entire past is not embodied in a situation; only the "final result" of the past, in some sense. Unlike von Neumann's model of extended games, the present model is not a tree, but an automaton (or a labeled directed graph). We can carry this process a step further and consider a situation as the "state of information" of a player; that is, a subset of the set of "actual situations." It would not be too difficult to show how a game with incomplete information can be converted into a "larger" game (with a larger number of situations) with complete information, in a way analogous to converting a nondeterministic automaton to a deterministic automaton. However, this generalization does not shed any further light on the methods of solution in the abstract, and is not pursued further in this book.

1.3. A SET-THEORETIC VIEW OF PATTERN RECOGNITION

The main purpose of this book is to consider certain methods for finding solutions to problems and games and their relationship to pattern recognition. This relationship can be discussed in a clear manner if both the activities (problem solving and pattern recognition) can be discussed within the same mathematical framework. As has been said before, the framework of elementary set theory is used in this book.

In their essence, the methods of problem solving will be taken to stem from the existence of certain basic subsets of the set S associated with a problem or game. Some such sets (like the winning situations, or the domain of applicability of different controls, etc.) are provided by the rules of the game itself. Certain others are suggested by the idea of a solution. To see this roughly (detailed discussions will appear later), we can imagine that one person who knows a winning strategy for the problem for every initial situation intends to transfer his knowledge to someone else. For every specific control he will have to define the set of situations in which that control is to be used. These sets (one set for each control) form one class of sets associated with the idea of solution. Other sets associated with the idea of solution are considered in the next chapter. Meanwhile, it is crucial to make the point that in all cases of interest the set S of situations is extremely large. Hence these sets cannot be exhibited by any practicable enumeration technique. It is this difficulty that holds up efforts at problem solving.

The difficulty, however, may not be insurmountable. It may be recalled that although the set of situations is large, no difficulty arises about its enumeration. Any chess player can recognize a chess position as a chess position. Similarly, the set of all "mates" (winning situations in chess) never have to be enumerated either: a mate is easily recognizable when it occurs. The rules of the game give us the controls, disturbances, and winning situation, not as enumerations but as "descriptions": methods by which members of these sets can be recognized when they arise. Similarly, any solution method, to be practicable, must be expressed in terms of the descriptions of the sets associated with the solution methods. The practicability of a strategy is strongly dependent on the language used for the description of the sets associated with the solution methods. We can change the language of description to change the practicability of various solution methods.

The difficulty of finding a solution of a game or problem lies in the fact that the language that is needed for practicable descriptions of the sets associated with the solution method is seldom identical to the one used in describing its rules (i.e., the controls and the winning, losing, and draw situations). Ideas regarding description languages are crucial here, as they are in any adequate theory of pattern recognition. In what follows, an approach to the formal definition of such terms as "description," "description language," "pattern," and so on is given.

As stated in Section 1.1, a pattern may be defined as a set of objects. We can consider the pattern of all the letters A projected on an array of photo cells, the pattern of all checker positions showing satisfactory center control [9], the pattern of all sets of theorems from which a desired theorem can be obtained by a single application of *modus ponens* [10], and so on.

It will be worthwhile to realize at the outset that when we try to develop a language for describing a class of patterns, we cannot seriously mean to be able to describe the class of all patterns (if we do try, we face immediate dilemmas, like "Does the set of all patterns that are not elements of themselves form a pattern?"). The class of patterns has to be restricted. The initial restriction made here is to a class of subsets of a given set, which we call the universe of discourse or simply the "universe." By definition, any object is taken to belong to the universe.

If the universe is finite, we can consider any subset of it to be described by a list of its elements; but if the subset (or pattern) is large, we cannot call such a description practicable. We have, at this point, to make some further restrictions: to assume some further structure for the universe.

Without loss of realism, we can make the assumption that there are certain general statements we can make about elements of the universe whose truth can be tested easily for any specific element of the universe. Such statements will be called *predicates*, in keeping with literature in symbolic logic [11]. The assumption is that, in addition to the universe, we are also given a set of predicates.

It has already been indicated that the description of a pattern yields a procedure that has the property: given an element of the universe, the application of the procedure determines whether the element belongs to the pattern or not. Clearly any pattern, each of whose elements satisfies a given predicate (which, in turn, is satisfied only by the elements of the pattern), is describable by that predicate. We can say, therefore, that our assumption has led us to a class of patterns that are "easily describable" in the sense that their descriptions are embodied by single predicates whose truths are easily tested for.

We can take the easily describable class of patterns as forming the generators of a Boolean algebra. The class of describable patterns may be restricted to the elements of this Boolean algebra. If we do this, we can make the rather trivial statement that a description language that incorporates the initial predicates and uses the logical connectives "or," "and," "not," "implies," and so on is able to describe any element of the class of patterns under consideration.

The major problem, however, is not so much of the possibility of description as of the efficiency of description. We need descriptions where the elementary predicates are combined in such a way that the resulting statements are not inordinately long. Also, we need the statements to be such that their truth and falsity can be tested for without an inordinate amount of processing. This once more restricts the class of easily describable patterns.

Logical connectives are not the only means by which the initial predicates can be combined. A large amount of work has gone into combining predicates by threshold gates [12], for instance. The patterns that yield short descriptions through single applications of threshold logic form a proper subclass of the class of all describable patterns. This class is much richer than the class obtainable through single uses of "or" or "and" gates. All describable patterns can be described by more than one application of threshold logic.

We can, in an informal way, define a description language to consist of a set of initial predicates and a set of connectives or modes of combination that can be used to combine the initial predicates to yield descriptions of describable patterns. The class of patterns easily describable by a given description language depends on the description language.

The class of patterns whose elements are to be described is determined by the problem that necessitates the recognition of elements of the patterns in the class. The basic problem then reduces to: "Given a class of patterns, develop a description language that yields short and easily processable descriptions for all patterns in the class."

At present, no practicable method for the solution of such a problem has been developed (as a matter of fact, solution methods for very few problems have been developed). However, a study of the problem in its formal aspect indicates the need for a uniform model of description languages in which different description languages can be embedded. This would make it possible to change one language to another, a definite necessity for the specification of the basic problem itself. In what follows, some of the basic building blocks for a generalized description language of this kind are specified.

Initially, some structure is assumed for the predicates of the language. It is assumed that each specifies the result of a test performed on an element of the universe. Each test breaks the universe up into disjoint equivalence classes, two elements of the universe being called equivalent if they yield the same results in the test. The elements of this partition are mapped one-to-one onto the set of results. The image of each element of the partition under this map is called the name of the element.

We can thus make two equivalent statements about an element u of the universe: (1) "The result of performing test P on u is p_1" or (2) "u belongs to the element p_1 of the partition P." For historical reasons the second form of the statement is adhered to.

On this basis we can define a pattern either as an element of a partition in a prespecified set of partitions or as obtained from other patterns by set-theoretic operations. In what follows, each partition is called an *input property* and the elements of a property are called its *values*. Any set of pairwise disjoint patterns whose union covers the universe is also called a property. By definition, any input property is a property, but not conversely.

An object is a pattern that is either contained in or disjoint from any value of any input property. It can be seen quite readily, then, that an object is contained in the intersection of a class of values of input properties. They can, therefore, be represented by a list of pairs of names, each pair consisting of the name of a property and the name of that value of this property to which the object belongs. For example, a typical object might be represented by $(P_1, p_{13}; P_2, p_{21}; P_3, p_{33})$; the object is a subset of the value p_{13} of the property P_1, the value p_{21} of P_2, and the value p_{33} of P_3.

Any pattern can be described by a Boolean expression involving values or a statement involving predicates of the form $P(u) = p$ where P is an input property. The problem of finding the simplest expression describing a pattern is a problem closely analogous to finding the simplest expression for a switching function (as can be seen, switching functions are special cases: each input property has two values). The solution depends basically on what is meant by "simple" and, as in the case of a switching function, the solution can be found only for some restricted definitions of simplicity.

Very often, after the simplest description for a pattern has been found, it is still so complex as to be unusable. At this point we can hope to find simpler descriptions if we use properties other than input properties in the description. To do this, we need to allow predicates of the form $u \in K$ where K is the value of some property other than an input property. Of course, to use such a description we need to invoke the description of K as a pattern. We thus obtain the analog of the Ashenhurst decomposition of a Boolean function [13]. Some of the techniques and terminologies associated with these problems are discussed in a later chapter.

The literature in the field of pattern recognition indicates that the only kind of switching functions that found use in the field till recently are those expressible as conjunctions and as threshold expressions. The largest effort in the practical field is spent on finding the "useful" properties that render the pattern expressible in one of these simple forms. Unfortunately, since

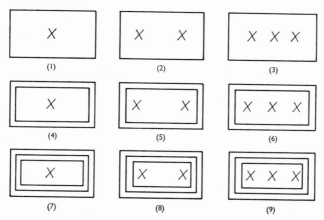

Figure I.I. A simple universe of discourse.

the methods used for finding properties are entirely *ad hoc*, they are seldom describable in a formal language. There is no uniform method for expressing the processes that yield values of these useful properties. If the problem is considered with the set-theoretic bias inherent in this book, a rather interesting uniformity emerges. We often find that the processes yielding the values of the useful properties really process the names rather than the denotations of the input properties and their values.

There is occasion later to discuss this kind of processing for some seemingly realistic situations. For the present we can consider the following artificial example, which is based on a rather well-known example used by Bruner [14].

Let the universe consist of the nine configurations shown in Figure 1.1. For convenience, we call the elements of this universe 1, 2, . . . , 9, as shown in the figure. Formally, the universe has two input properties, whose names are "crosses" and "borders." Each of the properties have three values, which have "one," "two," and "three" as names.

To give intuitive meaning to these properties and values, let the set $\{1, 4, 7\}$ be the value one of the property crosses. Similarly, let $\{4, 5, 6\}$ be the value two of the property borders.

This universe has the convenient property that every distinct element is the member of a distinct and unique object. As a result, every subset of the universe is a pattern. For the purposes of the present discussion, the pattern $\{4, 7, 8\} = A$ (say) may be considered. This set is described in three different ways: one using only input properties, one using properties other than input properties, and one using relationships between names of the values of properties. This is done to illustrate the three methods, rather than to exhibit the difference in their efficiency as description methods. Such difference can be exhibited conclusively only for larger universes; examples are given later when the description language is introduced formally.

One could describe the pattern A formally by the statement

$$x \in A \equiv (\text{crosses}(x) = \text{one}) \wedge ((\text{borders}(x) = \text{two}) \vee (\text{borders}(x) = \text{three}))$$
$$\vee ((\text{crosses}(x) = \text{two}) \wedge (\text{borders}(x) = \text{three}))$$

involving only predicates of the type $P(u) = p$.

The pattern A could also be described with statements of the type $u \in K$ as follows.

$$x \in A \equiv (x \in B) \wedge (x \in C) \wedge (x \in D),$$
$$x \in B \equiv (\text{crosses}(x) = \text{one}) \vee (\text{crosses}(x) = \text{two}),$$
$$x \in C \equiv (\text{crosses}(x) = \text{one}) \vee (\text{borders}(x) = \text{three}),$$
$$x \in D \equiv (\text{borders}(x) = \text{two}) \vee (\text{borders}(x) = \text{three}).$$

This form of description is of advantage only if the patterns B, C, and D can be involved in the description of many patterns other than A.

In many existing pattern recognition schemes, the switching function for a pattern is restricted to have some specific form. For instance, it may be restricted to have a form realizable by a single threshold gate or by a single "and" gate. If, for example, we make the restriction that A be described by a minterm expression, the second description above would be according to such a restriction. The patterns B, C, and D would be "useful features" for describing A. In most cases such features are obtained by processing the names of the values of the input properties and not in the form of a Boolean expression, as done here. It is desirable for the sake of uniformity and flexibility of the description language, however, to express such preprocessing of names in the same format as other descriptions.

To illustrate such a format, a third alternative description for the pattern A is presented. This example takes advantage of the fact that the names of the values of the two properties, crosses and borders, come from the set of numerals and the concept A can be described in English by saying "In any element of A, the number of crosses is less than the number of borders." The description language needs some method for expressing the relation "less than." (It is shown later how a relation can be expressed as a pattern in the universe of ordered n-tuples. This involves the introduction of several new universes. For the present purpose, only one new universe need be evoked.) This new universe is evoked to permit the expression of the symbols "one," "two," and "three" (the names of the values of the properties crosses and borders) as their binary counterparts. Each numeral has two properties, "head" and "tail," standing for the "twos place" and the "ones place" of their binary expansion. The values of both these properties will be called f and t. The numeral two, for example, will take the form (head, t; tail, f).

With this new universe in mind, we can describe the pattern A as follows.

$$x \in A \equiv (\text{head}(\text{border}(x)) = t) \wedge ((\text{head}(\text{crosses}(x)) = f)$$
$$\vee ((\text{tail}(\text{borders}(x)) = t) \wedge (\text{tail}(\text{crosses}(x)) = f))).$$

This description states, in effect, that a configuration belongs to A if and only if the twos place of the borders is t (it has two or three borders) and either the twos place of crosses is f (it has one cross) or otherwise the ones place of borders is t (it has three borders) and the ones place of crosses is f (it has fewer than three crosses). As before, the advantage of such a description becomes clear only in those cases where the universes involved are much larger. (There is occasion later to discuss this.) It may, however, be pointed out that even where such an advantage is obtainable, it is obtained at the expense of making the objects of the universe more complicated (imbuing the universe with greater structure). For example, as long as we used the symbols "one," "two," and "three" as values of crosses and borders, a typical object (8, say) of the universe would be (crosses, two; borders, three). When the values themselves are construed to come from the structured universe of binary numerals, the same object becomes (crosses, (head, t; tail, f); borders, (head, t; tail, t)).

The relationship between the richness of the description language and the facility of problem solving is discussed through some examples in later chapters. The present section concludes with the following remarks.

So far discussions have been limited to description of patterns. Given a description language, we want to construct a processor that can operate on objects to determine whether they are contained in any given pattern. This presupposes certain restrictions on the language. For instance, if the language is strong enough to describe recursively enumerable sets of objects, no processor of assured ability can be built.

Even assuming that we have a language that permits the construction of the corresponding processor, this would not solve the problem of pattern recognition. It appears from the literature that pattern recognition consists of forming rather than processing a description. What is generally envisaged as pattern recognition is the following phenomenon. A processor is presented with a set of objects, each of which is tagged to indicate whether or not it is contained in a given pattern. From these data, the processor is supposed to form a description (in some language) of a pattern that contains all the objects tagged as being contained in the given pattern and does not contain any object that is tagged as not being contained in the given pattern.

It is not overly difficult to build such a processor. The difficulty so far lies only in the simplicity of the generated description. This has been discussed before. However, another demand is often made on the description-generating processor. It is expected that the description constructed by it will be such that when an untagged new object is presented to the processor, it will fit the description if and only if it belongs to the given pattern. This property, called generalization ability, is clearly an impossible task in general, the only evidence presented to the processor about the pattern having been the tagged objects. As long as the tagged objects do not exhaust all objects in the universe of discourse, we can always have a number of distinct patterns satisfying the tagging of the elements. The processor builds the description of only one of these patterns; it would be self-defeating to form all the descriptions, and even that would not help in the recognition of later untagged elements.

The phenomenon of generalization has received some attention from statisticians [15]. Their studies seem to indicate that the number of tagged objects needed for establishing a degree of confidence in a description is strongly dependent on the usefulness of the features used and the resulting simplicity of description. There will be later occasion to comment on this matter in detail.

1.4. THE ARRANGEMENT OF THE BOOK

In the next chapter (Chapter 2) Marino's model is introduced formally and some of its important properties are discussed. It is then shown how some of the important concepts associated with the Marino model can be specialized to a model for problems. Some important classes of sets associated with solution methods are isolated and discussed. It is pointed out how some of these classes have already been used in some case studies reported in literature.

In Chapter 3 the Marino model is specialized to the case of two-person games and a discussion of solution methods similar to that in Chapter 2 is instituted.

As a prelude to Chapter 5 (on pattern recognition), Chapter 4 discusses in a precise and detailed manner the description language introduced in Section 1.3. This permits the discussion of similarities and differences between various pattern recognition languages and algorithms. Also, some work at the Case Western Reserve University is described that indicates how the use of pattern recognition techniques leads to efficient game-playing algorithms.

Chapter 2

PROBLEMS AND SOLUTION METHODS

2.1. INTRODUCTION

The main purpose of this chapter is to discuss problems as modeled by Windeknecht (these will be called W-problems in the future). However, since many ideas relevant to Marino's model are relevant to this as well as the next chapter, the next two sections of the present chapter are devoted to Marino's model (hereinafter called M-situations), some of its properties, and its relation to W-problems. An important theorem regarding M-situations (Theorem 2.1) deals with the existence of winning strategies in M-situations. Similar theorems will be shown to exist for W-problems and game situations (discussed in Chapter 3). These will be established by establishing W-problems and game situations as special cases of M-situations. To do this it is necessary to (1) set down the basic structure of M-situations, (2) put down the basic structure of W-problems and indicate their isomorphism with a special class of M-situations, and (3) set down the basic structure of game situations and indicate their isomorphism with another special class of M-situations. Section 2.2 formalizes the structure of M-situations. Section 2.3 elaborates the discussions envisaged in (2) above. The relationships between M-situations and game situations are discussed in Chapter 3.

In Sections 2.4 and 2.5 some well-known problems and puzzles are described as W-problems. In later sections, some methods for finding solutions to problems are discussed. It will be shown to what extent these methods have been approximated by some solution methods used in the literature.

2.2. SOME PROPERTIES OF M-SITUATIONS

In Chapter 1, the basic ideas underlying M-situations were clarified. In what follows, some of these ideas are made more precise. As said before, this formalism is essentially that of Marino, although a few minor changes have been made to bring it in line with the purposes of this book.

An *M-situation* is given by a 6-tuple $\langle S, C, D, M, S_W, S_L \rangle$ where S, C, and D are abstract sets and S_W and S_L are disjoint subsets of S. M is a subset of

$S \times C \times D \times S$ with the following properties:

M1 $(s_1, c_1, d_1, s_2) \in M$ and $(s_1, c_1, d_1, s_3) \in M$ implies $s_2 = s_3$.

This merely says that M is a function mapping a subset of $S \times C \times D$ into S. The reason it is not defined initially as a function is because M is not defined for the entire set $S \times C \times D$.

Before the next properties of the relation M are introduced, another definition will be needed. Given an M-situation and an element $c \in C$, we define the set

$$S_c = \{s \mid (\exists d)(\exists s')((s, c, d, s') \in M)\}.$$

Similarly, for each member $d \in D$ we can define

$$S_d = \{s \mid (\exists c)(\exists s')((s, c, d, s') \in M)\}.$$

It follows from the definition that if $(s, c, d, s') \in M$, then $s \in S_c \cap S_d$. However, in all M-situations the following assumption will also be made.

M2 If $s \in S_c \cap S_d$, then $(\exists s')((s, c, d, s') \in M)$.

For convenience as well as for motivation, members of S will be called *situations*; members of S_W and S_L will be called *winning situations* and *losing situations*, respectively; members of C will be called *controls*; and members of D will be called *disturbances*; $(s, c, d, s') \in M$ will often be expressed by saying "s' is the result of applying c and d to s" or $(c, d)(s) = s'$. Members of S_c will be called "situations to which c is applicable"; similarly with S_d. Situations to which no controls are applicable, if not winning or losing situations, will be called *draw situations* and denoted by S_D.

A function

$$P: S - (S_W \cup S_L \cup S_D) \to C$$

will be called a *control strategy* if

$$P(s) = c \quad \text{implies} \quad s \in S_c.$$

A *disturbance strategy* is defined similarly.

A winning strategy is one such that, no matter what strategy is chosen by the disturbing influence, any sequence of applications of controls and disturbances applied according to the strategies results in a winning situation. This can be expressed formally as follows.

Given an element $s_0 \notin S_W \cup S_L \cup S_D$, a control strategy P_C is called a *winning strategy* for s_0 if there exists an integer N such that for every disturbance strategy P_D there exists a sequence (c_1, d_1), (c_2, d_2), (c_3, d_3), . . . ,

(c_n, d_n) such that

$$1. \quad n \leq N;$$

$$2. \quad c_1 = P_C(s_0), \quad d_1 = P_D(s_0);$$

and for each i $(1 \leq i < n)$

$$c_{i+1} = P_C((c_i, d_i)((c_{i-1}, d_{i-1})(\cdots (c_1, d_1)(s_0) \cdots),$$
$$d_{i+1} = P_D((c_i, d_i)((c_{i-1}, d_{i-1})(\cdots (c_1, d_1)(s_0) \cdots);$$

and

$$3. \quad (c_n, d_n)((c_{n-1}, d_{n-1})) \cdots (c_1, d_1)(s_0) \cdots) \in S_W.$$

A control strategy P_C is called a *nonlosing strategy* for s_0 either if it is a winning strategy or if for no disturbance strategy P_D it is the case that there exists a sequence $\{(c_i, d_i)\}$ $(1 \leq i \leq n$, as before$)$ such that

$$c_1 = P_C(s_0), \quad d_1 = P_D(s_0);$$

and for each i $(1 \leq i < n)$

$$c_{i+1} = P_C((c_i, d_i)((c_{i-1}, d_{i-1})) \cdots (c_1, d_1)(s_0) \cdots),$$
$$d_{i+1} = P_D((c_i, d_i)((c_{i-1}, d_{i-1})) \cdots (c_1, d_1)(s_0) \cdots);$$

and

$$(c_n, d_n)((c_{n-1}, d_{n-1})) \cdots (c_1, d_1)(s_0) \cdots) \in S_L.$$

A situation for which a winning strategy exists is called a *forcing situation*. The set of all forcing situations is denoted by S_F. A situation for which a nonlosing strategy exists but no winning strategy exists is called a *neutral situation*.

The following theorem, which we state here without proof (a proof can be found in Marino's thesis), is of great interest.

THEOREM 2.1. *Given an M-situation, there exists a strategy that is a winning strategy for every forcing situation and a nonlosing strategy for every neutral situation.* ∎

This theorem, indeed, can be made stronger. It has been shown by Charles A. Dunning, in an unpublished paper, that the theorem remains true even where the upper bound N used in the definition of a winning strategy does not exist.

In the next section the definition of W-problems is introduced and related to that of M-situations. It may be worthwhile to mention at this point, however, that the word "strategy" here has been used in a somewhat specialized sense. Unlike its traditional usage in the field, a strategy is not a method for searching for the solution. In a later section the latter method is called a "search strategy." A strategy, as the term is used here, is the embodiment of the construction of a solution, correct or otherwise. A winning strategy is a method for embodying the construction of a "correct" solution. A search is really a method for changing strategies as defined here.

2.3. W-PROBLEMS AND M-SITUATIONS

A *W-problem* is given by a triple $\langle S, F_0, T \rangle$ where S is an abstract set, T a subset of S, and F_0 a set of functions from subsets of S into S

$$f \in F_0 \quad \text{implies} \quad f : S_f \to S \quad \text{and} \quad S_f \subseteq S.$$

Given a W-problem and $s_0 \in S$, a *winning solution* for s_0 is a sequence of functions $\{f_1, f_2, \ldots, f_n\}$ such that $f_i \in F_0$ for each i and such that

$$f_n(f_{n-1}(\cdots f_1(s_0) \cdots)) \in T$$

(*n* will be called the *length* of the solution).
A function

$$Q : \bigcup_{f \in F_0} S_f - T \to F_0$$

is called a *W-strategy* if and only if

$$Q(s) = f \quad \text{implies} \quad s \in S_f.$$

A W-strategy is *winning* for $s_0 \in S$ if there exists a winning solution $\{f_1, f_2, \ldots, f_n\}$ such that

$$f_1 = Q(s_0)$$

and for each i ($1 \le i \le n$)

$$f_{i+1} = Q(f_i(f_{i-1}(\cdots f_1(s_0) \cdots)).$$

To indicate the relationship between W-problems and M-situations we need a special class of M-situations, which will be defined next.
An M-situation is called *problemlike* if and only if

P1 $D = \{d'\}$, a unit set;

P2 $s \in S_c$ for some c implies $s \notin S_L$.

P3 $S_D = \varnothing$, the empty set.

Given a problemlike M-situation

$$R = \langle S, C, \{d'\}, M, S_W, S_L \rangle,$$

we can define a triplet

$$P(R) = \langle S, F_0, T \rangle$$

where $T = S_W$ and F_0 is a set of relations defined as follows:

$f \in F_0$ if and only if there exists a $c \in C$ such that, for all s, $s' \in S$, $(s, s') \in f$ if and only if $(s, c, d', s') \in M$.

It is not hard to see that $P(R)$ is a W-problem. S is an abstract set, and T is a subset of S. Each element $f \in F_0$ is a function since $(s, s') \in f$ and $(s, s'') \in f$ implies $(s, c, d', s') \in M$ and $(s, c, d', s'') \in M$ for some unique c whence, by M1, $s' = s''$. For each $c \in C$ there is a function $f_c \in F_0$ and these are the only members of F_0. Also, $S_{f_c} = S_c$. This can be seen by noting that $s \in S_c$ implies (due to the uniqueness of d') $s \in S_c \cap S_{d'}$ whence by definition there exists s' such that $(s, c, d', s') \in M$ whence f_c is defined for s, proving $S_c \subseteq S_{f_c}$. Similarly, if $s \in S_{f_c}$, then there is an s' such that $(s, c, d', s') \in M$ whence $s \in S_c$, proving the reverse inequality.

Given a W-problem

$$P = \langle S, F_0, T \rangle,$$

we can define a 6-tuple

$$R(P) = \langle S, C, \{d'\}, M, S_W, S_L \rangle$$

where

$$S_W = T,$$
$$S_L = S - \bigcup_{f \in F_0} S_f - S_W,$$

and C and M are composed as follows.

For each element of $f \in F_0$ there is an element $c_f \in C$ and these are the only elements of c. Also

$$(s, c_f, d', s') \in M \quad \text{if and only if} \quad f(s) = s'.$$

Situation $R(P)$ is a problemlike M-situation since S and C can be taken to be abstract sets, $D = \{d'\}$ satisfying P1. S_W and S_L are disjoint subsets of S by definition. M1 follows since f is a function for each c_f. M2 follows also since from the uniqueness of d', $s \in S_{c_f}$ implies and (trivially) is implied by $s \in S_{c_f} \cap S_{d'}$. Since it can also be seen quite easily that $S_f = S_{c_f}$, $s \in S_{c_f}$ also implies the existence of s' such that $f(s) = s'$ leading to $(s, c_f, d', s') \in M$. P2 can be seen to be satisfied since $s \in S_L$ shows $s \in S - \bigcup_{c \in C} S_c$; that is, $s \notin \bigcup_{c \in C} S_c$, proving the contrapositive of P2. To prove P3 we note that

$$S_D = S - \bigcup_{c \in C} S_c - S_L - S_W$$

and

$$S_L = S - \bigcup_{c \in C} S_c - S_W.$$

In what has gone before, two mappings have been defined, one from M-situations to W-problems and one from W-problems to M-situations. In what follows it is shown that these mappings are one-to-one and inverses of one another.

THEOREM 2.2.   *For all W-problems P and problemlike M-situations R*

$$P(R(P)) = P \quad \text{and} \quad R(P(R)) = R.$$

PROOF.   Let

$$P = \langle S, F_0, T \rangle,$$

$$R(P) = \langle S, C, \{d'\}, M, T, S - \bigcup_{c \in C} S_c - T \rangle,$$

and

$$P(R(P)) = \langle S, F'_0, T \rangle.$$

It is only required to show that $F_0 = F'_0$.

Let $f \in F_0$; then by definition of $R(P)$, there exists a $c_f \in C$ such that $S_{c_f} = S_f$ and $f(s) = s'$ if and only if $(s, c_f, d', s') \in M$. By construction of F'_0, there is an element $f' \in F'_0$ such that $S_{f'} = S_{c_f}$ and $f'(s) = s'$ if and only if $(s, c_f, d', s') \in M$. Hence, $f' = f$ showing that $F_0 \subseteq F'_0$. The reverse inequality follows similarly, proving that $F_0 = F'_0$.

Now let

$$R = \langle S, C, \{d'\}, M, S_W, S_L \rangle,$$

$$P(R) = \langle S, F_0, S_W \rangle,$$

and

$$R(P(R)) = \langle S, C', \{d'\}, M', S_W, S'_L \rangle.$$

That $C = C'$ and $M = M'$ will follow from the definition as in the previous case. To show that $S_L = S'_L$, it is recalled from P2 that $s \in S_L$ implies $s \notin \bigcup_{c \in C} S_c$ or $S_L \subseteq S - \bigcup_{c \in C} S_c$. However, since S_L and S_W are disjoint

$$S_L = S_L - S_W \subseteq S - \bigcup_{c \in C} S_c - S_W = S'_L.$$

Again, since by P3

$$S_D = S - \bigcup_{c \in C} S_c - S_L - S_W = \varnothing$$

we have

$$S_L \supseteq S - \bigcup_{c \in C} S_c - S_W = S'_L,$$

proving the reverse inequality.   ■

The R and P functions demonstrate that problemlike M-situations and W-problems are identical structures. However, they do not establish that the concept of a winning strategy as defined in the two structures is the same concept. To show this we introduce another definition.

Given a W-problem P and a W-strategy Q for P, we define a function $R(Q)$ from a subset of S into C in $R(P)$ as follows.

$$R(Q)(s) = c_f \quad \text{if and only if} \quad Q(s) = f.$$

It can be verified that $R(Q)$ is a control strategy for $R(P)$. $R(Q)(s) = c_f$ implies $Q(s) = f$. Since Q is a W-strategy, this implies $s \in S_f$ whence $s \in S_{c_f}$, showing that $R(Q)$ fulfills one condition for being a control strategy. To show that the domain of $R(Q)$ is indeed $S - S_W - S_L - S_D$, we note that the domain of Q is

$$\bigcup_{f \in F_0} S_f - S_W = \bigcup_{c \in C} S_c - S_W.$$

Now

$$S_L = S - \bigcup_{c \in C} S_c - S_W$$

whence

$$S - S_L = \left(\bigcup_{c \in C} S_c \right) \cup S_W$$

whence

$$S - S_L - S_W = \bigcup_{c \in C} S_c - S_W.$$

Since $S_D = \varnothing$ the domain of $R(Q)$, which coincides with the domain of Q, is indeed $S - S_W - S_L - S_D$.

We can now state and prove the following theorem, which is an important step toward the establishment of the analog of Theorem 2.1, in the case of W-problems.

THEOREM 2.3.   *Let Q be a W-strategy for the W-problem P. Let $R(Q)$ be the control strategy for $R(P)$ as defined. Then Q is a winning W-strategy for s_0 if and only if $R(Q)$ is a winning control strategy for s_0 in $R(P)$.*

PROOF.   We initially note from the construction of M that $s \in S_{d'}$ if and only if $s \in S_f$ for some $f \in F_0$. Hence, every disturbance strategy P_D has as its domain $\bigcup_{f \in F_0} S_f - S_W$ and $P_D(s) = d'$ for each s in this domain. This, then, is the only possible disturbance strategy.

Let now $R(Q)$ be a winning control strategy for s_0 in $R(P)$. Then there exists a sequence of controls $c_{f_1}, c_{f_2}, \ldots, c_{f_n}$ such that

$$c_{f_1} = R(Q)(s_0)$$

and for each $i < n$

$$c_{f_i} = R(Q)((c_{f_{i-1}}, d')((\cdots (c_{f_1}, d')(s_0)) \cdots)$$

and

$$(c_{f_n}, d')((c_{f_{n-1}}, d')((\cdots ((c_{f_1}, d')(s_0) \cdots) \in S_W.$$

This indicates that

$$f_n(f_{n-1}(\cdots f_1(s_0) \cdots) \in S_W,$$
$$f_1 = Q(s_0),$$

and

$$f_i = Q(f_{i-1}(\cdots f_1(s_0) \cdots)$$

for each $i \leq n$. Thus Q is a winning W-strategy for s_0 in P. The proof that $R(Q)$ is a winning control strategy for s_0 in $R(P)$ if Q is a winning W-strategy for s_0 is P follows in exactly the same way. It can also be shown that any strategy in $R(P)$ is $R(Q)$ for some strategy Q in P. ∎

It ought to be pointed out that, unlike the more general case of M-situations, no upper bound was assumed for the length of a winning solution. This indicates that in the case of problemlike M-situations the existence of the upper bound is redundant.

We can state without proving it that if there is a winning solution for s_0 in P, then there is a winning W-strategy for s_0 in P. We merely associate f_1 with s_0, f_2 with $f_1(s_0)$, and so on; the rest of the situations may have any value for the strategy.

Let $T' \subseteq S$ be the set of all situations in a W-problem such that $s \in T'$ if and only if there is a winning solution for s. Hence, there is a winning strategy for each element of T' in $R(P)$. Hence, each element of T' is a forcing state in $R(P)$. Also, it follows similarly that each forcing state in $R(P)$ is a member of T'. Hence, $S_F = T'$.

The important thing to note here is that by Theorem 2.1 there is a strategy $R(Q)$ in $R(P)$ that is a winning strategy for each $s \in T'$. Hence, there is a W-strategy that is winning for each element $s \in T'$. This fact yields some solidity to a rather meaningful theorem (Theorem 2.4) that will be indicated later. In the rest of this chapter some processes for finding winning strategies are discussed. To make this discussion meaningful, the next two sections introduce two problems that have been discussed in literature and show that these can be formalized as W-problems.

2.4. A SIMPLE EXAMPLE OF A W-PROBLEM: THE TOWER OF HANOI

In this and the next section, two problems are discussed as W-problems. In addition to motivating the use of W-problems, these also serve in future sections to illustrate some ideas developed in relation to solution methods. This section is devoted to describing the celebrated puzzle called the Tower of Hanoi [16, 17]. The puzzle is generally described as follows.

One is given a set of n disks (n may be any number: folklore attaches the value 64 to n; we will use smaller values) of unequal diameter. There are three long pins fixed upright on a board. Each disk has in its center a hole large enough to fit over any pin but not large enough to pass any other disk through it.

Initially, all the disks are threaded on one of the pins. They are arranged with the largest disk at the bottom and the smallest disk at the top; each disk rests on a larger one. It is required to transfer all the disks to another

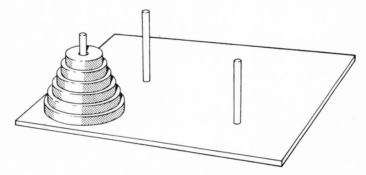

Figure 2.1.   The Tower of Hanoi.

pin by moving one disk at a time from one pin to another. The constraint is to be observed at all times that no disk should ever rest on any disk smaller than itself. Also, only the disks at the top position on any needle can be moved. The initial configuration is shown in Figure 2.1 to clarify the description (n has been taken to be 6 here. However, the value of n will not play any essential role in the formal representation of the problem).

To represent the Tower of Hanoi problem as a W-problem we may specify as follows. Each element of S consists of a sequence of three sequences of integers

$$s \in S \equiv s = \langle (x_{01}, x_{02}, \ldots, x_{0i_0}), (x_{11}, x_{12}, \ldots, x_{1i_1}), (x_{21}, x_{22}, \ldots, x_{2i_2}) \rangle.$$

These three sequences have the following properties.

H1 $i_0 + i_1 + i_2 = n$

(i.e., there are a total of n integers in the three sequences, each integer standing for a disk).

H2 $x_{ij} = x_{st}$ only if $i = s, j = t$

(i.e., the integers appearing in the sequences are distinct).

H3 $1 \leq x_{ij} \leq n$;

H4 $j > k$ implies $x_{ij} > x_{ik}$ for each i.

(i.e., larger integers appear after smaller ones in each sequence: smaller integers stand for larger disks).

The set F_0 consists of $2n$ functions, to be denoted by the generic name (k, m) where $1 \leq k \leq n$ and $m = +1$ or -1. The move (k, m) is the formal analog of moving the kth disk (in the order of size) from the top of any pile (or pin) either to the pile to the left or the one to the right, depending on the sign of m. The domain $S_{(k,m)}$ of the function (k, m) is defined as follows.

H5 $\langle (x_{01}, x_{02}, \ldots, x_{0i_0}), (x_{11}, x_{12}, \ldots, x_{1i_1}), (x_{21}, x_{22}, \ldots, x_{2i_2}) \rangle$

is an element of $S_{(k,m)}$ if and only if either $x_{0i_0} = k$ or $x_{1i_1} = k$ or $x_{2i_2} = k$ and if $x_{si_s} = k$, then $k > x_{ti_t}$ where $t = s + m$ (mod 3). The values of the functions are given as follows.

H6   If $s = \langle (x_{01}, x_{02}, \ldots, x_{0i_0}), (x_{11}, x_{12}, \ldots, x_{1i_1}), (x_{21}, x_{22}, \ldots, x_{2i_2}) \rangle$

is in the domain of (k, m) and $k = x_{ji_j}$ ($j = 0, 1, 2$), then

$(k, m)(s) = \langle (x'_{01}, x'_{02}, \ldots, x'_{0i_0'}), (x'_{11}, x'_{12}, \ldots, x'_{1i_1'}), (x'_{21}, x'_{22}, \ldots, x'_{2i_2'}) \rangle$

where $i'_t = i_t - 1$ if $t = j$; $i'_t = i_t + 1$ if $t = j + m$ (mod 3); $i'_t = i_t$ otherwise. Also

$$x'_{ti} = x_{ti} \quad \text{except when } t = j + m \text{ (mod 3) and } i = i'_t;$$

$$x'_{ti_{t'}} = k \quad \text{when } t = j + m \text{ (mod 3)}.$$

H7 T is specified to be the unit set consisting of $\langle \varnothing, (1, 2, \ldots, n), \varnothing \rangle$.

Interest is centered on specifying a winning solution for $\langle (1, 2, \ldots, n), \varnothing, \varnothing \rangle$.

As an example of a solution of the problem when $n = 3$, let us consider the following sequence of moves. The smallest disk is moved to the right pin, the second largest disk is moved to the left pin; the smallest disk is then moved right (from the right to the left pin "around the circle") to the top of the second largest pin. Then the largest disk is moved to the (now empty) right pin, the smallest disk moved right to the original (now empty) pin, the second largest disk is moved left (around the circle) to the top of the largest disk on the right pin, and the smallest disk moved right to the top of the pile.

The exhibition of this sequence of moves is formally equivalent to the statement that when $n = 3$

$$(3, +1), (2, -1), (3, +1), (1, +1), (3, +1), (2, -1), (3, +1)$$

is a solution, since

$(3, +1)((2, -1)((3, +1)((1, +1)((3, +1)((2, -1)((3, +1)$
$$(\langle(1, 2, 3), \varnothing, \varnothing\rangle))))))),$$
$(3, +1)((2, -1)((3, +1)((1, +1)((3, +1)((2, -1)(\langle(1, 2), (3), \varnothing\rangle)))))),$
$(3, +1)((2, -1)((3, +1)((1, +1)((3, +1)(\langle(1), (3), (2)\rangle)))))),$
$(3, +1)((2, -1)((3, +1)((1, +1)(\langle(1), \varnothing, (2, 3)\rangle))))),$
$(3, +1)((2, -1)((3, +1)(\langle\varnothing, (1), (2, 3)\rangle)))),$
$(3, +1)((2, -1)(\langle(3), (1), (2)\rangle))),$
$(3, +1)(\langle(3), (1, 2), \varnothing\rangle),$
$\langle\varnothing, (1, 2, 3), \varnothing\rangle.$

In a later section a winning strategy will be pointed out that yields this winning solution. Meanwhile, the next section formalizes the problem of finding proofs in propositional calculus. For this purpose the Russel–Whitehead version of the propositional calculus will be used, following Simon, Newell, and Shaw [61].

2.5. THE LOGIC THEORIST—ANOTHER EXAMPLE

As an introduction to formalizing the problem of finding proofs in propositional calculus as a W-problem, the exact model used in the Logic Theorist will be discussed here. This example will indicate the motivation for considering W-problems to have a possibly infinite F_0, as has been done in this book.

As in the literature, the alphabet of the propositional calculus will consist of (1) an infinite set of propositional variables, whose members will be denoted by lowercase Latin letters with integral subscripts if necessary; and (2) the symbols (,), $\sim$, $\vee$, and $\rightarrow$.

Well-formed formulas (wffs) are defined in the usual way as follows.

(i) Any propositional variable is a wff.

(ii) If A and B are wffs, then $\sim A$, $(A \vee B)$, $(A \rightarrow B)$ are wffs.

It is understood that A and B are metalinguistic variables standing for wffs. Also, in keeping with the literature, parentheses may be dropped when exhibiting a wff, it being understood that the resulting strings of characters are shorthands for wffs rather than wffs themselves.

A subset of the set of wffs is defined as the set of theorems as follows.

0. The following (called axioms) are theorems.

(i) $((p \lor p) \to p)$;

(ii) $(p \to (q \lor p))$;

(iii) $((p \lor q) \to (q \lor p))$;

(iv) $((p \lor (q \lor r)) \to (q \lor (p \lor r)))$;

(v) $((p \to q) \to ((r \lor p) \to (r \lor q)))$.

1. If $A(p)$ is a theorem in which the specific propositional variable p occurs, and B is any wff, then $A(B)$ is a theorem, where $A(B)$ is obtained from $A(p)$ by replacing every occurrence of p in $A(p)$ by an occurrence of B. This is the usual substitution rule.

2a. If $(\sim A \lor B)$ occurs anywhere in a theorem C, then D, obtained by replacing this occurrence in C by $(A \to B)$, is also a theorem.

2b. If $(A \to B)$ occurs in any theorem C, then D, obtained by replacing this occurrence in C by $(\sim A \lor B)$, is also a theorem. Postulates 2a and 2b are applications of the definition of "implication" in terms of "not" and "or."

3. If $(A \to B)$ is a theorem and A is a theorem, then B is a theorem. (The usual *modus ponens*.)

On the basis of these definitions, we can set up a W-problem as follows to represent the problems of finding the proofs of theorems.

Each situation s is a finite sequence of wffs $(s_1, s_2, \ldots, s_n)$. These wffs stand for the set of theorems proved at a certain stage of the proof procedure.

F_0 consists of four classes of functions, denoted by (i) $(i, A, B, 1)$ where i is an integer, A is a propositional variable, and B is a wff; (ii) $(i, j, 2a)$ where i and j are integers; (iii) $(i, j, 2b)$ where i and j again are integers; and (iv) $(i, j, 3)$ where i and j are integers. These stand for substitution, the "forward" and "backward" application of the definition of implication, and *modus ponens*, respectively. Formally, these functions are defined as follows.

(i) (Substitution) $s = (s_1, s_2, \ldots, s_n)$ is a member of $S_{(i,A,B,1)}$ if and only if $i \leq n$ and the wff s_i contains the propositional variable A. In this case

$$(i, A, B, 1)((s_1, s_2, \ldots, s_n)) = (s_1, s_2, \ldots, s_n, s_{n+1})$$

where s_{n+1} is obtained from s_i by replacing all occurrences of A by B.

(ii) (Definition-Application) $s = (s_1, s_2, \ldots, s_n)$ is a member of $S_{(i,j,2a)}$ if and only if $i \le n$ and there are at least j occurrences of wffs of the form $(\sim A \lor B)$ in s_i. In this case

$$(i, j, 2a)((s_1, s_2, \ldots, s_n) = (s_1, s_2, \ldots, s_n, s_{n+1})$$

where s_{n+1} is obtained by replacing the jth occurrence of $(\sim A \lor B)$ in s_i by $(A \to B)$.

(iii) (Definition-Application) $s = (s_1, s_2, \ldots, s_n)$ is a member of $S_{(i,j2b)}$ if and only if $i \le n$ and there are at least j occurrences of wffs of the form $(A \to B)$ in s_i. In this case

$$(i, j, 2b)((s_1, s_2, \ldots, s_n) = (s_1, s_2, \ldots, s_n, s_{n+1})$$

where s_{n+1} is obtained by replacing the jth occurrence of $(A \to B)$ in s_i by $(\sim A \lor B)$.

(iv) (*Modus Ponens*) $s = (s_1, s_2, \ldots, s_n)$ is a member of $S_{(i,j,3)}$ if and only if $i, j \le n$ and for some wffs A and B, s_i is $(A \to B)$ and s_j is A. In this case

$$(i, j, 3)((s_1, s_2, \ldots, s_n) = (s_1, s_2, \ldots, s_n, s_{n+1})$$

where s_{n+1} is B.

In (ii) and (iii) the occurrences of the sentence of the form $(\sim A \lor B)$ and $(A \to B)$ are ordered by the occurrences of the main connectives of these sentences, reading from left to right. As an example, in the wff

$$C = ((\sim(\sim a \lor (a \to b)) \lor (c \to (\sim d \lor e))) \to f)$$

the first occurrence of a wff of the form $(\sim A \lor B)$ is $(\sim a \lor (a \to b))$; the second occurrence is $(\sim(\sim a \lor (a \to b)) \lor (c \to (\sim d \lor e)))$; the third is $(\sim d \lor e)$. Similarly, the first occurrence of a sentence of the form $(A \to B)$ is $(a \to b)$; the second is $(c \to (\sim d \lor e))$; the third is C itself. Hence, if the situation s consists of the single element C, then

$$(1, 2, 2a)(s) = (((\sim(\sim a \lor (a \to b)) \lor (c \to (\sim d \lor e))) \to f),$$
$$((((\sim a \lor (a \to b)) \to (c \to (\sim d \lor e))) \to f))$$

while

$$(1, 3, 2b)(s) = (((\sim(\sim a \lor (a \to b)) \lor (c \to (\sim d \lor e))) \to f),$$
$$(\sim(\sim(\sim a \lor (a \to b)) \lor (c \to (\sim d \lor e))) \lor f)).$$

Finding a proof of B from the suppositions $A_1, A_2, \ldots, A_k$ (i.e., showing $A_1, A_2, \ldots, A_k \vdash B$) would correspond to the following W-problem. The term s_0 represents the sequence $(A_1, A_2, \ldots, A_k, X_1, X_2, \ldots, X_5)$ where $X_1, X_2, \ldots, X_5$ are the five axioms; T consists of the set of all sequences of wffs containing B. A winning solution would be a sequence $f_1, f_2, \ldots, f_n$ of functions such that the sequence

$$f_n(f_{n-1}(\ldots f_1((A_1, A_2, \ldots, A_k, X_1, X_2, \ldots, X_5))\ldots) \in T.$$

As an example, the winning solution of the W-problem corresponding to a proof of $((p \to \sim p) \to \sim p)$ from the axioms $(\vdash((p \to \sim p) \to \sim p))$ would be the sequence

$$(1, p, \sim p, 1), (6, 1, \text{2a}).$$

This can be seen as follows.

$$(6, 1, \text{2a})((1, p, \sim p, 1)((((p \lor p) \to p), (p \to (q \lor p)),$$
$$((p \lor q) \to (q \lor p)), ((p \lor (q \lor r)) \to (q \lor (p \lor r))),$$
$$((p \to q) \to ((r \lor p) \to (r \lor q))))))$$
$$= (6, 1, \text{2a})((((p \lor p) \to p), (p \to (q \lor p)), ((p \lor q) \to (q \lor p)),$$
$$((p \lor (q \lor r)) \to (q \lor (p \lor r))), ((p \to q) \to ((r \lor p) \to (r \lor q))),$$
$$((\sim p \lor \sim p) \to \sim p)))$$
$$= (((p \lor p) \to p), (p \to (q \lor p)), ((p \lor q) \to (q \lor p)),$$
$$((p \lor (q \lor r)) \to (q \lor (p \lor r))), ((p \to q) \to ((r \lor p) \to (r \lor q))),$$
$$((\sim p \lor \sim p) \to \sim p), ((p \to \sim p) \to \sim p)).$$

The last sequence contains the theorem to be proved as its last element.

It is to be noted that in the derivation above, the parentheses have been used with two purposes. One is the syntactic purpose as used to define well-formed formulas. The other is the usual mathematical use, in the enclosing of the argument of a function or the name of a function like $(1, 3, \text{2b})$. The latter use is metalinguistic here.

Two examples have been given, in this section and the previous one, of the representation of two problems as W-problems. In the next few sections various properties of winning strategies are discussed.

2.6. STRATEGIES AND THEIR DESCRIPTION

It is clear from the discussion in Section 2.3 that the solution for a W-problem can be found if a winning W-strategy is known. The idea of a strategy has been inherent in many works in artificial intelligence. However, the mere giving of a precise form to this idea does not shed any light on the basic question, "How is a winning strategy to be found?" In later sections various devices are suggested for the finding of strategies. Of course, these devices in their turn require the knowledge of other functions or sets. These functions, again, will have to be "found" for any given problem we are faced with. They are introduced in the hope that some of them will prove easier to deduce from the description of the problem or from "experience."

In this section attention is given to a different, though no less crucial, problem. "Even when we know a strategy, how can we make sure that it is easy to implement?" That is, in what form is a strategy to be represented in memory? Evidently, the strategy cannot be stored as a huge set of ordered pairs. It is essential that a small set of tests be specified to the computer. The value of the strategy for a situation (the control to be chosen) is determined on the basis of these tests. As can be seen from our discussion in Section 1.3, this is essentially a problem of description of sets. The details of the latter subject can only be discussed in a later chapter. For the present it is assumed only that some subsets of S are "easier" to describe than others. It is also assumed on the basis of the discussion in Chapter 1 that it is of use to be able to find a common description for all situations in S that yield the same value of the strategy.

Given a strategy Q, we can define the following relation E on $\bigcup_{f \in F_0} S_f - T$.

$$(s_1, s_2) \in E \quad \text{if and only if} \quad Q(s_1) = Q(s_2).$$

Clearly, this relation is an equivalence relation. This relation is precisely the relation $Q \circ Q^{-1}$ (the composition of Q with its inverse relation) and hence will be called the *kernel* of the strategy Q, following algebraic terminology [18].

The kernel of a strategy partitions the set $\bigcup_{f \in F_0} S_f - T$ into disjoint subsets called its equivalence classes. For a strategy to be practicable, each subset in this partition should be easily describable. For future purposes, the symbol $Q^{-1}(f)$ will be used to denote the set of all points s such that $Q(s) = f$. This, again, is standard algebraic notation. It follows immediately from definitions that

$$f_1 \neq f_2 \quad \text{implies} \quad Q^{-1}(f_1) \cap Q^{-1}(f_2) = \varnothing$$

and

$$\bigcup_{f \in F_0} Q^{-1}(f) = \bigcup_{f \in F_0} S_f - T,$$

establishing that the sets $\{Q^{-1}(f)\}$ are precisely the equivalence classes of $Q \circ Q^{-1}$.

A particularly easy description for these sets exists for the Tower of Hanoi problem. This is now set down as an example.

It will be recalled that in the Tower of Hanoi problem of Section 2.4, a situation consists of a sequence $\langle s_1, s_2, s_3 \rangle$ where each s_i $(i = 1, 2, 3)$ is a sequence of integers with certain properties. It will also be recalled that the controls are denoted by ordered pairs (k, m) where k is an integer and $m = \pm 1$. The domain $S_{(k,m)}$ of (k, m) has been previously defined. Also, it has been pointed out that there are n elements in the union of s_1, s_2, s_3, considered as sets. We now define a strategy Q:

$$Q(s) = (k, (-1)^{k+1})$$

if and only if

    (i) $s \neq \langle \varnothing, (1, 2, 3, \ldots, n), \varnothing \rangle$, and

    (ii) $s \in S_{(k,(-1)^{k+1})}$ and

    (iii) $s \notin S_{(i,(-1)^{i+1})}$ for any $i > k$.

Since in the case of the Tower of Hanoi $\bigcup_{f \in F} S_f = S$, the domain of Q ought to be $S - T$, which it is, by condition (i) above. Condition (ii) assures us that the strategy always chooses an applicable move. That Q is indeed a winning strategy for $s_0 = \langle (1, 2, 3, \ldots, n), \varnothing, \varnothing \rangle$ can be verified, in the case of $n = 3$, as follows.

$$Q(\langle (1, 2, 3), \varnothing, \varnothing \rangle) = (3, +1)$$

and

$$(3, +1)(\langle (1, 2, 3), \varnothing, \varnothing \rangle) = \langle (1, 2), (3), \varnothing \rangle.$$
$$Q(\langle (1, 2), (3), \varnothing \rangle) = (2, -1)$$

and

$$(2, -1)(\langle (1, 2), (3), \varnothing \rangle) = \langle (1), (3), (2) \rangle.$$
$$Q(\langle (1), (3), (2) \rangle) = (3, +1)$$

and

$$(3, +1)(\langle (1), (3), (2) \rangle) = \langle (1), \varnothing, (2, 3) \rangle.$$
$$Q(\langle (1), \varnothing, (2, 3) \rangle) = (1, +1)$$

and

$$(1, +1)(\langle (1), \varnothing, (2, 3) \rangle) = \langle \varnothing, (1), (2, 3) \rangle.$$
$$Q(\langle \varnothing, (1), (2, 3) \rangle) = (3, +1)$$

and

$$(3, +1)(\langle \varnothing, (1), (2, 3) \rangle) = \langle (3), (1), (2) \rangle.$$
$$Q(\langle (3), (1), (2) \rangle) = (2, -1)$$

and

$$(2, -1)(\langle (3), (1), (2) \rangle) = \langle (3), (1, 2), \varnothing \rangle.$$
$$Q(\langle (3), (1, 2), \varnothing \rangle) = (3, +1)$$

and

$$(3, +1)(\langle (3), (1, 2), \varnothing \rangle) = \langle \varnothing, (1, 2, 3), \varnothing \rangle.$$

The last situation is a winning situation. It will be noticed that the strategy Q has yielded the same solution as was exemplified in Section 2.4.

It can be shown by induction that Q is indeed the winning strategy for $(\langle(1, 2, \ldots, n), \varnothing, \varnothing \rangle)$ for all n. This will be indicated when the concept of subgoals is discussed later. It may be pointed out that Q is the winning strategy for all situations. For some situations, however, it may not yield the "shortest" solution in the sense that for these situations we can find shorter sequences of controls as solutions by violating the strategy Q. There are, again, other strategies for the Tower of Hanoi that are winning strategies only for some situations. There are others that yield the shortest solution for all situations. At present, it is not proposed to discuss these various strategies. It is, however, worthwhile to stress at this point that the strategy Q discussed here has been defined mostly in terms of statements that are needed for describing the problem itself. Only the concept of taking the powers of -1 was not a part of the concepts used in the description of the rules of the game. The others (the descriptions of $S_{(k,m)}$ and the concept of one integer being less than another) were inherent in the description of the problem. Free use was also made of logical quantification in defining the strategy but this was also used in the description of the problem. The significance of these facts has been touched upon in Chapter 1 and will be discussed again after the basis for description languages and their use in problem solving has been made clearer.

We conclude the present section by pointing out an important consideration regarding the search for a practicable strategy. In many real problems winning solutions are needed not for all possible situations, but for only a few situations. By the Marino theorem and Theorem 2.3, there is a winning strategy for the set of all situations for which a winning solution exists. However, it may be more advantageous to find a less "ambitious" strategy; one that is a winning strategy not for all possible situations but only for those situations for which a solution is needed. This will be clarified through a theorem. To introduce the theorem we need the following definition.

Given any subset $S_1 \subseteq T'$ let $\mathscr{P}(S_1)$ denote the set of all strategies that are winning strategies for every element of S_1: that is, $Q \in \mathscr{P}(S_1)$ if and only if for every $s \in S_1$, Q is a winning strategy for s.

THEOREM 2.4.   *If* $S_1 \subseteq S_2 \subseteq T'$, *then* $\mathscr{P}(S_1) \supseteq \mathscr{P}(S_2) \neq \varnothing$.

PROOF.   Let $Q \in \mathscr{P}(S_2)$. Then Q is a winning strategy for all elements of S_2. Since each element of S_1 is an element of S_2, Q is a winning strategy for every element of S_1. That is, $P \in \mathscr{P}(S_1)$.

That $\mathscr{P}(S_2) \neq \varnothing$ follows from Theorem 2.1, which states that $\mathscr{P}(T') \neq \varnothing$ and that $\mathscr{P}(S_2) \supseteq \mathscr{P}(T')$. ∎

The theorem gives us no assurance that if S_1 is a proper subset of S_2, then $\mathscr{P}(S_2)$ is a proper subset of $\mathscr{P}(S_1)$. This is in general not true, either. There are, however, many cases where choosing a proper subset of a set of situations yields a larger set of available winning strategies.

Let there be some evaluation function that associates with every subset of S a number that yields the "ease" with which it can be described. Then with each strategy Q we can associate a set of numbers each corresponding to the ease with which an equivalence class of its kernel $(Q \circ Q^{-1})$ can be described. The minimum of these numbers can be used as a measure of the "ease" with which Q can be used (this corresponds to the equivalence class of $Q \circ Q^{-1}$ "hardest" to describe). Associated with each subset S_1 of T', then, is a set of numbers, corresponding to the ease with which each strategy in $\mathscr{P}(S_1)$ can be used. Let the maximum of these be denoted by $E(S_1)$ (corresponding to the "easiest" possible strategy). Since, by Theorem 2.4 $S_1 \subseteq S_2$ implies $\mathscr{P}(S_2) \subseteq \mathscr{P}(S_1)$, it is not hard to see that $S_1 \subseteq S_2$ implies $E(S_1) \geq E(S_2)$. If it is required to find the best winning strategy only for all elements of S_1, it never increases the ease of applying the strategy by choosing one that is the best winning strategy for a set larger than S_1.

The foregoing gives plausible arguments for restricting one's ambition to find a winning strategy for the smallest set of situations one can "get away with." The arguments certainly are not rigorous. It has been assumed that all sets of numbers have maxima. It has been assumed that "ease" can be measured by numbers or at least by a linearly ordered set. It might be interesting to investigate the effect of relaxing these assumptions on the validity of the arguments. This will not be attempted here.

The ease of describing a strategy is only one of the problems associated with the concept of strategies. There still remains the problem of finding a strategy. In the following sections it will be pointed out that a winning strategy Q can be found if certain subsets of S (other than the equivalence classes of $Q \circ Q^{-1}$) can be easily described.

2.7. EVALUATIONS: A METHOD FOR DEFINING STRATEGIES

All the discussions thus far in this chapter lead to one important conclusion: "In a W-problem, a winning solution for s_0 can be found if we know the description of the equivalence classes of the kernel of some winning strategy for s_0." In the rest of this chapter, some similar statements are made and proved where the words "the equivalence classes of the kernel of some winning strategy for s_0," are replaced by the names of other classes of sets. A posteriori, these also yield methods for constructing winning strategies for s_0, and these constructions are discussed. The problem, "Given the definition of a class of sets, how does one construct their description?" is not discussed till after Chapter 3. Unfortunately, even there the discussion will have to be sketchy, and based on a single example.

A class of sets that readily comes to mind arises from our desire to know how "far" a situation is from the "nearest" winning situation. "Distance" may be defined as: "A situation s is at a distance i from the set of winning situations if there exists a winning solution for s of length i and if there is no winning solution of length less than i." If we denote by T_i the set of all situations at a distance i from the set winning situations, then we can construct the following alternative formal definition.

Let there be an enumerable class of sets defined as follows.

$$T_0 = T$$

and for all $i \geq 0$

$$T_{i+1} = \left\{ s \mid s \notin \bigcup_{k=0}^{i} T_k \text{ and } (\exists f)(f \in F_0 \text{ and } f(s) \in T_i) \right\}.$$

In words, a situation is in T_{i+1} if and only if there is a control that moves the situation to one in T_i and no control that moves it any "closer" to a winning situation.

It is clear from the definition that $i \neq j$ implies $T_i \cap T_j = \varnothing$. For assuming (without loss of generality) that $j < i$, we can obtain from the definition $T_i \subseteq S - \bigcup_{k<i} T_k \subseteq S - T_j$ if $j < i$.

The following theorem is evident from the initial definition of distance. However, the recursive definition, though easier to manipulate formally, is less transparent; it is therefore worthwhile to indicate the equivalence of the two definitions by proving the theorem.

THEOREM 2.5.   *In a W-problem $s_0 \in \bigcup T_k$ if and only if $s_0 \in T$ or a winning solution exists for s_0. That is,*

$$\bigcup_{k=1}^{\infty} T_k = T'.$$

PROOF.   We note initially that $s \notin \bigcup_{k=0}^{i} T_k$ and $(\exists f)(f \in F_0 \text{ and } f(s) \in T_i)$ implies $s \in T_{i+1}$ or

$$(\exists f)(f \in F_0 \text{ and } f(s) \in T_i) \rightarrow \left(\left(s \notin \bigcup_{k=0}^{i} T_k \right) \rightarrow s \in T_{i+1} \right)$$

or

$$(\exists f)(f \in F_0 \text{ and } f(s) \in T_i) \rightarrow \left(s \in \bigcup_{k=0}^{i} T_k \text{ or } s \in T_{i+1} \right)$$

or

$$(\exists f)(f \in F_0 \text{ and } f(s) \in T_i) \rightarrow s \in \bigcup_{k=0}^{i+1} T_k,$$

from which we obtain

$$(\exists f)\left(f \in F_0 \text{ and } f(s) \in \bigcup_{k=0}^{i} T_k \right) \rightarrow s \in \bigcup_{k=0}^{i+1} T_k.$$

We now prove by induction the following (yielding a stronger statement than the "if" part of the theorem).

If

$$f_n(f_{n-1}(\cdots f_1(s_0) \cdots)) \in T \qquad \text{then} \qquad s_0 \in \bigcup_{i=0}^{n} T_i.$$

For $n = 1$ we obtain $f_1(s) \in T = T_0$ yields $s \in \bigcup_{k=0}^{i} T_k$.

Let the theorem be true for $n = i$; that is, assume $f_i(f_{i-1}(\cdots f_1(s_0) \cdots)) \in T$ yields $s_0 \in \bigcup_{k=0}^{i} T_k$. Let $f_{i+1}(f_i(\cdots (f_1(s_0) \cdots)) \in T$ consider $f_1(s_0) = s_1$. We have

$$f_{i+1}(f_i(\cdots f_2(s_1) \cdots)) \in T,$$

yielding by induction hypothesis $s_1 \in \bigcup_{k=0}^{i} T_k$. Since $f_1(s_0) = s_1 \in \bigcup_{k=0}^{i} T_k$,

$$s_0 \in \bigcup_{k=0}^{i+1} T_k,$$

proving the theorem for all n.

To prove the converse, let $s_0 \in \bigcup_i T_i$. Then there exists an n such that $s_0 \in T_n$. The proof will be by induction on n, as before that either $n = 0$, or there exists a sequence $f_1 \cdots f_n$ of function F_0 such that $f_1(f_2(\cdots f_n(s_0)) \in T$. Let $n = 1$, then by definition there exists $f_1 \in F_0$ such that $f_1(s_0) \in T$.

Assume as induction hypothesis that if $s_i \in T_i$, then for some $f_1, \ldots, f_i$

$$f_1(f_2(\cdots f_i(s_0) \cdots)) \in T.$$

Let $s_0 \in T_{i+1}$. Let $f_{i+1}(s_0) \in T_i$; hence, there exists a sequence of functions $f_1 \cdots f_i$ such that

$$f_1(f_2(\cdots f_i(f_{i+1}(s_0) \cdots)) \in T,$$

proving the theorem for all n. ∎

The class of sets $\{T_i\}$ will be called *evaluations*.

A strategy Q will be called an *evaluating strategy* if and only if

$$s \in T_i \quad \text{implies} \quad Q(s)(s) \in T_{i-1}.$$

The following theorem is a special case of Theorem 2.1, relevant to W-problems and hence to problemlike M-situations.

THEOREM 2.6.   *An evaluating strategy is a winning strategy for every member of* $\bigcup_{i>0} T_i$.

PROOF.   Let $s \in \bigcup_{i>0} T_i$; then for some n, $s \in T_n$, $n > 0$.

If $n = 1$, then $Q(s)(s) \in T$, showing that Q is a winning strategy for T_1.
Let Q be a winning strategy for all $s \in T_i$. Let $s \in T_{i+1}$, then by definition of Q

$$Q(s)(s) \in T_i.$$

Since Q is a winning strategy for T_i, there exists a sequence $f_1, f_2, \ldots, f_i$ such that $f_i(f_{i-1} \cdots f_1(Q(s)(s)) \cdots) \in T$; and

$$f_k = Q(f_{k-1}(\cdots f_1(Q(s)(s)) \cdots)) \qquad \text{for each } k \leq i.$$

Hence, Q is a winning strategy for s.   ∎

The next theorem shows that we can make the statement, "If there is more than one evaluating strategy, then it is unnecessary to use any one of them consistently to arrive at a solution." Formally, it can be stated as follows.

THEOREM 2.7.   *Let* $\{S_\alpha\}$ *be a partition of* $\bigcup_{f \in F_0} S_f - T$. *Let* $\{Q_\beta\}$ *be a set of evaluating strategies. Let* $K: \{S_\alpha\} \to \{Q_\beta\}$ *associate a strategy with each class of the partition. Denote by* $K(S_\alpha)/S_\alpha$ *the restriction of* $K(S_\alpha)$ *to* S_α. *Then* $\bigcup_\alpha K(S_\alpha)/S_\alpha$ *is an evaluating strategy.*

PROOF.   Let $s \in S_\alpha$. Then $(\bigcup_\alpha K(S_\alpha)/S_\alpha)(s) = K(S_\alpha)(s)$. If $s \in T_i$, then, since $K(S_\alpha)$ is an evaluating strategy, $K(S_\alpha)(s)(s) \in T_{i-1}$. Hence, for all $s \in T_i$,

$$\bigcup_\alpha K(S_\alpha)/S_\alpha(s)(s) \in T_{i-1},$$

proving $\bigcup_\alpha K(S_\alpha)/S_\alpha$ is an evaluating strategy. That the domain of

$$\bigcup_\alpha K(S_\alpha)/S_\alpha$$

is as required for a strategy follows for the definition of $\{S_\alpha\}$.   ∎

In view of this theorem, it is now not necessary to know the description of the equivalence classes of the kernel of a specific evaluating strategy to apply it. All we need to know is that some evaluating strategy is being applied. To assure ourselves of that, we need to know the descriptions of the sets T_i instead. Knowing these descriptions, we can find a winning solution for s by finding out that $s \in T_i$ and obtaining control $f \in F_0$ such that $f(s) \in T_{i-1}$. If F_0 is a tractably small set, this can be done by enumeration. The resulting sequence of applications of controls will be according to some winning strategy and yield a solution. If F_0 be infinite, there is no claim that this method of constructing winning situations is in any way realistic.

If F_0 be finite, an evaluating strategy may be applied even without specific knowledge of all the T_i. Supposing that subsets of $S \times S$ can be described as easily in a description language as classes of subsets of S, we can define the following relation on S.

Let $G \subseteq T' \times T'$ have the property that $(s_1, s_2) \in G$ if and only if $s_1 \in T_i$ implies $s_2 \in T_{i-1}$.

If G is describable, that is, if given two elements of S, we can recognize whether they are related by G, then we can define an evaluating class of strategies as follows.

Let a strategy $Q \colon (\bigcup_{f \in F_0} S_f - T) \to F_0$ have the property that $Q(s) = f$ implies $(s, f(s)) \in G$. Clearly, such a strategy is an evaluating strategy. It should also be pointed out that the class of all relations G having the property described above is quite rich. It may, thus, be more reasonable to demand that one relation in this class be describable than to demand that an entire class $\{T_i\}$ of subsets of S be describable.

2.8. STRATEGIES BASED ON T'

The construction of evaluating strategies depends strongly on the availability of the description of each set T_i in an evaluation. In some special cases, it may be possible to develop a strategy with a much smaller repertoire of descriptions. In what follows a method for strategy construction will be discussed that merely needs a description of T'.

Given a W-problem $\langle S, F_0, T \rangle$ we can define a relation K' on S as

$$aK'b \text{ if and only if for some } f \in F_0, \, b = f(a).$$

Let K be the transitive closure of K'; K has the property that if aKb, then we can change situation a to situation b by the successive applications of controls.

A W-problem will be called *progressively finite* if and only if

F1 K is irreflexive; that is, no situation s is such that sKs (no "looping" is possible).

F2 There is no infinite chain $s_1, s_2, s_3, \ldots$ such that for each i $s_i K s_{i+1}$.

F1 says in effect that each action taken on the way to solving a problem is "irrevocable." In a way this is a very comforting situation, since no matter how "blindly" we apply controls, we never get "caught in a loop."

F2 essentially says that the process of applying controls always reaches a "dead end." This prevents our "going on forever" on an "open-ended path."

Neither the Tower of Hanoi problems nor the propositional calculus described in Section 2.4 is progressively finite. There will be occasion to exemplify the analogs of progressively finite problems in the next chapter, when the game of nim is discussed. For the present only some formal properties of progressively finite problems will be discussed.

The relation K, being irreflexive and transitive, is necessarily antisymmetric. That is, it has the two essential properties of a partial order. Every chain in this order, being finite, has a lower bound. Hence, the set of situations have a set of minimal elements.

The most useful thing about progressively finite W-problems is that a description of T' and (as a part of the problem specification) T is all that is needed to construct a winning strategy. To see this, we can define the following kind of strategy.

A strategy $Q: \bigcup_{f \in F_0} S_f - T \to F_0$ is called *cautious* if and only if

$$s \in T' \quad \text{implies} \quad Q(s)(s) \in T' \cup T.$$

Evidently, since every evaluating strategy is a cautious strategy, cautious strategies exist. However, the important thing to note is that every cautious strategy is a winning strategy, whether it is an evaluating strategy or not, as long as the problem is progressively finite. This can be seen in terms of the two following theorems.

THEOREM 2.8.   *Let P be a progressively finite W-problem. Let S_0 be the set of minimal elements of K. Then $S_0 - T \subseteq S - T'$.*

PROOF. $s \in S_0$ if and only if there is no $f \in F_0$ and no $s' \in S$ such that $f(s) = s'$. Hence,

$$S_0 = S - \bigcup_{f \in F_0} S_f.$$

This leads to

$$S - T' \supseteq S - \bigcup_{f \in F_0} S_f \supseteq S - \bigcup_{f \in F_0} S_f - T = S_0 - T. \quad \blacksquare$$

THEOREM 2.9.   *In a progressively finite W-problem every cautious strategy is a winning strategy for every element of T'.*

PROOF.   Let $s \in T'$ and Q a cautious strategy. Define a sequence $\{s_i\}$ of situations as follows.

$$s_0 = s;$$
$$s_{i+1} = Q(s_i)(s_i) \qquad \text{for all } i.$$

It is clear from the definition that for all i, $s_i K s_{i+1}$. Hence, the sequence $\{s_i\}$ is finite. Let s_t be the minimal element of this chain.

If $s_i \in T$ for some $i \leq t$, then the sequence $Q(s_0), Q(s_1) \cdots Q(s_{i-1})$ is a winning sequence showing that Q is a winning strategy for s_0. If $s_i \notin T$ for all $i \leq t$, then, since Q is a cautious strategy, $s_i \in T'$ for all $i \leq t$. Hence, $s_t \in T'$ in particular. However, $s_t \in S_0$, being a minimal element of K. Also, $s_t \notin T$, whence $s_t \in S_0 - T \subseteq S - T'$ by Theorem 2.7, which contradicts $s_t \in T'$.   ∎

It can be stated in a way analogous to the discussion at the end of the last section that for applying a cautious strategy, the description of the equivalence classes of its kernel need not be known. If we have a situation $s \in T'$ and choose $f \in F_0$ such that $f(s) \in T'$, we know that some cautious strategy is being applied. To prove this rigorously we would have to prove an analog of Theorem 2.7. This appears straightforward and need not be belabored here. Indeed, some may even argue that all this "rigorous rigmarole" (even if it is considered rigorous, there are many small points slurred over in the discussion) does not yield any results that could not be gleaned intuitively. Indeed, most rigorous discussions often take place only after some intuitive basis for them have been suggested. However, rigor has the advantage that through it we can clearly see the conditions under which the intuitively obtained results are valid. This gives a clearer insight into how an intuitively feasible operation may be improved when it is found to be unusable in reality. In our discussion of the general problem solver in the next section some of the possible reasons for the occasional failures of the GPS are discussed formally.

2.9.   STRATEGIES BASED ON SUBGOALS—THE GENERAL PROBLEM SOLVER

To discuss methods based on subgoals, it will be necessary to discuss evaluations based on sets other than T. One of the subgoal types used in the GPS [19] is "Apply operator f to situation s." This is a trivial operation if $s \in S_f$. Otherwise, we set up the subgoal "Transform s so that f can be applied." This is equivalent to solving a new problem, with S and F_0 the same as before but with T replaced by S_f. Any solution for this new problem may be discussed in terms of evaluations. It is probably not essential to use the idea of evaluations. At the present level of the author's understanding, however, any concept more general than evaluations is apt to be hard to handle. Moreover, workers using the idea of subgoals often have the idea of "reducing differences" implicitly in their argument. So the use of evaluation as a cornerstone of the theory of subgoals will probably not be an inherent limitation on the way workers in the field interpret the term "subgoals."

Given a W-problem and a subset $X \subseteq S$, we define a class of sets X_i as follows.

$$X_0 = X$$

and for all $i > 0$

$$X_{i+1} = \left\{ s \mid s \notin \bigcup_{k=0}^{i} X_k \text{ and } (\exists f)(f \in F_0 \text{ and } f(s) \in X_i) \right\}.$$

As in Section 2.7, we will denote $\bigcup_{i>0} X_i$ by X'.

We now define a set of subsets $(S_{fX})_{f \in F_0}$ of X', indexed by F_0, as: $s \in S_{fX}$ iff for some $i > 0$ $s \in X_i$ and $f(s) \in X_{i-1}$. The $(S_{fX})_{f \in F_0}$ are not necessarily pairwise disjoint. However, $\bigcup_{f \in F_0} S_{fX} = X'$. The class of sets $(S_{fX})_{f \in F_0}$ is a cover, rather than a partition on X'.

The GPS sets up the goal "Apply operator f to situation s" in view of the recognition of certain differences between the winning set (either T or S_g for some $g \in F_0$) and the "present situation." The extraction of this difference does not assure that $s \in S_f$. For the purposes of the present discussion the set S_{fX}^0 will denote the set of all situations s such that if the subproblem is "transform s to X," then the subgoal "apply f to s" will be set up.

Although the GPS is a scheme for directed search for a solution, we can envisage "difference tables" in the GPS that give rise to minimum search. A GPS-like algorithm is quoted late in this section that would be effective on such an optimal decision table. Our main purpose in this section is to set up certain conditions on the structure of the difference table (the sets S_{fX}^0) that are sufficient for the successful convergence of that algorithm. The sufficiency is exhibited with a series of lemmata. Later on there will be occasion to discuss how we can make modifications of the given algorithms to an exact replica of the GPS. It will be indicated how the convergence can be assured even for a slight relaxation of the axioms on S_{fX}^0. The axioms regarding the sets S_{fX}^0 will make explicit certain assumptions that are either tacitly made or hoped for in literature about the difference tables. It is considered useful to bring these "out in the open."

2. PROBLEMS AND SOLUTION METHODS

We assume initially, of course, that the difference table is such that if a situation can be transformed into a winning situation, the difference table will indicate some transformation for it. This is reflected later in axioms D1 and D3. Also, if a certain transformation is indicated, then if the transformation is applicable, the "distance" between the situation and the winning states is actually reduced. This is indicated in D2. This reduction may be considered inessential and it may be possible to prove convergence for a more relaxed condition: for the present this assumption is made as one of a set of sufficient condition only. D4, another important assumption (which, perhaps, may also be relaxed), indicates that if the application of a certain transformation f is indicated, then any other transformation used for making f applicable does not carry the situation away from the winning set.

One reason for setting up the assumptions formally is to indicate that the convergence of the GPS is difficult to assure intuitively. Hence, if relaxed assumptions are envisaged on intuitive grounds, the proof of the convergence of GPS will have to be carried out with a certain standard of rigor.

We concentrate on the following class of sets.

$$D = \{T\} \cup \{S_f \mid f \in F_0\}.$$

A class of sets $\{S^0_{fX} \mid f \in F_0, X \in D\}$ is now defined with the following properties.

D1   For each set $X \in D$, $X' = \bigcup_{f \in F_0} S^0_{fX}$.

D2 $S^0_{fX} \neq \varnothing$ implies $\varnothing \neq S^0_{fX} \cap S_f \subseteq S_{fX}$ for each $f \in F_0$, $X \in D$.

D3 $S^0_{fX} - S_f \subseteq \bigcup_{g \in F_0} S^0_{gsf}$.

D4 $s \in (S^0_{fX} - S_f) \cap X_i$, and $s \in S_g$ implies $g(s) \in S^0_{fX} \cap X_j$ where $j \leq i$.

An algorithm modeling the GPS (together with suggestions for making the model more realistic) will be given presently. Meanwhile, the following lemmata indicate some consequences of axioms D1–D4.

LEMMA 2.1.

$$S^0_{fS_f} = \varnothing.$$

PROOF. $S^\circ_{fS} \cap S_f \subseteq S_{fS_f}$ by D2. Hence, intersecting both sides with S_f, we have

$$S^0_{fS_f} \cap S_f \subseteq S_{fS_f} \cap S_f.$$

However, by definition $S_{fS_f} \subseteq S'_f$ and $S'_f \cap S_f = \varnothing$. Hence, $S^0_{fS_f} \cap S_f = \varnothing$. Contrapositive of D2 yields $S^0_{fS_f} = \varnothing$.   ∎

Given an element $s \in T'$, we can set up a sequence $\{X^i(s)\}$ of elements of D (called a *difference sequence*) as follows.

$$X^0(s) = T.$$

Since $s \in T'$ there is an element $f \in F_0$ such that $s \in S^0_{f X^0(s)}$ by D1; $X^1(s)$ is defined to be S_f. For all $i \geq 1$, $X^{i+1}(s)$ is defined if and only if $s \notin X^i(s)$. In this case $s \in S^0_{f X^{i-1}(s)} - X^i(s)$ where $X^i(s) = S_f$ for some $f \in F_0$. By D3 there exists a $g \in F_0$ such that $s \in S^0_{g X^i(s)}$. $X^{i+1}(s)$ is then defined to be S_g. Clearly, $g \neq f$, since in this case $s \in S^0_{f S_f}$, which contradicts Lemma 2.1.

A difference sequence is said to *end* at i if $X^{i+1}(s)$ is undefined.

Lemma 2.1 indicates that in any difference sequence two consecutive elements are never the same. The following lemma paves the way to a much stronger statement about difference sequences.

LEMMA 2.2.   *If $\{X^i(s)\}$ is a difference sequence where $X^j(s) = X^k(s)(j > k)$, then $\{Y^i(s)\}$ is also a difference sequence, where*

$$Y^i(s) = X^i(s) \quad \text{for } i \leq k,$$
$$Y^i(s) = X^{(i-k)+j}(s) \quad \text{for } i > k. \quad \blacksquare$$

The proof is left to the reader. It is also left to the reader to convince himself that on the basis of this lemma we can establish the existence of a difference sequence all of whose elements are distinct. If F_0 is finite, this would indicate the following.

PROPOSITION 2.1.   If F_0 is finite, then there exists an integer N such that for each $s \in T'$ there exists a difference sequence that ends at some $n \leq N$. $\blacksquare$

Instead of an assumption on the finiteness of F_0, we make the following much stronger assumption.

D5   There is an integer N such that for each $s \in T'$, all difference sequences end at some $n \leq N$.

On the basis of this stronger axiom, we can readily assert the following lemma, stronger than Lemmata 2.1 and 2.2.

LEMMA 2.3.   *In any difference sequence, all the elements are distinct.* $\blacksquare$

The proof follows trivially from the fact that if two elements $X^i(s)$ and $X^j(s)$ are the same, then the subsequence from $X^i(s)$ to $X^{j-1}(s)$ can be repeated an arbitrary number of times in a difference sequence, contradicting D5.

D5 was included among the axioms mainly to ensure the convergence of the algorithm to be indicated shortly. As will be pointed out later, the weaker statement in Proposition 2.1 is probably sufficient for a modified algorithm. Meanwhile, the following theorem, based on D1–D5 inclusive, indicates the convergence of the present algorithm.

THEOREM 2.10. *Let $s \in T'$ and $(T, S_{g_1}, S_{g_2}, \ldots)$ be a difference sequence for s. Then for all i, either $s \in S_{g_i}$ or there is a finite sequence $h_1, h_2, \ldots, h_r(h_j \in F_0)$ such that $h_r(h_{r-1}(\cdots h_1(s)) \cdots) \in S^0_{g_i S_{g_{i-1}}} \cap S_{g_i}$.*

PROOF. By D5, the sequence ends at some $i = n \leq N$. If $i = N$, then $s \in S_{g_i}$ and the theorem is true.

Let the theorem be true for $i = k$; $s \in S^0_{g_{k-1} S_{g_{k-2}}}$ by definition. If $s \in S_{g_{k-1}}$, there is nothing to prove. Otherwise, recall that $s \in S^0_{g_k S_{g_{k-1}}}$ by definition of difference sequence. Hence, by D1, $s \in (S_{g_{k-1}})'$. Let $s \in (S_{g_{k-1}})_p$. Then by induction hypothesis either $s \in S_{g_k}$, whence by D2, $s \in S_{g_k S_{g_{k-1}}}$ and hence, $g_k(s) \in (S_{g_{k-1}})_{p-1}$. Otherwise, there exists a sequence $h_1, h_2, \ldots, h_r$ such that $h_r(h_{r-1}(\cdots h_1(s) \cdots) \in S_{g_k}$. Also, by D4, for each $j \leq r$, $h_j(h_{j-1} \cdots h_1(s) \cdots) \in S^0_{g_k S_{g_{k-1}}} \cap (S_{g_{k-1}})_q$ for $q \leq p$. If for some j, $h_j(h_{j-1}(\cdots h_1(s) \cdots) \in S_{g_{k-1}}$, the proof is complete. Otherwise, let $h_r(h_{r-1}(\cdots h_1(s) \cdots) \in (S_{g_{k-1}})_q$. Then by D4 and D2 again $g_k(h_r(h_{r-1}(\cdots h_1(s) \cdots) \in (S_{g_{k-1}})_{q-1}$. Since $q - 1$ is strictly smaller than p, a finite number of repetitions of the process will yield a situation in $S^0_{g_{k-1} S_{g_{k-2}}} \cap S_{g_{k-1}}$. ∎

We can now state the basic result of this section. Let $s_0 \in T'$. By considering Theorem 2.10 we can see that if all the elements of a class of sets

$$\{S^0_{fX} \mid f \in F_0, X \in D\}$$

can be recognized, then the following process will generate a winning solution for s_0 in a finite number of steps.

1. Set $k = 1, j = 0, i = 0$, let $X^i = T$.

2. If $s_j \in X^i$, go to step 4.

3. If $s_j \notin X_i$, find f such that $s_j \in S^0_{fX}$; set $i = i + 1$, $X^i = S_f$. Return to step 2.

4. If $X^i = T$, stop.

5. If $X^i = S_f$, set $j = j + 1$, $s_j = f(s_{j-1})$, set $(\text{funct})_k = f$; set $k = k + 1$, $i = i - 1$. Return to step 2.

The foregoing method can be roughly described as follows. "Find a function g_1 appropriate to getting closer to the goal (reducing difference from the goal). If g_1 is applicable, apply it, and start with the resulting situation. If not, set up S_{g_1} as a new set of winning situations and start over again with a new g_2. Continue this till a point in S_{g_1} is reached. Then apply g_1 and start with the new situation." This sequence is very similar to the recursive use of the subgoal types of the GPS. The S^0_{fX} are the kernels of the map mapping every situation to some specific difference with X. The slight difference of the algorithm above from the GPS exists because in the algorithm, advantage has been taken of the rather strong axiom D5. If we relax the condition to the consequence of Proposition 2.1, a small modification can be made in the procedure to find a difference sequence of length less than or equal to N. It appears from a perusal of the flow charts of the GPS that the occasional "back-ups" are caused by such a search.

A class $\{S^0_{fX} \mid f \in F_0, X \in D\}$ always exists. If $S^0_{fT} = S_{fT}$ and $S^0_{fS_g} = S_{fS_g}$ for all f, $g \in F_0$, we have $X' = \bigcup_{f \in F_0} S_{fX}$ satisfying D1. D2 is satisfied since $S_{fX} \subseteq S_f$ for all X. D3 is satisfied since $S_{fX} - S_f$ is empty. D4 is also satisfied since the antecedent is false. D5 is satisfied for $N = 1$ since $X^1(s) = S_f$ implies $s \in S_{fT} \subseteq S_f$ hence, $X^2(s)$ is undefined. However, the set of classes of sets $\{S^0_{fX} \mid X \in D, f \in F_0\}$ may be much richer than those consisting of only the class $\{S_{fT} \mid f \in F_0\} \cup \{S_{fS_g} \mid f, g \in F_0\}$. Hence, for some of these classes $\{S^0_{fX}\}$ may be easier to describe in a given language than $\{S_{fT}\}$. Hence, the fact that the $\{S_{fT}\}$ are (at least conceptually) constructively defined, and that the $\{S^0_{fX}\}$ are not (D1–D5 are far from constructive definitions) so definable at present, does not preclude their usefulness.

The model above need not be the most faithful model of the GPS and more faithful models can be built. However, no matter what the model is, it may be worthwhile to consider the exact conditions (like D1–D5) under which the model can be used for finding winning solutions. Such an alternative set of conditions has recently been developed by Dr. George Ernst [62, 63].

When a GPS-like program meets with occasional failure, the need arises to modify the distance-transformation table. Such modifications may be made in a directed manner if we can pinpoint the failure to one or other of the conditions required for the convergence of the procedure for constructing winning solutions. Of course, to make such a process possible, it is necessary to understand the basic structure of the W-problem involved. Often this structure is ill understood and difficult to understand. No attempt is being made here to ignore the difficulty. However, the basic structures presented here do indicate some well-directed avenues that help to decide the directions in which understanding should be attempted.

2.10. SUNDRY REMARKS REGARDING THE SEARCH FOR WINNING SEQUENCES

In Sections 2.7 and 2.8 methods were developed for defining strategies in such a way that the use of the strategy did not require the recognition of the elements of their kernel. In Section 2.9, however, a procedure was described for constructing a winning sequence. It will be noticed that for finding an element f_k of the winning sequence we not only used the point s, but also kept in mind the previous procedures used in finding f_k (notice that in step 5, i was set to $i - 1$ after the finding of f_k, not to 1). It is possible to use GPS-like procedures for defining strategies (for instance, if $f \neq g$ implied $S^0_{fX} \cap S^0_{gX} = \varnothing$ for all X, we could easily transfer the control to 1 in the procedure); however, it is not clear that we should limit ourselves to the concept of strategies as a method for solution construction.

Two remarks connected with the Tower of Hanoi come to mind here. The reader may verify that the following procedure generates a winning solution for $\langle (1, 2, 3, \ldots, n), \varnothing, \varnothing \rangle$.

1. Apply $(n, (-1)^{n+1})$.

2. If the resulting state $= \langle \varnothing, (1, 2, \ldots, n), \varnothing \rangle$, stop.

3. In the resulting state $\langle (x_{01} \cdots x_{0i_0})(x_{11} \cdots x_{1i_1})(x_{21} \cdots x_{2i_2}) \rangle$, let $x_{ki_k} = n$. Find $\max_{m, j \neq k}(x_{ji_j}, x_{mi_m}) = x_{ti_t}$. Apply (x_{ti_t}, s), where s is such that $t + s \pmod 3 \neq k$. Return to step 1.

In words, "Move the smallest disk. Then make the only move possible without moving the smallest disk. Go back to moving the smallest disk. Always move the smallest disk in the same direction."

This procedure does not yield the winning solution for all situations, once in a while getting into a "loop." For the cases where it does yield a solution, however, the solution coincides with the one obtained by the strategy of Section 2.6.

In neither of the cases above was it clear how the procedure for obtaining the winning solution was discovered. The following considerations seem to lead to a more "natural" way of obtaining a solution.

We realize that, if the situation $\langle (1, 2, \ldots, n), \varnothing, \varnothing \rangle$ has to be converted into the situation $\langle 0, (1, 2, \ldots, n), \varnothing \rangle$ by applying controls as restricted by the rules given, it is necessary that 1 be "moved" from the first to the second position and for this all the other disks have to be in the third position.

Hence we must, sometime in the course of applying the controls, obtain the state $\langle(1), \varnothing, (2, 3, \ldots, n)\rangle$, which then is changed to $\langle\varnothing, (1), (2, 3, \ldots,)\rangle$. It is also clear that now the set of disks $(2, 3, \ldots, n)$ can be moved back to the second position: we can apply a sequence of controls very similar to the ones needed to move this set from the first to the third position. It is also clear that the problem of going from $\langle(1, 2, \ldots, n), \varnothing, \varnothing\rangle$ to $\langle(1), \varnothing, (2, 3, \ldots, n)\rangle$ is analogous to the problem of going from $\langle(1, \ldots, n-1), \varnothing, \varnothing\rangle$ to $\langle\varnothing, \varnothing, (1, 2, \ldots, n-1)\rangle$. These conditions lead naturally to the setting up of a recursive procedure, to be called "Move $(p, p + 1, \ldots, n)$ from position k to position l" $(k = 0, 1, 2; l = 0, 1, 2; l \neq k)$." The procedure is as follows.

"If $p = n$, move n from position k to position l (apply (n, t) where $k + t = l$ (mod 3)). If $p \neq n$, move $(p + 1, \ldots, n)$ from position k to position m $(m \neq k, l)$. Move p from position k to position l. Move $(p + 1, \ldots, n)$ from position m to position l."

The overall procedure then is "Move $(1, 2, \ldots, n)$ from position 0 to position 1."

What we have done above is to set up the idea of a "macro-control" $M(p, p + 1, \ldots, n; k, l)$, which consists of sequences of elementary controls. The sequence, as shown above in words, is generated by the following definitions.

1. $M(n; k; l) = (n, t)$ where $k + t = l$ (mod 3).

2. $M(p, p + 1, \ldots, n; k; l) = M(p + 1, \ldots, n; k; m)$

$$(p, t)M(p + 1, \ldots, n; m; l) \text{ where } m \neq k, l.$$

If we now expand $M(1, 2, 3; 0; 1)$ to generate a winning sequence for $\langle(1, 2, 3), \varnothing, \varnothing\rangle$, we obtain the following sequence.

$M(1, 2, 3; 0; 1)$

$\quad = M(2, 3; 0; 2)(1, +1)M(2, 3; 2; 1)$

$\quad = M(3; 0; 1)(2, -1)M(3; 1; 2)(1, +1)M(3; 2; 0)(2, -1)M(3; 0; 1)$

$\quad = (3, +1)(2, -1)(3, +1)(1, +1)(3, +1)(2, -1)(3, +1),$

yielding the same solution as in Section 2.4.

From here, it is a matter of perseverance to show why the strategy of Section 2.6 is a natural consequence of the foregoing recursive procedure. This will not be attempted here. However, the point has to be made that since the function $M(1, 2, \ldots, n; k; l)$ was not in the original repertoire of elementary statements used in describing the rules of the game, this does not throw any light on how we can mechanically generate this function from the original rules. For a discussion of these points see Amarel [20].

However, all these considerations do shed some light on what is often called "method of subgoal generation" in the literature. Here the term is used somewhat more strictly than is often the case, to give some concrete meaning to the discussion. The discussion, however, will remain informal.

Given a W-problem $\langle S, F_0, T \rangle$, an element $s_0 \in T_j$, and an integer $k < j$, T_k is called a *subgoal* for s_0. If $k < m < j$ and $T_m = \{s'\}$, a unit set, then the pair (s', T_k) is called a *subproblem* for s_0. In the case above of the Tower of Hanoi, the initial situation is an element of T_{2^n-1}; the only element of the T_{2^n-1-2} that need be considered is $\langle (1), \varnothing, (2, 3, \ldots, n) \rangle$. The attainment of this subgoal T_{2^n-1-2} leads to two successive subproblems $(\langle (1), \varnothing, (2, 3, \ldots, n) \rangle, T_{2^n-1-1})$ where $T_{2^n-1-1} = \{\langle \varnothing, (1), (2, 3, \ldots, n) \rangle\}$ and $(\langle \varnothing, (1), (2, 3, \ldots, n) \rangle, \{\langle \varnothing, (1, \ldots, n), \varnothing \rangle\})$. The advantage of this kind of breaking up of a problem into subproblems is evident in the case of the Tower of Hanoi: the successive steps in the breaking up exhibit the entire winning solution, as was indicated earlier in the construction of the "macro-moves." Whether this is feasible in all cases depends heavily on whether the language of discussion is strong enough to indicate that some of the subgoals are unit sets (i.e., when there are unit subgoals). Very little research has been done in this area, even though words like subgoal and subproblem have been around ever since the inception of the field. The reason for this situation may very well be that the advantages of precision of definitions have been consistently overlooked.

It ought to be pointed out that the idea of subgoals has meaning even when subgoals are not unit sets. The reason for this is as follow. Lets $s_0 \in T_j$ and $m < j$ and F_0 is a finite set of cardinality, say, k. Then there are at most k^{m-j} possible control sequences, at least one of which leads to a situation in T_m. From this situation, at least one of at most k^m sequences leads us to a winning situation. Hence, if s_0 can be recognized to be in T_j and T_m can be recognized, a total of at most $k^m + k^{j-m}$ systematic searches are necessary instead of the k^j searches that would be otherwise required in the absence of any knowledge about the T_j. Of course, all this search would be unnecessary if T_i could be recognized for each i.

In the previous sections, the entire idea of searches has been avoided. As indicated above, searches become necessary when any of the techniques discussed in the preceding sections (or similar techniques not discovered yet) cannot be applied because of our inability to recognize some of the sets involved.

At present very little is understood about optimal search procedures in the context discussed in this book. In what follows, a very informal approach is made toward setting up some ideas on the basis of which search may be discussed. It is pointed out at the outset, however, that a search cannot be carried out with confidence, even in principle, if there is no method for recognizing T', and unless the problem is progressively finite.

Given a W-problem (S, F_0, T), we can associate with each $s \in S$ a set, $F(s) = \{f \mid f \in F_0 \text{ and } s \in S_f\}$; $F(s)$, of course, is given by the rules of the problem. $K(s)$ denotes the set of all linear well-orderings on $F(s)$. Clearly, any element of $K(s)$ is a subset of $F(s) \times F(s)$ and hence, a subset of $F_0 \times F_0$. Let $B(F_0 \times F_0)$ denote the set of all subsets of $F_0 \times F_0$, that is, the set of all binary relations on F_0. By a *search strategy* is meant a function

$$S_T : S \rightarrow B(F_0 \times F_0)$$

such that $S_T(s) \in K(s)$ for every s. For some elements of s (when $s \in \bigcup_{f \in F_0} S_f$) $S_T(s)$ is the empty ordering.

On the assumption that F_0 is finite and T' is finite and recognizable and given any search strategy S_T, we can set up the following procedure for constructing a winning strategy for $s_0 \in T'$.

1. Set $i = 0$.

2. Set $X_i = S_T(s_i)$.

3. If $s_i \in T$, stop: indicating success.

4. If $s_i \notin T'$, set $i = i - 1$ if $i > 0$ and return to step 6. Otherwise, stop: indicating failure.

5. If $s_i = s_j$ for some $j < i$, set $i = i - 1$ if $i > 0$ and return to step 6. Otherwise, stop: indicating failure.

6. If X_i is empty, set $i = i - 1$ if $i > 0$ and return to step 6. Otherwise, stop: indicating failure.

7. Set $(\text{funct})_i$ = least element of X_i. Subtract $(\text{funct})_i$ from X_i and store result as X_i. Set $i = i + 1$, $(\text{funct})_{i-1}(s_{i-1}) = s_i$. Return to step 2.

Such a procedure (an exhaustive search determined by S_T) would stop after a finite time indicating success for all $s_0 \in T'$. In a progressively finite problem (see Section 2.8), even T' need not be recognized in step 4 for completion of the procedure. However, the crucial point here is that this finite procedure may turn out to be impossibly long if S_T is not well chosen.

If $S_T(s)$ turns out to be such that its least element turns out to be f where $s \in S_{fT}$, then an extremely rapid process will result.

We can say somewhat imprecisely that most methods developed by workers in the field consist of setting up efficient search strategies. Most methods dealing with problems of the W-problem type tend to set up sets like S_{fT}, S_{fX}^0, T_i, or T', as described in previous sections. These are set up generally from common sense (or "learned," as later chapters will indicate). However, it is kept in mind that the sets "guessed at" may not coincide with what they are supposed to be, so that when a certain control applied to a certain situation does not lead to a winning situation, we can "start over again" using a different control. This leads to something in the nature of a search strategy. In many cases, it has turned out that the search strategy so induced is better than what can be expected from an arbitrarily chosen search strategy.

Search strategies in the literature are often based on what are called "intermediate evaluations." From the point of view adopted in this book, the intermediate evaluation functions are merely alternative ways to form descriptions of the $\{T_i\}$ or of T'. This is discussed at some length in Chapter 3. It suffices to point out here that since intermediate evaluations are functions with the set of situations as their domain, their kernels define partitions on the situation set S.

There is a general belief often expressed in the literature that problems can be best attacked by "going backward" from the winning situation, that is, by successively generating members of T_1, T_2, T_3, and so on, till s_0 is located in some T_i. This belief would be valid if these sets did not grow exponentially with i. For instance, if the problem had the structure of a tree rooted at s_0 (i.e., if all situations $s \neq s_0$ were such that $s = f(s')$ for a unique f and s'), then such a generation method would be highly efficient. Exactly the opposite case would occur if each situation in T' was a member of S_f for only one f and each situation s was such that for each $f \in F_0$, there was a situation s' such that $f(s') = s$. Here, it might be better to "go forward," since the tree "fans backward."

The preceding paragraph indicates that search processes based on enumeration of situations can only succeed in very special cases. Methods for recognizing such special cases have not been developed. Nor have many methods been developed for constructing descriptions of the sets discussed in Sections 2.7, 2.8, and 2.9 from the description of the problem. It is becoming increasingly clear that the use of the proper description language is a very crucial matter here. This is discussed in somewhat greater depth in later chapters.

Before concluding this chapter and section it is worthwhile to point out that although a study of efficiencies of search strategies has not been made in a rigorous way, it may be extremely worthwhile doing. As clearer understandings develop of the sets discussed in this chapter and more are added to this repertoire, the effect of errors in recognizing these sets may become clearer.

Chapter 3

GAMES AND SOLUTION METHODS

3.1. INTRODUCTION

In the preceding chapter M-situations were introduced as formal structures and the ideas of forcing situations and neutral situations were introduced, as well as the idea of winning and nonlosing strategies. Also, an important theorem (Theorem 2.1) was quoted regarding the existence of winning and nonlosing strategies.

The general model was then specialized to yield a class of structures that had one-to-one correspondences to W-problems. Also, it was shown that winning strategies of these special M-situations could be utilized for constructing W-strategies for the corresponding W-problems and hence, for constructing winning solutions. It was indicated how W-problems are adequate formal models for many problems studied in the field of artificial intelligence. A number of alternative methods of constructing winning solutions for W-problems were then discussed.

A similar sequence of discussions is undertaken in the present chapter, which deals with the formal model of a wide class of two-person board games. As is well known, the classical model of games can be specialized to cover exactly the same situations. Many of the formal notions introduced are superficially analogous to those introduced in Chapter 2: however, it is not clear that the ideas in Chapter 2 would be special cases of ideas developed in the present chapter. Such relationships are not discussed. Also, as before, no attempts are made to derive results as special cases of results obtainable for M-situations, even though it may be possible to do so in some cases.

In the next section the special class of M-situations is introduced as models of game situations and the special properties of winning strategies pertaining to these models are discussed. In Section 3.3 specific board games are formalized to conform to the structure of these special classes. In later sections methods for the construction of winning strategies are considered. Here, as in the previous chapters, the importance of the language for describing certain sets of situations is kept in mind.

53

3.2. GAME SITUATIONS AND STRATEGIES

In a general M-situation, a control and a disturbance are applied simultaneously to a situation. In a board game, only one player moves while the other player stays inactive. This special situation may be formalized as follows.

A *basic game situation* is an M-situation $\langle S, C, D, M, S_W, S_L \rangle$ with two prespecified elements $c_0 \in C$ and $d_0 \in D$ (called *inaction*) such that

G1 $S_c \cap S_d \neq \varnothing$ implies either $c = c_0$ or $d = d_0$ but not both. The following facts are worth noticing.

LEMMA 3.1.

$$\text{(i) } S_{c_0} = \bigcup_{d \neq d_0} S_d; \qquad \text{(ii) } S_{d_0} = \bigcup_{c \neq c_0} S_c.$$

PROOF.   Let $s \in S_{c_0}$; then by definition there exist a $d \in D$ and $s' \in S$ such that $(s, c_0, d, s') \in M$ whence $s \in \bigcup_{d \in D} S_d$. However, $s \notin S_{d_0}$ since $S_{c_0} \cap S_{d_0} = \varnothing$ by G1. Hence, $S_{c_0} \subseteq \bigcup_{d \neq d_0} S_d$.

Conversely, if $s \in S_d$ where $d \neq d_0$, then by the same argument as above there exists a c such that $s \in S_d \cap S_c$. However, since $d \neq d_0$, by G1 $c = c_0$. Hence, $s \in S_{c_0}$. Hence, $S_{c_0} \supseteq \bigcup_{d \neq d_0} S_d$.

The second part follows similarly.   ∎

LEMMA 3.2.

(i) $s \in S_{c_0}$ and $c \neq c_0$ implies $s \notin S_c$;

(ii) $s \in S_{d_0}$ and $d \neq d_0$ implies $s \notin S_d$.

PROOF.   By Lemma 3.1, $s \in S_c$ and $c \neq c_0$ implies $s \in S_{d_0}$, but this implies $s \in S_{c_0} \cap S_{d_0}$, which contradicts G1.

The second part follows similarly.   ∎

The lemmata above indicate that $\bigcup_{c \in C} S_c$ has a partition consisting of S_{c_0} and $\bigcup_{c \neq c_0} S_c$. The same set $\bigcup_{c \in C} S_c$ coincides by definition of M-situations with $\bigcup_{d \in D} S_d$. This in its turn has a partition coinciding with the previous partition, S_{d_0} coinciding with $\bigcup_{c \in C} S_c$ and $\bigcup_{d \neq d_0} S_d$ coinciding with S_{c_0}.

In the board games of interest here, the following facts are also taken to be true. The players play alternately. The game stops whenever a win or a loss is reached. The opponent ("disturbance") cannot make a final move into a win and the player cannot make a final move into a loss. To say this formally, the idea of a basic game situation is further specialized for our purposes in the following way. A basic game situation will be called a *game situation* if it obeys the following additional axioms.

G2 $S_W \cup S_L \subseteq S - \bigcup_{c \in C} S_c = S - \bigcup_{d \in D} S_d$.

G3 $s \in S_{c_0} \cap S_d$ implies $(c_0, d)(s) \in S - S_W - S_{c_0}$.

G4 $s \in S_c \cap S_{d_0}$ implies $(c, d_0)(s) \in S - S_L - S_{d_0}$.

It is possible that the major points that will be made about game situations can be made with much weaker assumptions than made here. However, this fact will not be emphasized further in this book. In the next paragraph a somewhat simpler-looking structure that has many properties in common with game situations is introduced.

A *board game* is given by the 5-tuple $\langle S, G, F, W, L \rangle$ where S is an abstract set, F and G sets of functions from subsets of S into S ($h \in F \cup G \to h$: $S_h \to S$ and $S_h \subseteq S$), and W, L subsets of S, with the following properties.

B1 $(\bigcup_{f \in F} S_f) \cap (\bigcup_{g \in G} S_g) = \varnothing$.

B2 $W \cap L = \varnothing$.

B3 $W \cup L \subseteq S - \bigcup_{f \in F} S_f - \bigcup_{g \in G} S_g$.

B4 $s \in S_f$ and $f \in F$ implies $f(s) \in S - \bigcup_{f \in F} S_f - L$.

B5 $s \in S_g$ and $g \in G$ implies $g(s) \in S - W - \bigcup_{g \in G} S_g$.

Given a game situation $R = \langle S, C, D, M, S_W, S_L \rangle$, we define a 5-tuple $B(R) = \langle S, F, G, W, L \rangle$ as follows.

1. $W = S_W; L = S_L$.

2. For each $c \in C$, there is a unique element $f_c \in F$ such that $f_c = (c, d_0)$ and these are the only members of F. For each $d \in D$ there is a unique element $g_d \in G$ such that $g_d = (c_0, d)$ and these are the only members of G; f_{c_0} and g_{d_0} are not defined since $(c_0, d_0)(s)$ is not defined.

THEOREM 3.1. *Given a game situation R, $B(R)$ is a board game.*

PROOF. S is a set and W and L are subsets of S as required by the definition of a board game. B2 is satisfied since S_W and S_L are disjoint by definition of an M-situation. It is clear from the construction of $B(R)$ that $\bigcup_{f \in F} S_f = (\bigcup_{c \in C} S_c) \cap S_{d_0}$. However, since $S_{d_0} = \bigcup_{c \neq c_0} S_c$ by Lemma 3.1, we have $\bigcup_{f \in F} S_f = \bigcup_{c \neq c_0} S_c$. Similarly, $\bigcup_{g \in G} S_g = \bigcup_{d \neq d_0} S_d$. Hence, $(\bigcup_{f \in F} S_f) \cap (\bigcup_{g \in G} S_g) = \bigcup_{\substack{c \neq c_0 \\ d \neq d_0}} (S_c \cap S_d) = \varnothing$ (by G1), proving B1.

Now

$$\bigcup_{c \in C} S_c = S_{c_0} \cup \left(\bigcup_{c \neq c_0} S_c \right) = \left(\bigcup_{d \neq d_0} S_d \right) \cup \left(\bigcup_{c \neq c_0} S_c \right)$$

$$= \left(\bigcup_{f \in F} S_f \right) \cup \left(\bigcup_{g \in G} S_g \right).$$

Similarly

$$\bigcup_{d \in D} S_d = \left(\bigcup_{f \in F} S_f \right) \cup \left(\bigcup_{g \in G} S_g \right),$$

whence G2 reduces to B3.

Again, $s \in S_c$ implies $s \in S_c \cap S_{d_0}$ and $f_c(s) = (c, d_0)(s)$. By G3, $f_c(s) \in S - S_W - S_{d_0} = S - W - \bigcup_{f \in F} S_f$, proving B5. Similarly, G4 yields B4. ∎

Given a board game $B = \langle S, F, G, W, L \rangle$, we define a 6-tuple $R(B) = \langle S, C, D, M, S_W, S_L \rangle$ as follows.

1. $S_W = W; S_L = L$.

2. For each $f \in F$ there is a unique element $c_f \in C$. In addition, there is an element $c_0 \in C$. These are the only elements of C. Similarly, the only elements of D are d_0 and a unique element d_g for each $g \in G$.

3. $(s, c, d, s') \in M$ if and only if either (a) $c = c_0$, $d = d_g$ for some $g \in G$ and $s' = g(s)$, or (b) $c = c_f$ for some $f \in F$, $d = d_0$, and $s' = f(s)$.

The following lemma is useful for tying together the next theorem.

LEMMA 3.3. *If B is a board game $\langle S, F, G, W, L \rangle$, then the following is true for $R(B)$.*

(i) $S_{c_0} = \bigcup_{g \in G} S_g = \bigcup_{d \neq d_0} S_d$;

(ii) $S_{d_0} = \bigcup_{f \in F} S_f = \bigcup_{c \neq c_0} S_c$;

(iii) $\bigcup_{c \in C} S_c = \left(\bigcup_{f \in F} S_f \right) \cup \left(\bigcup_{g \in G} S_g \right) = \bigcup_{d \in D} S_d$.

PROOF OF (i). Let $s \in S_{c_0}$. Then there exists $d \in D$, $s' \in S$ such that $(s, c_0, d, s') \in M$. By construction $d = d_g$ for some $g \in G$ and $s' = g(s)$ so that $s \in S_g \subseteq \bigcup_{g \in G} S_g$. If $s \in S_g$, then $(s, c_0, d_g, g(s)) \in M$ whence $s \in \bigcup_{d \neq d_0} S_d$. Hence $S_{c_0} \subseteq \bigcup_{g \in G} S_g \subseteq \bigcup_{d \neq d_0} S_d$.

Again, let $s \in \bigcup_{d \neq d_0} S_d$; hence, in particular $s \in S_{d_g}$. There exists $c \in C$ and $s' \in S$ such that $(s, c, d_g, s') \in M$. Hence, $c = c_0$; that is, $s' = g(s)$, whence $s \in \bigcup_{g \in g} S_g$. Also, if $s \in S_g$, then $(s, c_0, d_g, g(s)) \in M$ whence $s \in S_{c_0}$. Hence, $S_{c_0} \supseteq \bigcup_{g \in G} S_g \supseteq \bigcup_{d \neq d_0} S_d$.

Part (ii) is proved similarly.

Part (iii) follows since

$$\bigcup_{c \in C} S_c = S_{c_0} \cup \left(\bigcup_{c \neq c_0} S_c \right) = \left(\bigcup_{g \in G} S_g \right) \cup \left(\bigcup_{f \in F} S_f \right)$$

$$= \bigcup_{d \neq d_0} S_d \cup S_{d_0} = \bigcup_{d \in D} S_d. \quad \blacksquare$$

THEOREM 3.2. *Given a board game B, $R(B)$ is a game situation.*

PROOF. Let $(s, c, d, s') \in M$ and let $(s, c, d, s'') \in M$. If $c = c_0$, and $d = d_g$, then $s' = g(s) = s''$. If $c = c_f$, $d = d_0$, then $s' = f(s) = s''$. This proves M1. To prove M2 assume $s \in S_c \cap S_d$. By Lemma 3.3 $(\bigcup_{d \neq d_0} S_d) \cap (\bigcup_{c \neq c_0} S_c) = (\bigcup_{f \in F} S_f) \cap (\bigcup_{g \in G} S_g) = \varnothing$ by B1; hence, either $c = c_0$ or $d = d_0$. Also by Lemma 3.3 and B1 $S_{c_0} \cap S_{d_0} = \varnothing$ (this proves G1). If $s \in S_c \cap S_d$, then by G1 (already proved) either $c = c_0$, $d = d_g$ whence $(s, c_0, d, g(s)) \in M$ or $c = c_f$ and $d = d_0$ whence again $(s, c, d, f(s)) \in M$ in both cases, proving M2. G2 follows since

$$S_W \cup S_L = W \cup L \subseteq S - \bigcup_{f \in F} S_f - \bigcup_{g \in G} S_g \quad \text{(by B3)}$$

$$= S - \left(\left(\bigcup_{f \in F} S_f \right) \cup \left(\bigcup_{g \in G} S_g \right) \right)$$

$$= S - \bigcup_{c \in C} S_c = S - \bigcup_{d \in D} S_d.$$

To show G3 we note that $s \in S_{c_0} \cap S_d$ implies $s \in S_g$ where $d = d_g$. Hence by B5, $(c_0, d)(s) = g(s) \in S - W - \bigcup_{g \in G} S_g = S - S_W - S_{c_0}$. G4 follows similarly from B4. $\blacksquare$

It is also interesting to note the following.

THEOREM 3.3. *If B is a board game and R a game situation, then*

$$B = B(R(B)) \quad and \quad R = R(B(R)).$$

PROOF. Let

$$B = \langle S, F, G, W, L \rangle,$$

$$R(B) = \langle S, C, D, M, S_W, S_L \rangle,$$

$$B(R(B)) = \langle S, F', G', W, L \rangle.$$

Let $f \in F$ and $f(s) = s'$. Then there exists a $c_f \in C$ such that $(s, c_f, d_0, s') \in M$, that is, $(c_f, d_0)(s) = s'$ whence $f_{c_f}(s) = s'$. Hence, $f \subseteq f_{c_f}$. Again, if $f_{c_f}(s) = s'$, then $(c_f, d_0)(s) = s'$; that is, $(s, c_f, d_0, s') \in M$, which implies $f(s) = s'$; that is $f_{c_f} \subseteq f$, showing $f = f_{c_f}$. Hence $F \subseteq F'$.

Let now $f \in F'$ and $f = f_c$ where $c \in C$. If $f_c(s) = s'$, then $(s, c, d_0, s') \in M$ whence $c = c_f{}'$, for some $f' \in F$ such that $f'(s) = s'$ whence $f \subseteq f'$. Again if $f'(s) = s'$, then $(s, c_f{}', d_0, s') = (s, c, d_0, s') \in M$ or $f_c(s) = s'$. That is, $f' \subseteq f$ or $f' = f$. This shows $F' = F$.

The equality of G' and G can be proved analogously. This shows $B(R(B)) = B$.

Let now

$$R = \langle S, C, D, M, S_W, S_L \rangle,$$

$$B(R) = \langle S, F, G, W, L \rangle,$$

$$R(B(R)) = \langle S, C', D', M', S_W, S_L \rangle.$$

The set F has a unique element f_c for each element $c \in C$ where $c \neq c_0$ and C' has a unique element c_{f_c} for each element $f_c \in F$ and an additional element c_0. Hence the mapping $c \to c_{f_c}$ between C and C' is one-to-one onto. So is the mapping $d \to d_{g_d}$ from D to D'. Denoting d_{g_d} by d and c_{f_c} by c, these maps may be considered as identity maps.

Let $(s, c, d, s') \in M$; by G1, either $c = c_0$ or $d = d_0$ but not both. Let $c = c_0$ then $g_d(s) = s'$. Hence, $(s, c_0, d_{g_d}, s') \in M'$. Since $d_{g_d} = d$, $(s, c, d, s') \in M'$. Similarly if $d = d_0$, $(s, c, d, s') \in M'$. Hence, $M \subseteq M'$.

Let now $(s, c, d, s') \in M'$. Either $c = c_0$ or $d = d_0$ by construction of $R(B(R))$ from $B(R)$. If $c = c_0$, then $d = d_g$ for some $g \in G$ and $g(s) = s'$. From construction of $B(R)$ from R this is true only if $(c_0, d)(s) = s'$; that is, $(s, c_0, d, s') = (s, c, d, s') \in M$. Similarly, if $d = d_0$, $(s, c, d, s') \in M$. Hence, $M' \subseteq M$. ■

3.3. WINNING SOLUTIONS IN BOARD GAMES

Theorem 3.3 establishes the similarity of structure between board games and game situations. Most of the present chapter deals with board games. In the rest of this section the concepts of winning solution and winning strategies for board games are introduced.

Given an element $s_0 \in \bigcup_{f \in F} S_f$, a sequence $\mathscr{F} = (f_1, f_2, \ldots, f_n; f_i \in F$ for all $1 \leq i \leq n)$, and a sequence $\mathscr{G} = (g_1, g_2, \ldots, g_{n-1}; g_i \in G$ for all i, $1 \leq i < n)$, $\mathscr{G}$ will be called *compatible* with $\mathscr{F}$ if and only if

$$f_1(s_0) \in S_{g_1}, \qquad g_1(f_1(s_0)) \in S_{f_2},$$

$$f_2(g_1(f_1(s_0))) \in S_{g_2}, \qquad g_2(f_2(g_1(f_1(s_0)))) \in S_{f_3},$$

$$\cdots,$$
$$\cdots,$$
$$\cdots,$$

for all $i < n - 1$

$$f_{i+1}(g_i(f_i \cdots g_1(f_1(s_0))) \cdots) \in S_{g_{i+1}};$$
$$g_{i+1}(f_{i+1} \cdots g_1(f_1(s_0) \cdots)) \in S_{f_{i+2}}.$$

Given $s_0 \in \bigcup_{f \in F} S_f$ and $\mathscr{F} = (f_1, \ldots, f_2; f_i \in F$ for all i, $1 \leq i \leq n)$, $\mathscr{F}$ will be called a *winning solution* for s_0 if for each $\mathscr{G} = (g_1, g_2, \ldots, g_{n-1};$ $g_i \in G$ for all i, $1 \leq i < n)$ compatible with $\mathscr{F}$

$$f_n(g_{n-1}(f_{n-1} \cdots g_1(f_1(s_0)) \cdots) \in W.$$

As was indicated in Chapter 1, the demand for a situation s_0 to have a winning solution is an extremely restrictive one, corresponding to the demand for an open-loop control. The next few definitions introduce the less demanding idea of winning strategies.

A function $Q_F: \bigcup_{f \in F} S_f \to F$ is called a *board control strategy* if for all s, $Q_F(s) = f$ implies $s \in S_f$. Similarly a function $Q_G: \bigcup_{g \in G} S_g \to G$ is called a *board disturbance strategy* if for all s, $Q_G(s) = g$ implies $s \in S_g$.

A board control strategy Q is called *winning* for $s_0 \in S$ if there exists an integer N such that for every board disturbance strategy Q_G there exist sequences $(f_1, f_2, \ldots, f_n; f_i \in F$ for all i, $1 \leq i \leq n)$ and $(g_1, g_2, \ldots, g_{n-1};$ $g_i \in G$ for all i, $1 \leq i < n)$ such that

(i) $n \leq N$;

(ii) $Q_F(s_0) = f_1$, $\quad Q_G(f_1(s_0)) = g_1$,

$\quad Q_F(g_1(f_1(s_0))) = f_2$, $\quad Q_G(f_2(g_1(f_1(s_0)))) = g_2$,

for all $i < n - 1$

$$Q_F(g_i(f_i \cdots g_1(f_1(s_0) \cdots) = f_{i+1};$$
$$Q_G(f_{i+1}(g_i \cdots (g_1(f_1(s_0) \cdots) = g_{i+1};$$
$$Q_F(g_{n-1}(f_{n-1}(\cdots g_1(f_1(s_0) \cdots) = f_n$$

and

(iii) $f_n(g_{n-1}(f_{n-1} \cdots g_1(f_1(s_0)) \cdots) \in W.$

For the sake of brevity (i) may be expressed by saying "the sequences $\mathscr{F}$ and $\mathscr{G}$ have lengths n and $n - 1$"; (ii) may be expressed by saying "the sequences $\mathscr{F}$ and $\mathscr{G}$ are dictated by Q_F and Q_G"; (iii) may be expressed by saying "the sequences $\mathscr{F}$ and $\mathscr{G}$ end s_0 in W."

The reason for calling a demand for winning solutions stronger than a demand for winning strategies can be brought out by asking two questions:

1. If there is a winning solution for s_0, is there a winning board control strategy for s_0?

2. If there is a winning board control strategy for s_0, is there a winning solution for s_0?

The answer to both these questions is "no" in general. In what follows a sufficient condition will be set forth for the answer to question 1 to be "yes." (A necessary and sufficient condition can be developed with some effort, but is not worth doing.) A counterexample will indicate that the condition is not sufficient for the answer to the second question to be "yes."

A board game will be called *free* if for all $f, f' \in F$ and $s \in S$, $f(s) \in S_g$ implies $g(f(s)) \in S_{f'}$ or $g(f(s)) \in L$.

THEOREM 3.4.   *If in a free board game there is a winning solution for s_0, there is a winning board control strategy for s_0.*

PROOF.   Let $\mathscr{F} = (f_1, f_2, \ldots, f_n)$ be a winning solution for s_0. Let Q_G be a board disturbance strategy. Define a sequence $\mathscr{G}_{Q_G} = (g_1, g_2, \ldots, g_{n-1})$ as follows.

$$g_1 = Q_G(f_1(s_0))$$

and for all $i < n$

$$g_i = Q_G(f_i(g_{i-1}(f_{i-1} \cdots g_1(f_1(s_0)) \cdots).$$

Sequence $\mathscr{G}_{Q_G}$ is compatible with $\mathscr{F}$, since by definition of strategy

$$f_i(g_{2-1}(f_{i-1} \cdots g_1(f_1(s_0)) \cdots) \cdots) \in S_{g_i}$$

and, since the board game is free,

$$g_{i-1}(f_{i-1} \cdots g_1(f_1(s_0)) \cdots) \in S_{f_i}.$$

Define a sequence of situations $T^{Q_G} = (s_0{}^{Q_G}, s_1{}^{Q_G}, \ldots, s_{n-1}{}^{Q_G})$ as follows.

$$s_0{}^{Q_G} = s_0$$

and for each $i < n$

$$s_i{}^{Q_G} = g_i(f_i(s_{i-1}^{Q_G})).$$

With each element $s \in \bigcup_{f \in F} S_f$ associate a subset $F_s \subseteq F$ as follows.

$$F_s = \{f_{i+1} \mid s = s_i^{Q_G} \text{ for some strategy } Q_G\}.$$

Define $Q_F : \bigcup_{f \in F} S_f \to F$ as follows.

$$Q_F(s) = f_k$$

where k is the largest integer such that $f_k \in F_s$. $Q_F(s) = f_i$ if F_s is empty and $s \in f_i$ and $s \notin f_j$ for $j < i$.

It will be shown that Q_F is a winning strategy for s_0. The proof is by induction on n, the number of components in $\mathscr{F}$.

If $n = 1$, $f_n(s_0) \in W$. In this case $T^{Q_G} = \{s_0\}$ for all Q_G whence $Q_F(s_0) = f_1$. Hence, Q_F is a winning strategy for s_0.

Let now the theorem be true for $n < j$. Let $Q_F(s_0) = f_{k+1}$. Then $(f_{k+2}, \ldots, f_n)$ is a winning solution for all $g_{k+1}(f_{k+1}(s_0))$ such that $f_{k+1}(s_0) \in S_{g_{k+1}}$ and hence, Q_F is a winning strategy for s_0. ∎

The converse of this theorem is not true. Consider a board game as follows.

$$S = (A, B, C, E, F, G, H, I, J, K, L),$$

$$L = \varnothing, \quad W = (K, M),$$

$$F = (a, b, c), \quad G = (\alpha, \beta, \gamma),$$

$$S_a = S_b = S_c = (A, B, C, E, F),$$

$$S_\alpha = (G, H, I), \quad S_\beta = (G, J, I), \quad S_\gamma = (H, J).$$

Table 3.1

x	$a(x)$	$b(x)$	$c(x)$	y	$\alpha(y)$	$\beta(y)$	$\gamma(y)$
A	I	G	J	G	C	A	—
B	I	J	H	H	E	—	F
C	H	I	J	I	A	B	—
E	J	K	I	J	—	C	B
F	M	J	I				

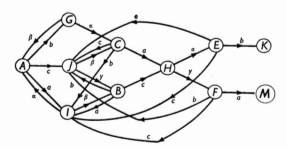

Figure 3.1. An illustration of a pathological game.

The functions $a, b, c, \alpha, \beta, \gamma$ are given in tabular form in Table 3.1 and graphically in Figure 3.1. It can be seen by inspection that there is no winning solution for A. However, the strategy Q_F shown in Table 3.2 is a winning strategy for A.

Table 3.2

x	$Q_F(x)$
A	c
B	c
C	a
E	b
F	a

The concepts of strategy in board games and game situations are closely related and this enables us to indicate a theorem analogous to Theorem 2.1 for board games.

Given a control strategy P_C in a game situation R, we define a relation $B(P_C) \subseteq S \times F$ as follows.

$$(s, f) \in B(P_C) \quad \text{if and only if} \quad P_C(s) \neq c_0 \quad \text{and} \quad f = f_{P_C(s)}.$$

Similarly, given a disturbance strategy P_D in a game situation R, we define a relation $B(P_D) \subseteq S \times G$ as

$$(s, g) \in B(P_D) \quad \text{if and only if} \quad P_D(s) \neq d_0 \quad \text{and} \quad g = g_{P_D(s)}.$$

The following lemmata can be proved readily.

LEMMA 3.4.   *If P_C and P_D are control and disturbance strategies in a game situation R, then*

(i) *$B(P_C)$ is a board control strategy in $B(R)$;*
(ii) *$B(P_D)$ is a board disturbance strategy in $B(R)$.*

PROOF.   Only (i) will be proved. The proof of (ii) follows identically.

To show that $B(P_C)$ is a function $B(P_C): \bigcup_{f \in F} S_f \to F$ let $(s, f) \in B(P_C)$, then $P_C(s) \neq c_0$, whence $s \in \bigcup_{c \neq c_0} S_c = \bigcup_{f \in F} S_f$ whence the domain of $B(P_C)$ is contained in $\bigcup_{f \in F} S_f$. Again, if $s \in \bigcup_{f \in F} S_f$, then $s \in \bigcup_{c \neq c_0} S_c \subseteq \bigcup_{c \in C} S_c$. Hence, $P_C(s)$ is defined and $P_C(s) \neq c_0$. If $P_C(s) = c$, then $(s, f_c) \in B(P_C)$. Hence, $\bigcup_{f \in F} S_f$ is contained in the domain of $B(P_C)$. Hence, the domain of $B(P_C)$ coincides with $\bigcup_{f \in F} S_f$. If $(s, f) \in B(P_C)$ and $(s, f') \in B(P_C)$ and $P_C(s) = c$, then $f' = f_c$ and $f = f_c$ by definition of $B(P_C)$. Since f_c is unique, $f = f'$ showing that $B(P_C)$ is a function.

Let now $B(P_C)(s) = f$, then $P_C(s) = c$ where $f = f_c$. Since $s \in S_c$ by definition of control strategy and $S_c = S_{f_c}$, $s \in S_f$, fulfilling the condition for $B(P_C)$ being a board control strategy.   ∎

LEMMA 3.5. (i) *The mapping $P_C \to B(P_C)$ is one-to-one onto the set of all board control strategies of $B(R)$. Similarly,* (ii) *the mapping $P_D \to B(P_D)$ is a one-to-one map onto the set of all board disturbance strategies of $B(R)$.*

PROOF. Let P_C and P'_C be two distinct control strategies, so that for at least one $s \in \bigcup_{c \in C} S_c$, $P_C(s) \neq P'_C(s)$. Since $P_C(s) = c_0$ for all $s \in S_{c_0}$; this implies $s \notin S_{c_0}$. Hence, both $B(P_C)(s)$ and $B(P_C)(s')$ are defined. Let $P_C(s) = c \neq c' = P'_C(s)$. By definition of $B(P_C)$ and $B(P'_C)$

$$B(P_C)(s) = f_c; \qquad B(P'_C)(s) = f_{c'}.$$

But the map $c \to f_c$ is one-to-one by definition, hence, $c \neq c'$ implies $f_c \neq f_{c'}$. Hence, $B(P_C) \neq B(P_{C'})$.

To show that every board control strategy Q_F is equal to $B(P_C)$ for some control strategy P_C, we construct the control strategy as follows.

(i) $P_C(s) = c$ if and only if $Q_F(s) = f_c$;
(ii) $P_C(s) = c_0$ if and only if $s \in \bigcup_{g \in G} S_g$;
(iii) $P_C(s) =$ undefined otherwise.

P_C is a control strategy, since $P_C(s)$ is defined for $\bigcup_{f \in F} S_f = \bigcup_{c \neq c_0} S_c$ by construction (i) and over S_{c_0} by condition (ii). Also, if $P_C(s) = c$, then $Q_F(s) = f_c$. $Q_F(s) = f_c$ indicates $s \in S_{f_c} = S_c$. Also, $P_C(s) = c_0$ only if $s \in S_{c_0}$. Again, $Q_F = B(P_C)$ by construction. ∎

The most important thing to notice about the mapping $P_C \to B(P_C)$ is given by the next theorem.

THEOREM 3.5. *In a game situation R, P_C is a winning control strategy for $s_0 \in \bigcup_{c \neq c_0} S_c$ if and only if $B(P_C)$ is a winning board control strategy for s_0 in $B(R)$.*

PROOF. Let P_C be a winning control strategy for s. Then there exists an integer N such that given any disturbance strategy P_D, there exists a sequence $(c_1, d_1) \cdots (c_n, d_n)$ such that $n \leq N$ and

$$c_1 = P_C(s_0), \qquad d_1 = P_D(s_0),$$

for each $i < n$;

$$c_{i+1} = P_C((c_i, d_i)((c_{i-1}, d_{i-1})(\cdots (c_1, d_1)(s_0)) \cdots)),$$
$$d_{i+1} = P_C((c_i, d_i)((c_{i-1}, d_{i-1})(\cdots (c_1, d_1)(s_0)) \cdots)),$$

and

$$(c_n, d_n)((c_{n-1}, d_{n-1})(\cdots (c_1, d_1)(s_0)) \cdots) \in W.$$

Since $s_0 \in \bigcup_{c \neq c_0} S_c$, $c_1 \neq c_0$. Also, $d_1 = d_0$. Also, since

$$(c_n, d_n)((c_{n-1}, d_{n-1})(\cdots (c_1, d_1)(s_0)) \cdots) \in W,$$

we obtain, from the contrapositive of G3, that

$$((c_{n-1}, d_{n-1}) \cdots (c_1, d_1)(s_0)) \cdots) \in S_c \cap S_{d_0}$$

for some $c \in C$. Hence, $d_n = d_0$. Hence,

$$c_1, c_3, \ldots, c_n \neq c_0, \qquad c_2 = c_4 = \cdots = c_{n-1} = c_0,$$

$$d_1 = d_3 = \cdots = d_n = d_0, \qquad d_2, d_4, \cdots, d_{n-1} \neq d_0,$$

indicating that n is an odd integer; let $n = 2m_0 - 1$.

Set $f_{c_{2m-1}} = f_m$ for each $m \leq m_0$ and $g_{d_{2m}} = g_m$ for each $m < m_0$. By definition of $B(R)$ we obtain for each $m \leq m_0$

$$(c_{2m-1}, d_{2m-1}) = (c_{2m-1}, d_0) = f_m$$

and for each $m < m_0$

$$(c_{2m}, d_{2m}) = (c_0, d_{2m}) = g_m,$$

reducing the equation

$$(c_n, d_n)((c_{n-1}, d_{n-1})(\cdots (c_1, d_1)(s_0) \cdots) \in W$$

to

$$f_{m_0}(g_{m_0-1}(\cdots g_1(f_1(s_0)) \cdots) \in W.$$

Also, for each even i

$$c_{i+1} = P_C((c_{i-1}, d_{i-1})(\cdots (c_1, d_1)(s_0)) \cdots)$$

reduces to

$$f_{(i/2)+1} = P_C(g_{i/2}(f_{i/2-1} \cdots g_1(f_1(s_0)) \cdots)),$$

and for each odd i

$$d_{i+1} = P_D((c_i, d_i)(\cdots (c_1, d_1)(s_0)) \cdots)$$

reduces to

$$g_{(i+1)/2} = P_C(f_{i-1/2}(g_{i-1/2}(\cdots g_1(f_1(s_0) \cdots)).$$

However, by definition of $B(P_C)$

$$P_C(s) = c_{i+1}$$

if and only if $B(P_C)(s) = f_{(i/2)+1}$ since $c_{i+1} \neq c_0$. Similarly,

$$P_D(s) = d_{i+1}$$

if and only if $B(P_D)(s) = g_{(i+1)/2}$. Hence, we obtain

$$Q_F(s_0) = f_1, \qquad Q_G(f_1(s_0)) = g_1,$$

and for all $i < (n + 1)/2 = m_0$

$$B(P_C)(g_i(f_i(\cdots g_1(f_1(s_0)\cdots) = f_{i+1},$$
$$B(P_D)(f_{i+1}(g_i \cdots g_1(f_1(s_0)\cdots) = g_{i+1},$$

and

$$B(P_C)(g_{m_0-1}(f_{m_0-1}\cdots g_1(f_1(s_0)\cdots) = f_{m_0}.$$

Since P_C is a winning strategy, $B(P_C)$ is such that for any board disturbance strategy $B(P_D)$ a sequence $f_1, f_2, \ldots, f_{m_0}$ and a sequence $g_1, g_2, \ldots, g_{m_0-1}$ will exist having the foregoing properties. $B(P_C)$, hence, is a winning board control strategy. ∎

The proof of the "if" part of the theorem is left to the reader. The theorem leads to the following interesting corollary analogous to a weak form of Theorem 2.1.

COROLLARY 3.1. *In a board game B there exists a board control strategy that is winning for every element $s \in \bigcup_{f \in F} S_f$ such that a winning strategy for s exists.*

PROOF. If $s \in \bigcup_{f \in F} S_f$ in B, then $s \in \bigcup_{c \neq c_0} S_c$ in $R(B)$. If a winning board control strategy exists for s in B, then by Theorem 3.5 a winning control strategy exists for s in $R(B)$. Hence, the set of all $s \in \bigcup_{f \in F} S_f$ for which a winning board control strategy exists is a subset of the set of all $s \in S$ for which a winning control strategy exists. Hence, it follows a fortiori from Theorem 2.1 that there exists a strategy P_C in $R(B)$ that is a winning control strategy for all elements of this set. By a second application of Theorem 3.5, $B(P_C)$ will be a winning strategy for all the elements of this set. ∎

As indicated in Section 2.2, Theorem 3.5 can be strengthened to include a definition of a winning strategy, both for board games and M-situations, in which no upper bound need exist for the lengths of winning sequences. This also has been established by Charles A. Dunning.

It will be noted that Corollary 3.1 neglects to make any statements regarding nonlosing strategies. It seems apparent that a stronger form for Corollary 3.1 could be obtained. However, since most of the later discussion in this book is directed toward winning board control strategies for members of $\bigcup_{f \in F} S_f$ in board games, extensions to such stronger forms may not be relevant at present.

A discussion regarding strategies and their descriptions similar to that in Section 2.6 is pertinent here. Corresponding to each strategy Q_F, $Q_F \circ Q_F^{-1}$ again defines a partition of $\bigcup_{f \in F} S_f$. As pointed out before, the major problem regarding the applicability of any winning strategy (even when it is definable) pertains to the ease with which the elements of the corresponding partition can be described. Also, if we are interested in only a small subset of situations, we have a greater freedom of choice between alternative strategies of varying ease of applicability.

The major problem regarding winning strategies, of course, remains how to find a winning strategy. As in Chapter 2, the later sections of the present chapter deal with certain aspects of this problem as applied to board games. Initially, however, a few well-known games are described in the general format of board games. This is also in keeping with what was done in Chapter 2.

3.4. THE NIM CLASS OF GAMES—AN EXAMPLE

This and the next section describe two classes of well-known games. As in Chapter 1, the examples serve to illustrate that the formal model of board games is suitable for representing well-known games and to provide vehicles for discussion in later chapters.

The first class of games can be described in general terms as follows. One has a number of piles of sticks on the table. Each player in his turn removes a number of sticks from each pile, obeying certain restrictions (for instance, "not more than one stick from each pile," "sticks to be removed only from one pile," and the like). The first player to pick the last stick in the piles wins. (In some variants of the games the person who takes the last stick loses: but the difference is not essential and in this book the rule will be as stated initially.) Specific games in this class are distinguished by the number of piles, the number of sticks on each pile initially, and (in a more fundamental way) the constraints on the way the sticks can be removed by each player.

The set S of situations in all of these games is characterized by a set of ordered pairs (I, p); p determines which player is to move (this will be formally stated presently), and I is a sequence of n nonnegative integers, where n is the number of piles and each integer in the sequence denotes the number of sticks in each pile. Any situation $s \in S$, then, has the form $((i_1, i_2, \ldots, i_n), p)$ where i_k is an integer for each k ($1 \leq k \leq n$) and p is either the integer 0 or the integer 1.

Each element of the set of functions F has the form $(x, 0)$ where x is a sequence of n nonnegative integers $x = (x_1, x_2, \ldots, x_n)$. Unlike the sequence I, however, where any sequence of integers is permitted, x has to satisfy some criterion according to the rules of the game. We will specify this criterion in general by a statement that x must satisfy, that is, such that $\alpha(x)$

is satisfied by any x such that $(x, 0)$ is a member of F, and for all x that satisfies α, $(x, 0)$ is a member of x.

Similarly, each element of the set of functions G has the form $(x, 1)$ where x is a sequence of n nonnegative integers $x = (x_1, x_2, \ldots, x_n)$ satisfying some criterion β.

For any element $(x, p) \in F \cup G$, $S_{(x, p)}$ is defined as follows.

$$S_{(x, p)} = \{(I, p) \mid i_k \geq x_k \text{ for each } k \ (1 \leq k \leq n)\}$$

and for each $(I, p) \in S_{(x, p)}$

$$(x, p)((I, p)) = ((i'_1, i'_2, \ldots, i'_n), p + 1 \ (\text{mod } 2))$$

where for each k $(1 \leq k \leq n)$

$$i'_k = i_k - x_k.$$

The set W consists of the single element $((0, 0, \ldots, 0), 1)$ and L of the single element $((0, 0, \ldots, 0), 0)$; α and β are so chosen that B3 is always satisfied. It is left to the reader to verify that B1, B2, B4, and B5 are satisfied by any specification in the class defined above. The descriptions of some specific games follow.

The simplest subclass of games in this class occurs when $n = 1$, $\alpha \equiv \beta \equiv (0 < x_1 \leq k)$ with a specific k. A typical game of this class may be "There are 15 sticks in a pile. Each player in his turn takes away at least 1 and at most 3 sticks from the board. The player who leaves an empty pile wins." Here the initial state is taken to be $((15), 0)$ or $((15), 1)$, depending on who plays first.

A specific game in the larger class that is easy to analyze is one in which $n = 2$ and $\alpha \equiv \beta \equiv ((x_1 \leq 1) \text{ and } (x_2 \leq 1) \text{ and } (x_1 + x_2 \neq 0))$. With the initial state $((5, 3), 0)$ the game is described as follows. "There are two piles, with 5 and 3 sticks. Each player, in his turn, picks up at least one stick, but not more than 1 from each pile. The player who leaves both piles empty wins."

In one of the most well-known subclasses of this class of games, $\alpha \equiv \beta \equiv (\exists x_i)(x_i > 0 \text{ and } j \neq i \rightarrow x_j = 0)$; that is, sticks are removed from one and only one pile. The well-known game of nim belongs to this class; in this specific game $n = 3$, and the initial state is $((3, 5, 7), 0)$ or $((3, 5, 7), 1)$, depending on who plays first. It will also be of interest to consider a more general subclass of this class of games where

$$\alpha \equiv \beta \equiv (\exists x_1)(k \geq x_i > 0 \qquad \text{and} \qquad j \neq i \rightarrow x_j = 0).$$

These games will be referred to as various methods for finding strategies are developed in later sections.

3.5. THE TIC-TAC-TOE-LIKE GAMES—ANOTHER EXAMPLE

The class of games discussed in this section is of interest because a close examination of them brings out in a convincing and nontrivial way the close relationship that exists between the efficiencies of solutions and description languages. The class of games is described here without any reference to the description language. A few well-known members of this class are then exhibited. The significance of the description languages to this class of games will be discussed later.

All the games in this class can be visualized as played on a board consisting of a finite number of "cells." Two classes of subsets of cells are predefined, which we shall call $\mathscr{A}$ and $\mathscr{B}$. The members of $\mathscr{A}$ are denoted by A (with or without subscripts) and are called "winning files for X"; members of $\mathscr{B}$ are denoted by B (with or without subscripts) and called "winning files for Y."

In the beginning, each cell is unmarked. The players play alternately. The first player, in his turn, marks some previously unmarked cell with an "X"; the second player, in his turn, marks some previously unmarked cell with a "Y." The first player wins if, on making his mark, a configuration of marks is produced such that some winning file for X has an "X" on each of its cells. The second player wins if, on making his mark, a configuration is produced such that some winning file for Y has a "Y" on each of its cells.

Formally, with each game will be associated a finite set N and two class $\mathscr{A}$ and $\mathscr{B}$ such that

$$A \in \mathscr{A} \quad \text{implies} \quad A \subset N,$$

$$B \in \mathscr{B} \quad \text{implies} \quad B \subset N.$$

We can assume, without losing any essential aspect of the games, that no member of $\mathscr{A}$ is a proper subset of any other member of $\mathscr{A}$; and similarly for $\mathscr{B}$. Another set with three elements $\{X, Y, \Lambda\}$ will also be used in specifying any game in the class.

Given N, $\mathscr{A}$, $\mathscr{B}$ for a game, we define a board game as follows. Any situation s is a function from N into $\{X, Y, \Lambda\}$ such that the number of cells mapped into X is equal to or one more than the number of cells mapped into Y. Denoting the cardinality of set P by $|P|$, we may say the foregoing formally as

$s \in S$ if and only if $s \in \{X, Y, \Lambda\}^N$ and $((|s^{-1}(X)| = |x^{-1}(Y)|)$ or $(|s^{-1}(X)| = |x^{-1}(Y)| + 1))$;

$s \in W$ if and only if $|s^{-1}(X)| = |s^{-1}(Y) + 1|$, there exists an unique file $A \in \mathscr{A}$ such that $A \subseteq s^{-1}(X)$ and there is no file $B \in \mathscr{B}$ such that $B \subseteq s^{-1}(Y)$;

$s \in L$ if and only if $|s^{-1}(X)| = |s^{-1}(Y)|$, there exists an unique file $B \in \mathscr{B}$ such that $B \subseteq s^{-1}(Y)$ and there is no file $A \in \mathscr{A}$ such that $A \subseteq s^{-1}(X)$.

Each element of F is denoted by the pair (n, X) where n is an element of N. Every element of G is denoted by a pair (n, Y) where n is an element of N.

$s \in S_{(n, X)}$ if and only if $s \in S - L$, $|s^{-1}(X)| = |s^{-1}(Y)|$, and $s(n) = \Lambda$. In this case $(n, X)(s) = s'$ where $s'(m) = s(m)$ if $m \neq n$ and $s'(n) = X$.

$s \in S_{(n, Y)}$ if and only if $s \in S - W$, $|s^{-1}(X)| = |s^{-1}(Y)| + 1$ and $s(n) = \Lambda$. In this case $(n, Y)(s) = s'$ where $s'(m) = s(m)$ if $m \neq n$ and $s'(n) = Y$.

As in the last section, it is left to the reader to verify that B1–B5 are satisfied by any board game as just defined. In what follows some well-known games in this class are described.

The most well-known subclass of this class of games is the "m^n tic-tac-toe games." "Naughts and crosses" or 3^2 tic-tac-toe is the most popular one among young children; 4^3 tic-tac-toe, a game sophisticated enough to be played by adults, sells under the trade name Qubic.

In general m^n tic-tac-toe game the set N consists of n-tuples of integers, each element of the n-tuple being a nonnegative integer less than m; S, then, is a prespecified subset of $\{X, Y, \Lambda\}^{m^n}$.

The classes $\mathscr{A}$ and $\mathscr{B}$ coincide in this class of games and consist in the set of n-tuples defined as follows.

$$A \in \mathscr{A} \equiv A = \{(f_1(s), f_2(s), \ldots, f_n(s)) \mid 0 \leq s < m\}$$

and each $f_i(s)$ is either a constant between 0 and $m - 1$ inclusive or $f_i(s) = s$ or $f_i(s) = m - 1 - s$: but not all f_i can be constant functions.

Basically, the preceding formalism states that a set is a file if it consists of m cells in a straight line. The idea can be exemplified by the picture (Figure 3.2) of a Qubic ($4 \times 4 \times 4$ tic-tac-toe) board and two files on it, as shown by the two parallelepipeds drawn with dotted lines. One consists of the 4 cells $\{(0, 0, 0), (1, 1, 0), (2, 2, 0), (3, 3, 0)\}$, which can be represented by $\{(s, s, 0) \mid 0 \leq s < 4\}$. The other consists of the cells $\{(1, 0, 2), (1, 1, 2), (1, 2, 2), (1, 3, 2)\}$, which can be represented by $\{(1, s, 2) \mid 0 \leq s < 4\}$. The set represented by $\{(s, 2, 3 - s) \mid 0 \leq s < 4\}$ consists of the cells $\{(0, 2, 3), (1, 2, 2), (2, 2, 1), (3, 2, 0)\}$.

The files in m^n tic-tac-toe are easier to describe intuitively for small values of n. However, something like the formal description given above (which is just a parametric definition of straight lines in a "hypercubic lattice") is essential for machine representation. This particular representation of files as n-tuples of functions has been found useful in certain combinatorial

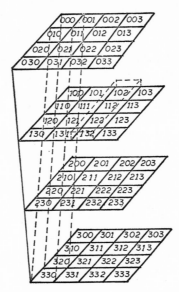

Figure 3.2. The 4^3 tic-tac-toe game.

problems associated with the multiplicity of various classes of files in general m^n tic-tac-toe games.

Another well-known game in the tic-tac-toe-like class is Go-moku (also known as Renjyu, Pegetty, and 5-place tic-tac-toe). The set N consists of cells in a 19×19 board as in a 19^2 tic-tac-toe game. However, the files, instead of being sets of 19 elements, are sets of 5 elements in a line anywhere on the board. Thus, the files in $\mathscr{A}$ and $\mathscr{B}$ consist of sets of the form $\{(f_1(s), f_2(s)) \mid 0 < s \leq 5\}$ where f_1 and f_2 have the form $K, K + s, K - s$ where K is any nonnegative integer less than 16 and more than 4: it being specified that both f_1 and f_2 are not constant functions.

In a third class of games the set N consists of arcs in a specified graph with two designated nodes. The class $\mathscr{A}$ consists of all paths between the designated points and $\mathscr{B}$ the class of all minimal sets of arcs whose removal separates the designated points. This is often described by saying that the first player, in his turn renders an arc invulnerable while the second player, in his turn, removes one of the vulnerable arcs. The game continues till either an invulnerable path is established between the two designated nodes or the nodes have been separated. In the first case the first player wins; in the second, the second player wins.

Games in this class are called Shannon games, after their originator. Lehman has recently given a characterization of the class of networks for which there is a winning strategy for the initial configuration [21]. The strategy given by him is characterized differently from the general strategy for tic-tac-toe-like games discussed later in this book.

The most important difference between the Shannon games and the m^n tic-tac-toe games is that in the former the classes $\mathscr{A}$ and $\mathscr{B}$ are described

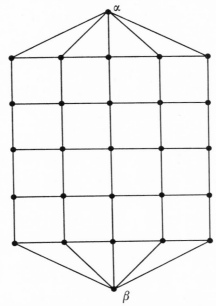

Figure 3.3. The Shannon game for Bridg-it.

in a much more complicated way. This fact has a rather strong impact on the way Shannon games are played.

A specific Shannon game is commercially available under the name Bridg-it. It consists of the network shown in Figure 3.3, with the nodes α and β predesignated. The actual Bridg-it board and the way the game is described appear different from the foregoing. However, Busacker and Saaty have pointed out that if α and β are joined by an extra arc, then the dual of the resulting graph is isomorphic to the resulting graph and the dual of the cut sets of this graph are paths between two specific points of the dual graph (joining the nodes corresponding to the regions separated by the extra line) with the arc dual to the extra line removed [22]. In the commercial game, the two opposing players play on the two dual graphs.

Another important game in the larger class of tic-tac-toe-like games is the game of hex. The set N consists of hexagons on a honeycomb structure as shown in Figure 3.4. The class $\mathscr{A}$ has as members all paths connecting the top edge to the bottom edge. The class $\mathscr{B}$ consists of all paths connecting the left edge to the right edge. Figure 3.4 exhibits a winning position.

Before leaving the subject it may be worthwhile to point out that every game in this class can be considered a subgame of a larger game in another

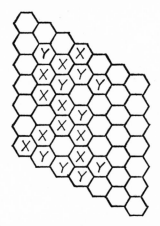

Figure 3.4.   A winning situation in 7 × 7 hex.

class, a description of which is introduced here. This embedding will bring out certain essential symmetries between the control and disturbance that will be of interest in a later section.

The specification starts with the same triple, N, $\mathscr{A}$, and $\mathscr{B}$; the situations are ordered pairs $\{s, p\}$ where $p = 0$ or $p = 1$ and $s \in \{X, Y, \Lambda\}^N$ without any restriction on s. Elements of F and G again have forms (n, X) and (n, Y); their definitions, however, are changed slightly:

$(s, p) \in S_{(n,X)}$ if and only if $s \in S - L$, $s(n) = \Lambda$, and $p = 0$. In this case $(n, X)(s, 0) = (s', 1)$ where $s'(m) = s(m)$ if $m \neq n$ and $s'(n) = X$;

$(s, p) \in S_{(n,Y)}$ if and only if $s \in S - W$, $s(n) = \Lambda$, and $p = 1$. In this case $(n, Y)(s, 1) = (s', 0)$ where $s'(m) = s(m)$ if $m \neq n$ and $s'(n) = Y$.

Also, W and L are slightly redefined: $(s, p) \in W$ if and only if $p = 1$, there exists an unique file $A \in \mathscr{A}$ such that $A \subseteq s^{-1}(X)$, and there is no file

$B \in \mathscr{B}$ such that $B \subseteq s^{-1}(Y)$; $(s, p) \in L$ if and only if $p = 0$, there exists an unique file $A \in \mathscr{A}$ such that $A \subseteq s^{-1}(Y)$, and there is no file $B \in \mathscr{B}$ such that $B \subseteq s^{-1}(X)$.

The reader should convince himself that in the original version of the game the first component of all situations were restricted to the set of first components of all situations (s, p) of the new version that could be attained from $((\Lambda, \Lambda, \ldots, \Lambda), 0)$.

In Section 3.9 certain subsets of S associated with winning strategies of tic-tac-toe-like games will be pointed out and the merits and drawbacks of the resulting strategies will be discussed.

3.6. EVALUATING STRATEGIES IN BOARD GAMES

The practical utility of a winning control strategy is intimately related to the ease with which the blocks of its kernel are amenable to easy description. Any comment that can be made regarding this matter has already been made in Section 2.6. It is, therefore, germane to move directly to the discussion of various methods for finding winning strategies. The discussion in this section follows roughly the same lines as Sections 2.7 and 2.8. Because of the important role played by the disturbance in a board game, however, there is more to say about evaluations in board games.

Given a board game, we can define readily two classes of sets $\{W_i \,|\, i > 0\}$ and $\{L_i \,|\, i > 0\}$ as follows.

$s \in W_1$ if and only if there exists an $f \in F$ such that $f(s) \in W$.

$s \in W_{i+1}$ if and only if $s \notin W_k$ $(k \leq i)$ and there exists an $f \in F$ such that $s \in S_f$, $f(s) \in \bigcup_{g \in G} S_g$, and for every $g \in G$ such that $f(s) \in S_g$, $g(f(s)) \in W_k$ $(k \leq i)$.

$s \in L_1$ if and only if there exists $g \in G$ such that $g(s) \in L$.

$s \in L_{i+1}$ if and only if $s \notin L_k$ $(k \leq i)$ and there exists a $g \in G$ such that $s \in S_g$, $g(s) \in \bigcup_{f \in F} S_f$, and every $f \in F$ such that $g(s) \in S_f$, $f(g(s)) \in L_k$ $(k \leq i)$.

It is clear that $\bigcup_{k \geq 1} W_k \subseteq \bigcup_{f \in F} S_f$ and $\bigcup_{k \geq 1} L_k \subseteq \bigcup_{g \in G} S_g$. The following also can be shown readily.

THEOREM 3.6. (i) If $s \in \bigcup_{k \leq 1} W_k$, then there exists an $f \in F$ such that $s \in S_f$ and $f(s) \notin \bigcup_{k \geq 1} L_k$.

(ii) If $s \in \bigcup_{k \geq 1} L_k$, then there exists $g \in G$ such that $s \in S_g$ and $g(s) \notin \bigcup_{k \geq 1} W_k$.

PROOF. Let $s \in W_k \subseteq \bigcup_{k \leq 1} W_k$. The proof is by induction over k.

If $s \in W_1$, then there exists an $f \in F$ such that $f(s) \in W \subseteq S - \bigcup_{g \in G} S_g$. Since $f(s) \notin \bigcup_{g \in G} S_g$ and $\bigcup_{k \geq 1} L_k \subseteq \bigcup_{g \in G} S_g$, $f(s) \notin \bigcup_{k \geq 1} L_k$.

Let the theorem be true for $s \in W_i$ $(i \leq k)$. Let $s \in W_{k+1}$. Then there exists an $f \in F$ such that $f(s) \in \bigcup_{g \in G} S_g$ and for all g such that $s \in S_g$, $g(f(s)) \in W_i$ $(i \leq k)$. If $f(s) \in \bigcup_{k \geq 1} L_k$, let $f(s) \in L_p$. Then there exists a g such that $g(f(s)) \in \bigcup_{f \in F} S_f$ and for all f' such that $g(f(s)) \in S_{f'}$, $f'(g(f(s))) \in \bigcup_{k \geq 1} L_k$. However, $g(f(s)) \in W_i$ $(i \leq k)$, whence by induction hypothesis there exists an $f' \in F$ such that $s \in S_{f'}$ and $f'(g(f(s))) \notin \bigcup_{k \geq 1} L_k$. This leads to a contradiction. ■

Part (ii) can be proved similarly.

The sets $\{L_i\}$ and $\{W_i\}$ will be called *W-evaluations* and *L-evaluations*, respectively. This idea of evaluations follows the mode set by Chapter 2. However, because the structure of board games is richer than that of *W*-problems, some further classes of sets related to evaluations can be utilized for the construction of strategies. Before taking up such further structures in detail, however, the results analogous to those in Chapter 2 will be set down. Theorems analogous of Theorems 2.5 and 2.6 will be seen to hold true for board games, again as special cases of Theorem 2.1. In view of the more general structure of board games as compared to *W*-problems, it will be more meaningful and easier to prove these analogs in somewhat stronger forms. For this, a few more initial definitions are in order.

Given a board game $\langle S, G, F, W, L \rangle$ and an element $s_0 \in \bigcup_{f \in F} S_f$ such that a winning board control strategy Q_F exists for s_0, we have a positive integer N such that for every board disturbance strategy Q_G there exist sequences $(f_1, f_2, \ldots, f_n \mid f_i \in F)$ and $(g_1, g_2, \ldots, g_{n-1} \mid g_i \in G)$, which fulfills the condition set out in Section 3.3. The integer n (less than or equal to N) is determined by s_0, Q_F, and Q_G and is denoted by $n(s_0, Q_F, Q_G)$ to emphasize this dependence. In view of Q_F being a winning strategy, $n(s_0, Q_F, Q_G) \leq N$ for every disturbance strategy Q_G. Hence, a least upper bound $n(s_0, Q_F)$ exists for the set of integers $\{n(s_0, Q_F, Q_G) \mid Q_G \text{ is a board disturbance strategy}\}$. In symbols

$$n(s_0, Q_F) = \operatorname*{lub}_{Q_G} \{n(s_0, Q_F, Q_G)\} \leq N.$$

Since the set of integers $n(s_0, Q_F, Q_G)$ is finite, this bound is attained by some Q_G.

The greatest lower bound of $n(s_0, Q_F)$ over all winning strategies for s_0 is denoted by $n(s_0)$.

$$n(s_0) = \operatorname*{glb}_{Q_F} \{n(s_0, Q_F) \mid Q_F \text{ is a winning strategy for } s_0\}.$$

Again, since the set $n(s_0, Q_F)$ is finite, this bound is attained by some Q_F. The following lemma will be useful.

LEMMA 3.6. *In a board game, let there be a winning strategy for $s_0 \in \bigcup_{f \in F} S_f$ and let $n(s_0) = n(s_0, Q_F) = n(s_0, Q_F, Q_G)$ for some control strategy Q_F and disturbance strategy Q_G. Let $s_1 = Q_F(s_0)(s_0)$ and $s' = Q_G(s_1)(s_1)$. Then $n(s') \leq n(s_0) - 1$.*

PROOF. It can be seen initially that Q_F is a winning strategy for s'. If it is not a winning strategy, there exists a disturbance strategy Q'_G such that there are no sequence $\mathcal{F}$ and $\mathcal{G}$ of length $n(s')$ and $n(s') - 1$ dictated by Q_F and Q'_G that end s' in W. If we now define a new strategy Q''_G such that $Q''_G(s_1) = Q_G(s_1)$ and $Q''_G(s) = Q'_G(s)$ for all situations $s(\neq s_1)$ for which Q'_G is defined, then there will be no $\bar{f}$, $\bar{g}$ of lengths $n(s_0)$ and $n(s_0) - 1$ dictated by Q_F and Q''_G that end s_0 in W. This contradicts the hypothesis that $n(s_0, Q_F)$ by Q_F and Q''_G that end s_0 in W. This contradicts the hypothesis that

$$n(s_0, Q_F) = n(s_0).$$

Given that there is a winning strategy for s', if $n(s') \leq n(s_0) - 1$, then for every winning control strategy Q'_F, $n(s', Q'_F) \geq n(s_0)$. Hence, there is a disturbance strategy Q'_G such that $n(s', Q'_F, Q'_G) \geq n(s_0)$. A fortiori there is a disturbance strategy Q'_G such that $n(s', Q_F, Q'_G) \geq n(s_0)$. Define a strategy Q''_G such that $Q''_G(s_1) = Q_G(s_1)$ and $Q''_G(s)$ for all $s(\neq s_1)$ for which Q'_G is defined. Then $n(s_0, Q_F, Q''_G) \geq n(s_0) + 1$. But $n(s_0) = n(s_0, Q_F, Q_G) \geq n(s_0, Q_F, Q''_G)$, leading to a contradiction. ■

We can easily prove the following on the basis of this.

LEMMA 3.7. *If in a board game $n(s_0) = k$, then*

$$s_0 \in \bigcup_{i=1}^{k} W_i.$$

PROOF. Let $n(s_0) = 1$. Then there exists a function $f \in F$ such that $f(s) \in W$. Hence, $s_0 \in W_1 = \bigcup_{i=1}^{1} W_i$.

Let now the theorem be true for $n(s_0) = k$. Let $n(s_0) = k + 1$. Then there exists a control strategy Q_F such that for every disturbance strategy Q_G, $n(s_0, Q_F, Q_G) \leq k + 1$. Let $Q_F(s_0)(s_0) = s_1$ and $Q_G(s_1)(s_1) = s'$. Then by Lemma 3.6 $n(s') = k_0 \leq k$. Hence, by the induction hypothesis, $s' \in \bigcup_{i=1}^{k_0} W_i \subseteq \bigcup_{i=1}^{k} W_i$. Hence, by definition, $s_0 \in \bigcup_{i=1}^{k+1} W_i$. ■

This leads immediately to the following corollary.

COROLLARY 3.2.   *If there is a winning control strategy for* $s_0 \in \bigcup_{f \in F} S_f$, *then* $s_0 \in \bigcup_i W_i$.

PROOF.   Let $n(s_0) = k$. Then $s_0 \in \bigcup_{i=1}^{k} W_i \subseteq \bigcup_i W_i$.   ■

Analogous to the case of W-problems, the idea of W-evaluations is of utility in the description of strategies. A strategy Q_F will be called evaluating if $s \in W_k$ ($k > 1$) and $Q_F(s) = f$ implies that for all $g \in G$ such that $f(s) \in S_g$, $g(f(s)) \in \bigcup_{k=1}^{k-1} W_i$, and $s \in W_1$ and $Q_F(s) = f$ implies $f(s) \in W$.

THEOREM 3.7.   *An evaluating strategy is a winning strategy for every* $s \in \bigcup_{f \in F} S_f$ *for which a winning strategy exists.*

PROOF.   If there is a winning control strategy for s, then $s \in \bigcup_i W_i$. Let $s \in W_k$. Let Q_F be an evaluating strategy and Q_G any disturbance strategy.

If $k = 1$, then $Q_F(s)(s) \in W$, indicating that Q_F is a winning strategy.

Let the theorem be true for $s \in \bigcup_{i=1}^{k} W_i$. Let $s \in W_{k+1}$. Then by definition of evaluating strategies if $Q_F(s)(s) = s_1$ and $Q_G(s_1)(s_1) = s'$, then $s' \in \bigcup_{i=1}^{k} W_k$. By induction hypothesis there exists sequence $(f_1, \ldots, f_n)$ and $(g_1, g_2, \ldots, g_{n-1})$ dictated by Q_F and Q_G such that $f_n(g_{n-1}(\cdots g_1(f_1(s') \cdots))$ $\in W$. Hence,

$$f_n(g_{n-1}(\cdots g_1(f_1(Q_G(s_1)(Q_F(s)(s)) \cdots) \in W.$$

Since Q_G is arbitrary, Q_F is a winning strategy for s.   ■

We can also prove an analog of Theorem 2.7 regarding evaluating strategies to show that if in every situation we apply a move dictated by some evaluating strategy, the resulting behavior of the game corresponds to that dictated by an evaluating strategy. The theorem and its proof are omitted since these are exact analogs of Theorem 2.7 and no new difficulty is created by the relaxed structure of board games.

The idea of evaluations and evaluating strategies are analogs of the similar idea for W-problems. However, certain classes of sets exist for board games whose descriptions also help in the construction of winning strategies and whose analogs do not exist for W-problems. These will now be discussed, for their role in strategy construction as well as for bringing the theory in line with certain graph-theoretic concepts that will be of value in later discussions.

We can define a class of subsets $\{K_i\}$ of $\bigcup_{g \in G} S_g$: $s \in \bigcup_{g \in G} S_g$ is a member of K_1 if and only if for all g such that $s \in S_g$, $g(s) \in W_1$; $s \in \bigcup_{g \in G} S_g$ is a member of K_i ($i > 1$) if and only if for all g such that $s \in S_g$, $g(s) \in \bigcup_{k=1}^{i} W_k$ and $s \notin \bigcup_{k=1}^{i-1} K_k$.

The following are easy to see.

LEMMA 3.8. $s \in W_k$ if and only if there exists an $f \in F$ such that $f(s) \in K_{k-1}$ and there is no $f \in F$ such that $f(s) \in K_j$ ($j < k - 1$). ∎

The proof will be omitted.

THEOREM 3.8. Given an $s \in \bigcup_{f \in F} S_f$ if there exists an $f \in F$ such that $f(s) \in K_i$ and no $f' \in F$ such that $f'(s) \in K_j$ ($j < i$), then $f = Q_F(s)$ for some evaluating strategy Q_F. ∎

The proof of this follows from Lemma 3.8. The importance of $\{K_i\}$ for the construction of winning strategies lies in the fact that if we have descriptions of K_i for every i, then we can construct evaluating strategies also.

Before going on to another very important property of the class $\{K_i\}$ in the next section, it is useful to indicate an analog of cautious strategies in board games. For this we need the following definition.

Given a board game, we define a relation $R \subseteq S \times S$ as follows.
sRs' if and only if there exists an $h \in F \cup G$ such that $h(s) = s'$.

A board game is called *progressively finite* if and only if there is no infinite chain $s_1, s_2, \ldots$, ($s_i \in S$) such that for each i, $s_i R s_{i+1}$.

A board control strategy is called *cautious* if and only if for each $s \in \bigcup_i W_i$, $Q_F(s) = f$ is such that either $f(s) \in W$ or $f(s) \in \bigcup_{g \in G} S_g$ and for all $g \in G$ such that $f(s) \in S_g$, $g(f(s)) \in \bigcup_i W_i$. Evidently every evaluating strategy is a cautious strategy. However, we can say more.

THEOREM 3.9. If a board game is progressively finite, then a cautious strategy is a winning strategy for every element $s_0 \in \bigcup_i W_i$.

PROOF. Let Q_F be a cautious control strategy. For any arbitrary control strategy Q_G, define a sequence $s_0, s_1, s_2, \ldots$ such that for each i

$$s_{i+1} = Q_F(s_i)(s_i) \qquad \text{if } i \text{ is even,}$$
$$s_{i+1} = Q_G(s_i)(s_i) \qquad \text{if } i \text{ is odd.}$$

Evidently, in this sequence $s_i R s_{i+1}$ for every i. Since the game is progressively finite, this chain has a last element s_k. Now $s_k \notin \bigcup_{g \in G} S_g$ since otherwise $Q_G(s_k)$ would be defined and s_k would not be the last element of the chain. Similarly, $s_k \notin \bigcup_{f \in F} S_f$.

If $s_{k-1} \in \bigcup_{g \in G} S_g$, then $Q_F(s_{k-2})(s_{k-2}) = s_{k-1}$ and hence, $k - 2$ is even. However, since $s_0 \in \bigcup_i W_i$ and S_F is cautious, $s_j \in \bigcup_i W_i$ for all even j. Hence, $s_{k-2} \in \bigcup_i W_i$. Hence, by definition of a cautious strategy $s_k \in \bigcup_i W_i$, which contradicts s_k being the last element of the chain. Hence, $s_{k-1} \notin \bigcup_{g \in G} S_g$. Also, $k - 1$ is then even. So $s_{k-1} \in \bigcup_i W_i$. Then $s_k \in W$ or $s_k \in \bigcup_{g \in G} S_g$. But $s_k \notin \bigcup_{g \in G} S_g$. Hence, $s_k \in W$.

Since Q_G is arbitrary, Q_F is a winning strategy. ∎

This theorem is an analog of Theorem 2.9 and indicates that in a finitely progressive game we can construct a winning strategy whenever we have a description of $\bigcup_i W_i$.

It can also be seen quite easily that a cautious strategy can also be constructed from a knowledge of $\bigcup_i K_i$.

THEOREM 3.10.   *In a progressively finite board game if* $s \in \bigcup_{f \in F} S_f$ *and there exists an* $f \in F$ *such that* $f(s) \in \bigcup_i K_i$, *then* $f = Q_F(s)$ *for some cautious strategy* Q_F.

PROOF.   Let $f(s) \in K_k$. Then, for every $g \in G$ such that $f(s) \in S_g$, $g(f(s)) \in \bigcup_{i=1}^{k-1} W_i \subseteq \bigcup_i W_i$. Hence, $Q_F(s) = f$ for some cautious strategy Q_F.   ∎

Some of the foregoing theorems could have been strengthened. Also, some further theorems can be added regarding the relationships between W_i and K_i. Also, analogs of these theorems exists for $\{L_i\}$, the L-evaluations. For the present purposes, however, these are not of immediate importance. In the next section certain well-known graph-theoretic properties of $\bigcup_i K_i$ are introduced that lead to important methods for construction of winning strategies. In these, attention will be mostly limited to progressively finite board games.

3.7.   STRATEGIES BASED ON GRAPH DECOMPOSITION

Most of the results in this section are interpretations of well-known results in graph theory [23]. These interpretations have been aided by certain elementary concepts of automata theory [24]. It is strongly surmised by the author that the extension of the techniques discussed in this section will be of help in developing new methods of problem solution.

The introduction of some graph-theoretic notions are in order. A *graph* is given by a pair $\langle S, R \rangle$, where S is an abstract set and $R \subseteq S \times S$. Clearly, for a board game $\langle S, F, G, W, L \rangle$, if R is defined as in the preceding section, then $\langle S, R \rangle$ defines a graph. Given a subset $S' \subseteq S$, $R(S')$ is the set of all elements related by R to elements of S'. In symbols

$$R(S') = \{s \mid (\exists s')(s' \in S' \quad \text{and} \quad s'Rs)\}.$$

For simplicity, $R(\{s\})$ will be denoted by $R(s)$.

Given a graph $\langle S, R \rangle$, a subset $S' \subseteq S$ is called a *kernel* if

$$s \notin S' \quad \text{implies} \quad R(s) \cap S' \neq \varnothing$$

and

$$s \in S' \qquad \text{implies} \qquad R(s) \cap S' = \varnothing.$$

Given a graph $\langle S, R \rangle$, an integer-valued function $M: S \to N$ mapping S into nonnegative integers is called a *Grundy function* if it has the property $M(s) = n$ implies, for all $s' \in R(s)$, $M(s') \neq n$ and for each integer $m < n$ there exists an $s' \in R(s)$ such that $M(s') = m$.

THEOREM 3.11 (Berge). *If the graph $\langle S, R \rangle$ corresponding to a board game $\langle S, F, G, W, L \rangle$ possesses a Grundy function M, then the set*

$$S' = \{s \mid M(s) = 0\}$$

is a kernel.

PROOF. If $s \in S'$, then $M(s) = 0$. Then for all $s' = h(s)\{h \in F \cup G\}$, $M(s') \neq 0$; that is, $h(s) \notin S'$. Also, if $s \notin S'$, then $M(s) \neq 0$. Then there exists at least some $h \in F \cup G$ such that $M(h(s)) = 0$; that is, $h(s) \in S'$. ∎

The next theorem, like the last one, is an obvious specialization of a general theorem in graph theory. We initially introduce another definition: A progressively finite graph $\langle S, R \rangle$ is called *progressively bounded* if for each $s \in S$ there is an integer $N(s)$ such that all chains of R starting at s have a length less than N.

THEOREM 3.12. *If a board game $\langle S, F, G, W, L \rangle$ is progressively bounded and $\langle S, R \rangle$ is its corresponding graph, then $\langle S, R \rangle$ has an unique Grundy function M.*

PROOF. Define a subset T of S as

$$T_0 = S - \bigcup_{f \in F} S_f - \bigcup_{g \in G} S_g.$$

By definition, if $s \in T_0$ and M is a Grundy function, $M(s) = 0$. Also, T is nonempty by definition.

Since the graph $\langle S, R \rangle$ is progressively bounded for every $s \in S$, there is an integer $N(s)$ such that any chain starting at s has length less than or equal to $N(s)$. The lengths of all chains starting at s are thus bounded above and hence, there is a chain of maximal length starting at s. Let the length of the chain of maximal length be $k(s)$. It will be proved by induction that for all integers n if $k(s) = n$, then the value of the Grundy function of s is defined, finite, and unique.

If $k(s) = 1$, then there exists a function $h \in F \cup G$ such that $h(s) \in S - \bigcup_{f \in F} S_f - \bigcup_{g \in G} S_g$ and there is no function $h \in F \cup G$ such that $h(s) \in \bigcup_{h \in F \cup G} S_h$, because if there were, there would be a chain starting at s of length greater than 1. Since $h(s) \in T_0$, $M(h(s)) = 0$, hence, $M(s) = 1$. Hence, if $K(s) = 1$, then the Grundy function of s is defined.

Let the theorem be true for all s such that $k(s) \leq n$. Let $k(s) = n + 1$. Then for any $h \in F \cup G$ such that $s \in S_h$, $k(h(s)) \leq n$ since otherwise there would be a chain starting at s of length greater than $n + 1$. Since the set of values $M(s')$ for all s' with $k(s) \leq n$ is defined and finite, we have a unique integer $M(s)$ such that $M(s) \neq M(s')$ for all s' such that $s' = h(s)$ for some $h \in F \cup G$, and for each $k < M(s)$ there is an s' such that $s' \in h(s)$ for some $h \in F \cup G$ and $M(s')$. ∎

The next theorem exhibits the relationship between the class $\{K_i\}$ and the graph-theoretic concepts developed earlier.

THEOREM 3.13.   *In a progressively bounded board game* $\langle S, F, G, W, L \rangle$ *let* S' *be the set of all points for which the Grundy function* M *has value* 0. *Then*

$$S' \cap \left(\bigcup_{g \in G} S_g \right) \supseteq \bigcup_i K_i.$$

Moreover, if $W \cup L = S - \bigcup_{f \in F} S_f - \bigcup_{g \in G} S_g$ *and if for each* $s \in S$ *the set* $G_s = \{g \mid g \in G \text{ and } s \in S_g\}$ *is finite, then*

$$S' \cap \left(\bigcup_{g \in G} S_g \right) = \bigcup_i K_i.$$

PROOF.   Let $s \in K_k$. It will be shown by induction on k that $M(s) = 0$.

It is clear that if $s \in W_1$, then $M(s) > 0$, since there is an $f \in F$ such that $f(s) \in W$ and hence, $M(f(s)) = 0$. Now if $s \in K_1$, then $R(s) \subseteq W_1$. Hence, for all g such that $s \in S_g$, $M(g(s)) > 0$. Hence, $M(s) = 0$.

Let the theorem be true for $s \in K_i$. If $s \in W_{i+1}$, then $M(s) > 0$ since there is an $f \in F$ such that $F(s) \in K_i$ (by Lemma 3.8) and hence, $M(f(s)) = 0$. Let $s \in K_{i+1}$; then by definition, for every $g \in G$ such that $s \in S_g$, $g(s) \in \bigcup_{j=1}^{i+1} W_j$, whence $M(s) = 0$.

Hence, $\bigcup_i K_i \subseteq S'$. Also, by definition $\bigcup_i K_i \subseteq \bigcup_{g \in G} S_g$. Hence, the first part of the theorem follows.

For the second part of the theorem, let $s \in S' \cap (\bigcup_{g \in G} S_g)$. Define any control strategy Q_F such that for all $s \in \bigcup_{f \in F} S_f$, if $M(s) \neq 0$, $Q_F(s)(s) \in S'$. Since S' is a kernel, such a strategy exists. Let Q_G be any disturbance strategy. Let $Q_G(s)(s) = s'$. Define the sequence $h_1, h_2, \ldots$ of members of F and G as follows.

$$h_1 = Q_F(s'), \qquad h_2 = Q_G(h_1(s')),$$

and in general

$$h_{2i+1} = Q_F(h_{2i}(h_{2i-1}, \ldots, h_1(s'), \ldots)),$$
$$h_{2i} = Q_G(h_{2i-1}, \ldots, h_1(s'), \ldots).$$

Since the game is progressively finite, such a sequence must end. Let h_m be the last element of the sequence. Then $h_m \notin G$. If it were, then

$$M(h_m(h_{m-1} \cdots h_1(s') \cdots) = 0$$

and $h_{m-1} \in F$. But by the definition of h_{m-1} and the property of Q_F,

$$M(h_{m-1}(\cdots h_1(s')) = 0.$$

This leads to a contradiction. Hence, $h_m \in F$ and $h_m(h_{m-1} \cdots (h_1(s') \cdots) \in S - \bigcup_{f \in F} S_f - \bigcup_{g \in G} S_g = W \cup L$ and by B4, $h_m(h_{m-1} \cdots (h_1(s') \cdots) \notin L$. Hence, $h_m(h_{m-1} \cdots (h_1(s') \cdots) \in W$. Since Q_G is arbitrary, Q_F is a winning strategy for s'. Hence, $s' \in \bigcup_i W_i$ by Corollary 3.2. Let $s' \in W_j$. Since $s' = g(s)$ for an arbitrary g such that $s \in S_g$, we obtain that if $s \in S' \cap (\bigcup_{g \in G} S_g)$, then for a $g \in G$ such that $s \in S_g$, $g(s) \in W_j$ for some j.

Given $s \in S' \cap (\bigcup_{g \in G} S_g)$, define the set of integers

$$N_s = \{j \mid (\exists g)(s \in S_g \text{ and } g(s) \in W_j)\}.$$

Since by assumption there is only a finite set of disturbances $g \in G$ such that $s \in S_g$, N_s is a finite set. Let k be the maximum of N_s. Then for all g such that $s \in S_g$, $g(s) \in \bigcup_{i=1}^{k} W_i$. Hence, $s \in \bigcup_{i=1}^{k} K_i$. This proves

$$S' \cup \left(\bigcup_{g \in G} S_g \right) \subseteq \bigcup_i K_i$$

and with the reverse inequality proven in the first part of the theorem it proves the second part of the theorem. ∎

A board game will be called *Grundy tractable* if and only if it is progressively finite, if $W \cup L = S - \bigcup_{f \in F} S_f - \bigcup_{g \in G} S_g$, and for any $s \in \bigcup_{g \in G} S_g$ the set $G_s = \{g \mid g \in G \text{ and } s \in S_g\}$ is finite. The calculation of the Grundy function in a Grundy-tractable board game leads to a mode of description for $\bigcup_i K_i$ and hence, to the construction of winning strategies. However, the method for calculating the Grundy function as indicated in Theorem 3.12 is certainly not a very practicable one. Practicable methods are available for a certain class of board games, which will now be discussed.

A board game $\langle S, F, G, W, L \rangle$ will be called *graph interpretable* if and only if there exists an abstract set Ω, a set H of functions mapping subsets of Ω into Ω (i.e., $h \in H$ implies $h: S_h \to \Omega$ where $S_h \subseteq \Omega$) and a subset T of Ω such that

Gr1 $S = \Omega \times \{0, 1\}$.

Gr2 (i) $W = \{(s, 1) \mid s \in T\}$;
   (ii) $L = \{(s, 0) \mid s \in T\}$.

Gr3   (i) $h \in H$ if and only if there exists an $f \in F$ such that $s \in S_h$ if and
              only if $(s, 0) \in S_f$ and $f(s, 0) = (h(s), 1)$;
         (ii) $h \in H$ if and only if there exists a $g \in G$ such that $s \in S_h$ if and
              only if $(s, 1) \in S_g$ and $g(s, 1) = (h(s), 0)$.

Gr4   (i) $(s, k) \in S_f$ and $f \in F$ implies $k = 0$;
         (ii) $(s, k) \in S_g$ and $g \in G$ implies $k = 1$.

A graph-interpretable game is played as follows. A directed graph is
placed on the table and a counter is placed on one of the nodes. Each player
in his turn moves the counter from one node to an adjacent node. Any
player who lands the counter on any of a set of prespecified "winning"
nodes wins. It will be shown later (Theorem 3.16) that many games can be
considered graph interpretable.

The rest of the discussion in this section is restricted to graph-interpretable
games, particularly Grundy tractable graph-interpretable games. Obviously,
a graph-interpretable game is completely specified by the triple $\langle \Omega, H, T \rangle$
and defines a graph $\langle \Omega, \bigcup_{h \in H} h \rangle$. The Grundy function M of this graph
has the property that $s \in T$ implies $M(s) = 0$.

Given a finite set of graph-interpretable games $\{\langle \Omega_i, H_i, T_i \rangle \mid 1 \leq i \leq n\}$,
a graph-interpretable game $\langle \Omega, H, T \rangle$ is called the *sum* of $\{\langle \Omega_i, H_i, T_i \rangle\}$ if
and only if

S1 $\Omega = \Omega_1 \times \Omega_2 \times \cdots \times \Omega_n$.

S2 $h \in H$ and $h(s_1, \ldots, s_n) = (s_1', \ldots, s_n')$ if and only if there is a unique
         positive integer $i \leq n$ and a member $h_i \in H_i$ such that

$$s_j' = s_j \quad \text{if } j \neq i; \qquad s_i' = h_i(s_i).$$

S3 $T = T_1 \times T_2 \times \cdots \times T_n$.

The game on a sum graph is played by placing all the graphs on the table
with a counter on each. Moves consist of moving the counter on exactly one
graph. In a winning situation, each counter is on a winning node of its graph.

It will be shown in Theorem 3.17 that many games are interpretable as
sum games. Meanwhile, the following facts have to be established.

THEOREM 3.14.   *Given a finite set* $\{\langle \Omega_i, H_i, T_i \rangle\}$ *of Grundy-tractable graph-
interpretable games, their sum is Grundy tractable.*

PROOF.   For each i, $W_i \cup L_i = S_i - \bigcup_{f \in F_i} S_f - \bigcup_{g \in G_i} S_g$, since the game
$\langle \Omega_i, H_i, T_i \rangle$ is Grundy tractable. If now $s \in \Omega_i - \bigcup_{h \in H_i} S_h$, then there is no
$f \in F_i$ such that $(s, 0) \in S_f$ and by definition no $g \in G_i$ such that $(s, 0) \in$
S_g. Hence, $(s, 0) \in S_i - \bigcup_{f \in F_i} S_f - \bigcup_{g \in G_i} S_g$. Hence, $(s, 0) \in L_i$ or $s \in T_i$.

Hence, $T_i \supseteq \Omega_i - \bigcup_{h \in H_i} S_h$. That $T_i \subseteq \Omega_i - \bigcup_{h \in H_i} S_h$ follows from B3. Hence, for each i, $T_i = \Omega_i - \bigcup_{h \in H_i} S_h$. Let $\langle \Omega, H, T \rangle$ be the sum of $\langle \Omega_i, H_i, T_i \rangle$ $(i = 1, 2, \ldots, n)$. If $(s_1, s_2, \ldots, s_n) \in T$, then for each i, $s_i \in \Omega_i - \bigcup_{h \in H_i} S_h$. Hence, there is no $h \in H$ such that $s \in S_h$. Hence, $T \subseteq \Omega - \bigcup_{h \in H} S_h$. Similarly, if $(s_1, s_2, \ldots, s_n) \in \Omega - \bigcup_{h \in H} S_h$, then for each i, $s_i \in \Omega_i - \bigcup_{h \in H_i} S_h$. Since $T_i = \Omega_i - \bigcup_{h \in H_i} S_h$, $s_i \in T_i$. Hence, $(s_1, \ldots, s_n) \in T_1 \times T_2 \times \cdots \times T_n = T$. Hence, $\Omega - \bigcup_{h \in H} S_h \subseteq T$. This with the previous inequality shows $T = \Omega - \bigcup_{h \in H} S_h$. Hence, $W \cup L = (\bigcup_{s \in T} \{(s, 0)\}) \cup (\bigcup_{s \in T} \{(s, 1)\}) = S - \bigcup_{f \in F} S_f - \bigcup_{g \in G} S_g$.

Let $s \in \bigcup_{g \in G} S_g$. Hence, $s = (s, 1)$ for some $s = (s_1, s_2, \ldots, s_n) \in \Omega$ and for some $i(i \leq i \leq n)$, $s_i \in \bigcup_{h \in H_i} S_{h_i}$. Since the game $\langle \Omega_i, H_i, T_i \rangle$ is Grundy tractable, the set $\{h \mid h \in H_i \text{ and } s \in S_h\}$ is finite. Hence, the set of $h \in H$ such that $(s_1, s_2, \ldots, s_n) \in S_h$ is finite. Hence, the set of $g \in G$ such that $(s, 1) \in S_g$ is finite.

To show that $\langle \Omega, H, T \rangle$ is progressively finite, we assume to the contrary that there exists an infinite sequence $h^1, h^2, \ldots$ of functions in H such that for an $s \in \Omega$, $s \in S_{h^1}$, and in general $h^{i-1}(h^{i-2}(\cdots h^1(s) \cdots)) \in S_{h^i}$.

We say that $\langle \Omega_k, H_k, T_k \rangle$ occurs in h^i if the kth component of

$$h^{i-1}(\cdots h^1(s) \cdots)$$

and the kth component of $h^i(h^{i-1}(\cdots h^1(s) \cdots))$ are distinct. Since one game $\langle \Omega_k, H_k, T_k \rangle$ occurs in h^i for every i and there are only n games, some game $\langle \Omega_k, H_k, T_k \rangle$ must occur in h^i for an infinite subsequence $h^{i_1}, h^{i_2}, \ldots$ of $\{h^i\}$. Then the kth component s' of $h^{i_1-1}(h^{i_1-2} \cdots h^1(s) \cdots)$ belongs to $S_{h_{i_1}}$ for some $h_{i_1} \in H_k$ and the kth component of $h^{i_1}(h^{i_1-1}(\cdots h^1(s) \cdots))$ is $h_{i_1}(s')$ and is identical to the kth component of $h^{i_2-1}(h^{i_2-2}(\cdots h^1(s) \cdots))$ and is a member of $S_{h_{i_2}}$ for some $h_{i_2} \in H_k$. We thus obtain an infinite sequence $h_{i_1}, h_{i_2}, \ldots$, of members of H_k such that some element s' of Ω_k belongs to $S_{h_{i_1}}$, and for each p, $h_{i_p-1}(h_{i_p-2} \cdots h_{i_1}(s') \cdots) \in S_{h_{i_p}}$. This contradicts the assumption that $\langle \Omega_k, H_k, T_k \rangle$ is Grundy tractable and hence, progressively finite. ∎

The importance of the sum of graph-interpretable games stems from the fact that if the Grundy functions of the components are known, then the Grundy function of the sum can be calculated quite readily.

To indicate the method of this calculation we need to define a special binary operation $\oplus$ between nonnegative integers. Let a and b be two such integers. Let

$$a = a_0 + a_i 2 + a_i 2^2 + \cdots + a_m 2^m, \qquad a_i = 0 \text{ or } 1,$$
$$b = b_0 + b_i 2 + b_i 2^2 + \cdots + b_n 2^n, \qquad b_i = 0 \text{ or } 1;$$

that is, let $a_m a_{m-1} \cdots a_0$ and $b_n b_{n-1} \cdots b_0$ be the binary representation of a and b. We can assume without loss of generality that $m = n$ and that some of the leading binary digits are 0.

We define

$$c = (a \oplus b) = c_0 + c_1 2 + c_2 2^2 + \cdots + c_m 2^m$$

where for each i, $c_i = a_i + b_i$ (mod 2).

It can be seen easily that the $\oplus$ operation is a group operation on integers, with 0 as the unit element and every integer its own inverse.

The following theorem indicates the use of the $\oplus$ operator in the calculation of the Grundy function of sums of games.

THEOREM 3.15.   *Let $\langle \Omega_i, H_i, T_i \rangle$, $i = 1, 2, \ldots, n$, be a collection of graph-interpretable Grundy-tractable games and let M_i be their Grundy functions. We define M on their sum as follows.*

$$M((s_1, \ldots, s_n)) = M_1(s_1) \oplus M_2(s_2) \oplus \cdots \oplus M_n(s_n).$$

M is a Grundy function on the sum.

PROOF.   Let $M((s_1, s_2, \ldots, s_n)) = k$ and let $M_i(s_i) = n_i$. We have to show that for all $h \in H$ such that $(s_1, \ldots, s_n) \in S_h$, $M(h((s_1, s_2, \ldots, s_n))) \neq k$ and for each integer $m < k$ there exists an $h \in H$ such that $(s_1, \ldots, s_n) \in S_h$ and $M(h((s_1, \ldots, s_n))) = m$.

Let $k = k_0 + k_1 2 + \cdots + k_t 2^t$ and for each i, $n_i = n_{i0} + n_{i1} 2 + \cdots + n_{it} 2^t$. Let $h((s_1, s_2, \ldots, s_n)) = (s_1', s_2', \ldots, s_n')$. Then there exists a j such that $s_i = s_i'$ for all $i \neq j$ and $s_j' = h_j(s_j)$ for some $h_j \in H_j$. Then $M_j(s_j') \neq n_j$. Now $M((s_1', s_2', \ldots, s_n')) = n_1 \oplus n_2 \oplus \cdots \oplus n_{j-1} \oplus M_j(s_j') \oplus n_{j+1} \oplus \cdots \oplus n_n$ and $M((s_1, s_2, \ldots, s_n)) = k = n_1 \oplus n_2 \oplus \cdots \oplus n_j \oplus \cdots \oplus n_n$, whence

$$M((s_1, s_2, \ldots, s_n)) + M((s_1', s_2', \ldots, s_n')) = n_j \oplus M_j(s_j').$$

Since $M_h(s_j') \neq n_j$, $M((s_1, s_2, \ldots, s_n)) \neq M((s_1', s_2', \ldots, s_n'))$, proving that for all h such that $(s_1, s_2, \ldots, s_n) \in S_h$,

$$M(h((s_1, s_2, \ldots, s_n))) \neq M((s_1, s_2, \ldots, s_n)).$$

Let $m < k$. Let $m = m_0 + m_1 2 + \cdots + m_t 2^t$. There must be at least one j such that $m_j \neq k_j$ since $m \neq k$. Let j_0 be the largest such integer. Since $m < k$, $m_{j_0} = 0$ and $k_{j_0} = 1$. Since $k_{j_0} = 1$, there is an i_0 such that $n_{i_0 j_0} = 1$. Define an integer $n_{i_0}' = n_{i_0 0}' + n_{i_0 1}' 2 + \cdots + n_{i_0}' 2^t$ as

$$n_{i_0 j}' = n_{i_0 j} \quad \text{if } m_j = k_j;$$

$$n_{i_0 j}' = n_{i_0 j} + 1 \text{ (mod 2)} \quad \text{if } m_j \neq k_j.$$

Since $m_j = k_j$ for $j > j_0$ and $m_{j_0} \neq k_{j_0}$ and $n_{i_0 j_0} = 1$, we have

$$n'_{i_0 j} = n_{i_0 j} \qquad \text{for } j > j_0.$$

Also,

$$n'_{i_0 j_0} < n_{i_0 j_0} \qquad \text{since} \quad n'_{i_0 j_0} = 0.$$

Hence, $n'_{i_0} < n_{i_0}$. Moreover, for each $j < t$,

$$k_j = n_{1j} + n_{2j} + \cdots + n_{(i_0-1)j} + n_{i_0 j} + n_{(i_0+1)j} + \cdots + n_{nj} \pmod 2.$$

Consider

$$p_j = n_{1j} + n_{2j} + n_{(i_0-1)j} + n'_{i_0 j} + n_{(i_0+1)j} + \cdots + n_{nj} \pmod 2$$

whence $p_j + k_j = n_{i_0 j} + n'_{i_0 j}$, whence $p_j = k_j$ if and only if $n_{i_0 j} = n'_{i_0 j}$ (i.e., if and only if $m_j = k_j$). Hence, $p_j = m_j$ for every j. Hence,

$$m = n_1 \oplus n_2 \oplus \cdots \oplus n_{(i_0-1)} \oplus n'_{i_0} \oplus n_{(i_0+1)} \oplus \cdots \oplus n_n.$$

Since $n'_{i_0} < n_{i_0} = M_{i_0}(s_{i_0})$, there exists an $s'_{i_0} \in \Omega_{i_0}$ and an $h \in H_{i_0}$ such that $M_{i_0}(s'_{i_0}) = n'_{i_0}$ and $h(s_{i_0}) = s'_{i_0}$. Hence, there exists an $h' \in H$ such that $h((s_1, s_2, \ldots, s_n)) = (s_1, s_2, \ldots, s_{i_0-1}, s'_{i_0}, s_{i_0+1}, \ldots, s_n)$ and

$$M((s_1, s_2, \ldots, s_{i_0-1}, s'_{i_0}, s_{i_0+1}, \ldots, s_n)) = m. \quad \blacksquare$$

If we are given a graph-interpretable game $\langle \Omega, H, T \rangle$ that is the sum of a finite number of graph-interpretable Grundy-tractable games, we can calculate the Grundy function of $\langle \Omega, H, T \rangle$, identify the set $\bigcup_i K_i$ for it, and construct a winning strategy. This requires a knowledge of the Grundy functions of each component. However, since the component games have far fewer states, their Grundy functions may be calculated by the exhaustive technique indicated in Theorem 3.12.

This technique of construction for winning strategies, of course, is limited to graph-interpretable games that can be decomposed into Grundy-tractable games. In what follows, conditions will be set down for the graph-interpretability of board games and decomposability of graph-interpretable games.

THEOREM 3.16.   *A board game* $\langle S, F, G, W, L \rangle$ *is graph interpretable if and only if there are two subsets* S_0, S_1 *of* S *and two one-to-one onto maps*

$$\alpha: S_0 \to S_1, \qquad \beta: F \to G$$

such that

(i) $L \subseteq S_0$, $W \subseteq S_1$;

(ii) $\bigcup_{g \in G} S_g \subseteq S_1$, $\bigcup_{f \in F} S_f \subseteq S_0$;

(iii) $\alpha^{-1}(S_g) = S_{\beta^{-1}(g)}$, $\alpha(S_f) = S_{\beta(f)}$;

(iv) $\alpha^{-1}(f(s)) = \beta(f)(\alpha(s))$, $\alpha(g(s)) = \beta^{-1}(g)(\alpha^{-1}(s))$ *for each* $f \in F$, $g \in G$
and any $s \in S$ *for which either side of the equation is defined;*

(v) $\alpha(L) = W$;

(vi) $S_0 \cup S_1 = S$.

PROOF. Let $\langle S, F, G, W, L \rangle$ be graph interpretable. There exists a set Ω, a set H of partial functions mapping subsets of Ω into Ω, and a subset T of Ω satisfying Gr1–Gr4. Define $S_0 = \{(s, 0) \mid s \in \Omega\}$ and $S_1 = \{(s, 1) \mid s \in \Omega\}$. Then (vi) is satisfied.

Define $\alpha(s, 0) = (s, 1)$ for each element of S_0. This is one-to-one from S_0 onto S_1. Also, $(s, k) \in S_g$ for $g \in G$ implies $k = 1$, whence $(s, k) \in S_1$. Hence, $\bigcup_{g \in G} S_g \subseteq S_1$. Similarly, $\bigcup_{f \in F} S_f \subseteq S_0$, satisfying (ii).

$$W = \{(s, 1) \mid s \in T\} \subseteq \{(s, 1) \mid s \in \Omega\} = S_1.$$

Similarly, $L \subseteq S_0$, proving (i).

If $(s, 0) \in L$, then $s \in T$ and $\alpha(s, 0) = (s, 1)$, whence

$$\alpha(s, 0) \in \{(s, 1) \mid s \in T\} = W.$$

Hence, $\alpha(L) \subseteq W$. It can be shown similarly that $\alpha^{-1}(W) \subseteq L$, proving (v).

For each $f \in F$ there exists an $h \in H$ and $g \in G$ such that $S_f = \{(s, 0) \mid s \in S_h\}$ and $S_g = \{(s, 1) \mid s \in S_h\}$, $f(s, 0) = (h(s), 1)$ and $g(s, 1) = (h(s), 0)$. If we define $\beta(f) = g$, the resulting β is one-to-one onto. Also, (iii) and (iv) will be satisfied by this β.

Let now $\langle S, F, G, W, L \rangle$, S_0, S_1, α, and β be as defined by (i) through (vi). Then we can define Ω, H, and T as follows: $\Omega \subseteq S \times S$ such that $(s_0, s_1) \in \Omega$ if and only if $s_1 = \alpha(s_0)$. Hence, $s_0 \in S_0$ and $s_1 \in S_1$. Denote s_0 by $\{(s_0, s_1), 0\}$ and s_1 by $\{(s_0, s_1), 1\}$. Since α is one-to-one onto, and because of (vi), if $s \in S$, then either $s \in S_1$ and $s = \{(\alpha^{-1}(s), s), 1\}$ or $s \in S_0$ and $s = \{(s, \alpha(s)), 0\}$. Hence, $S = \Omega \times \{0, 1\}$, satisfying Gr1.

$s \in L \subseteq S_0$ if and only if $\alpha(s) \in W \subseteq S_1$. Define by T the set of all pairs $(s, \alpha(s))$ such that $s \in L$. Then $s \in T$ if and only if $(s, 0) \in L$ and $(s, 1) \in W$. This establishes Gr2.

$H \subseteq \{h \mid h : \Omega_h \to \Omega\}$ is constructed as follows. Let $f \in F$ and $s \in S_f$. Then by (ii) and the construction of Ω, $s = \{(s, \alpha(s)), 0\}$. By (iii) $\alpha(s) \in S_{\beta(f)}$. Define h so that

$$S_h = \{(s, \alpha(s)) \mid s \in S_f\} = \{(s, \alpha(s)) \mid \alpha(s) \in S_{\beta(f)}\}$$

and $h(s, \alpha(s)) = (\beta(f)(\alpha(s)), f(s))$; $h(s, \alpha(s)) \in \Omega$ since by (iv) $\alpha(\beta(f)(\alpha(s))) = f(s)$. Also, $f(s) = (h(s, \alpha(s)), 1)$. This establishes first part of Gr3 and Gr4. The second parts follow similarly. ∎

This theorem is included to show clearly what kind of symmetry is demanded of a graph-representable game. The definition, based on the existence of the Ω graph, did not clarify the structure sufficiently.

It is worthwhile pointing out here that the nim-type games are graph interpretable. This follows from the definition of graph-interpretable games, the role of Ω being played by the set of sequences I (see Section 3.4). The reader can verify that conditions G1–G4 are satisfied.

The tic-tac-toe-like games are graph interpretable also if there is a permutation P on N such that $A \in \mathscr{A}$ if and only if there exists a $B \in \mathscr{B}$ such that $n \in A$ if and only if $P(n) \in B$. In this case we can set $S_0 = \{(s, p) \mid p = 0\}$ and $S_1 = \{(s, p) \mid p = 1\}$. The function α may be defined as follows: $\alpha((s, 0)) = (s', 1)$ where $s'(P(n)) = X$ if $s(n) = Y$, $s'(P(n)) = Y$ if $s(n) = X$ and $s'(P(n)) = s(n)$ otherwise; β is defined by $\beta(n, X) = (P(n), Y)$. At this point it may not be worthwhile proving formally that the partition S_0, S_1 and the maps α and β satisfy conditions (i)–(vi) in Theorem 3.16. However, the reader will do well to convince himself, at least intuitively, that this is so. It can be strongly surmised that games like chess and checkers are also graph representable in this sense.

THEOREM 3.17. *A graph-representable game $\langle \Omega, H, T \rangle$ is isomorphic to the sum of a set of n graph-representable games $\{\langle \Omega_i, H_i, T_i \rangle \mid 1 \leq i \leq n\}$ if and only if there exists a set of n equivalence relations $\{E_i \mid 1 \leq i \leq n\}$ on Ω and a set of disjoint subsets $\{H'_i \mid 1 \leq i \leq n\}$ of H such that*

(i) $\cup H'_i = H$;
(ii) $\cap E_i = I$, *the identity relation on Ω;*
(iii) *For any $s_1 s_2 \cdots s_n (s_i \in \Omega)$ there exists $s \in \Omega$ such that $s_i E_i s$ for each i.*
(iv) $s \notin T$ *implies that for some E_i, $sE_i s'$ implies $s' \notin T$.*
(v) $sE_i s'$ *implies $s \in S_h$ if and only if $s' \in S_h$ for all $h \in H'_i$ and $h(s)E_i h(s')$ for all h such that $s \in S_h$ and $s' \in S_h$.*
(vi) $h \in H'_i$ *implies, for all $s \in S_h$, $h(s)E_j s$ for all $j \neq i$.*

PROOF. The sufficiency is proved by constructing $\langle \Omega_i, H_i, T_i \rangle$ and an isomorphism as follows. Let Ω_i be the set of equivalence classes of E_i. Since by condition (ii), Theorem 3.17, $\cap E_i = I$, there is at most one situation s in a set $e_1 \cap e_2 \cap \cdots \cap e_n$ where $e_i \in \Omega_i$ for each i. Also, there is at least one element in $e_1 \cap e_2 \cap \cdots \cap e_n$. This can be seen as follows. Since the sets $e_1, e_2, \ldots, e_n$ are nonempty, there exist elements $s_i \in e_i$ for each i. By (iii) there exists an $s \in S$ such that $sE_i s_i$ for each i, $s \in e_i$ for each i and hence $s \in e_1 \cap e_2 \cap \cdots \cap e_n$.

Set up the following map from $\Omega_1 \times \Omega_2 \times \cdots \times \Omega_n$ to Ω.

$$\varphi(e_1, e_2, \ldots, e_n) = s$$

where s is the unique element of $e_1 \cap e_2 \cap \cdots \cap e_n$. This map is one-to-one onto.

Define T_i to be the set of equivalence classes containing some element of T. Let $s \in T$; then if $s \in e_i$ and e_i is an equivalence class of E_i, $e_i \in T_i$. Hence, $s \in T$ implies $s \in e_1 \cap e_2 \cap \cdots \cap e_n$ when $e_i \in T_i$ for each i. Hence,

$$s = \varphi(e_1, e_2, \ldots, e_n) \in \varphi(T_1 \times T_2 \times \cdots \times T_n).$$

Hence, $T \subseteq \varphi(T_1 \times T_2 \times \cdots \times T_n)$. If $s \notin T$, then by (iv) there is an i such that $s \in e_i$ and for all $s' \in e_i$, $s' \notin T$. Hence, $e_i \notin T_i$. Hence,

$$s \notin \varphi(T_1 \times T_2 \times \cdots \times T_n),$$

whence $S - T \subseteq \varphi\{\Omega_1 \times \Omega_2 \times \cdots \times \Omega_n - T_1 \times T_2 \times \cdots \times T_n\}$, proving $T \supseteq \varphi(T_1 \times T_2 \times \cdots \times T_n)$. With the previous inequality this proves $T = \varphi(T_1 \times T_2 \times \cdots \times T_n)$.

Define H_i as follows. For every $h' \in H'_i$, define a function $h \in H_i$ such that if $s \in S_{h'}$, then the equivalence class e_i of E_i containing s is in S_h and $h(e_i)$ is the equivalence class containing $h'(s)$. By (v), this determines the function h unequivocally. For all E_j ($j \neq i$), if e_j is the equivalence class of E_j containing s, then by (vi) e_j is also the equivalence class containing $h'(s)$. Hence, $h'(s)$ is in the intersection of the equivalence classes of E_j ($j \neq i$) containing s, and the equivalence class of E_i containing $h'(s)$. Hence, if

$$s = \varphi(e_1, e_2, \ldots, e_n)$$
$$h'(s) = \varphi(e_1, e_2, \ldots, h(e_i), \ldots, e_n)$$

showing that $\langle \Omega, H, T \rangle$ is isomorphic to the sum of $\{\langle \Omega_i, H_i, T_i \rangle\}$.

To show necessity, let $\langle \Omega, H, T \rangle$ (considered isomorphic to itself) be the sum of $\{\langle \Omega_i, H_i, T_i \rangle\}$. Define $(s_1, s_2, \ldots, s_n)E_i(s'_1, s'_2, \ldots, s'_n)$ if and only if $s_i = s'_i$. Clearly $(s_1, s_2, \ldots, s_n)(\cap E_i)(s'_1, s'_2, \ldots, s'_n)$ if and only if $s_i = s'_i$ for every i. This establishes (ii).

Since $T = T_1 \times T_2 \times \cdots \times T_n$, by S3 $(s_1, s_2, \ldots, s_n) \notin T$ implies $s_i \notin T_i$ for some i. Hence, for any $(s'_1, s'_2, \ldots, s'_n)$, $s_i = s'_i$ implies $(s'_1, s'_2, \ldots, s'_n) \notin T$. Hence, (iv) follows.

Now for every $h \in H$ there is a unique integer i ($1 \leq i \leq n$) such that $h(s_1, \ldots, s_n) = (s'_1, s'_2, \ldots, s'_n)$ implies $s_i \in S_h$, for some $h' \in H_i$, $s'_i = h'(s_i)$ and $s'_j = s_j$ for all $j \neq i$. Define the class of subsets H'_i as $h \in H'_i$ if and only if the corresponding $h' \in H_i$. Since there is a unique i with this property for every element of H, the subsets H'_i are disjoint. Since an i exists for every element $h \in H$, (i) follows. Also, if $(s_1, s_2, \ldots, s_n)E_i(s_1', s_2', \ldots, s_n')$, then $s_i = s_i'$. Hence, if $(s_1, s_2, \ldots, s_n) \in S_h$ for $h \in H_i'$, then $s_i \in S_{h'}$ for $h' \in H_i$; hence, $(s_1', s_2', \ldots, s_n') \in S_h$ also. Again, $h((s_1, s_2, \ldots, s_n)) = (s_1, s_2, \ldots, s_{i-1},$ $h(s_i), s_{i+1}, \ldots, s_n)$ and $h((s_1', \ldots, s_n')) = (s_1', s_2', \ldots, s_{i-1}', h(s_i), s_{i+1}', \ldots, s_n')$ whence $h((s_1, s_2, \ldots, s_n))E_i h(s_1', s_2', \ldots, s_n')$. Also, $h((s_1, s_2, \ldots, s_n)) =$ $(s_1, s_2, \ldots, h(s_i), \ldots, s_n)$, so that $h((s_1, s_2, \ldots, s_n))E_j(s_1, s_2, \ldots, s_n)$ for all $j \neq i$. This establishes (v) and (vi).

Let there be n elements $s_1, s_2, \ldots, s_n$ in Ω. Denote these by $(s_{11} \cdots s_{1n},$ $(s_{21} \cdots s_{2n}) \cdots (s_{n1} \cdots s_{nn})$, respectively. Let $s' = (s_{11}, s_{22}, \ldots, s_{nn})$. Then $s_i E_i s_i'$ for each i. This establishes (iii). ∎

It must be emphasized at this point that for any application of Theorem 3.16 or 3.17 to be practicable, we must have descriptions of the blocks of the partitions referred to in these theorems. This again necessitates the use of a language in which such descriptions can be expressed by tractably short expressions. It is indicated in the next section how some of the nim-type games shown in Section 3.4 are sum decomposable. In these cases, the description of the equivalence classes of E_i are particularly simple.

In what follows, some of the ideas developed in this and the preceding sections are exemplified for the nim class of games. Some discussions of the tic-tac-toe class of games are included in Section 3.9. (The ideas of Section 3.9 are useful again in Chapter 5.)

3.8. SOME EXAMPLES OF STRATEGY CONSTRUCTION

Concentrating attention on the nimlike games, we can quite easily construct a winning strategy for the first game in the examples for all states $(i, 0)$ where $i \neq 0 \pmod{k + 1}$. It can be seen that $\bigcup_i K_i = ((k + 1)p, 1)$ for any integer $p > 0$. This is because for all $(x_1, 1) \in G$ such that $x_1 \leq k$, $(x_1, 1)((k + 1)p, 1) = ((k + 1)p - x_1, 0)$. If we choose $(k + 1 - x_1, 0) \in F$, we obtain $(k + 1 + x_1, 0)((k + 1)p - x_1, 0)$ $((k + 1)(p - 1), 1)$. If $p = 1$, the resulting situation is a member of W, so that $(x_1, 1)((k + 1), 1) \in W_1$ for all $(x_1, 1)$ satisfying condition α. The result follows by induction on p. Hence, in any situation $(i, 0)$ if $i \neq 0 \pmod{k + 1}$, we can choose an integer $x \equiv i \pmod{k + 1}$ such that $0 < x \leq k$ and such that $(x, 0)(i, 0) \in \bigcup_i K_i$. Since the game is obviously progressively bounded, this yields a winning control strategy for the set of situations mentioned.

For future discussions, it is worthwhile pointing out that the Grundy function M of the graph of this game is definable as the smallest integer $M(i)$ such that $M(i) \equiv i \pmod{k + 1}$. Figure 3.5 indicates this fact for a game

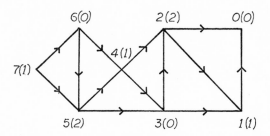

Figure 3.5.   Grundy function of the 7-stick nim.

with $i \leq 7$ for all nodes and $k = 2$. The numeral at each node indicates the value of i and the numeral in parentheses indicates the value of the Grundy function.

The game with $n = 2$ cited in Section 3.4 is also analyzable in terms of the Grundy function. However, this does not shed any further light on the contents of this book. It will be analyzed in an entirely *ad hoc* manner.

It can be seen in this case that the situations $((2p, 2q), 1)$ belong to $\bigcup_i K_i \cup W$ for all p, q. For $q = p = 0$, the situation belongs to W. Also, for all p and q the only situations to which the disturbance can move are $((2p - 1, 2q), 0)$, $((2p, 2q - 1), 0)$, and $((2p - 1, 2q - 1), 0)$, from which the control can move to $(2(p - 1), 2(q - 1), 0)$. For $p = q = 1$ and $p = 0$, $q = 1$ and $p = 1$, $q = 0$, then $((2p, 2q), 1)$ is a member of K_1. The result follows by induction.

We can express the results above by saying that if the control can reduce the situation to the case where both heaps are even, then the disturbance has to reduce at least one heap to an odd number from which the control can move always to a "both even" situation.

In both of the cases above the descriptions of $\bigcup_i K_i$ was expressible in a language containing predicates involving ideals of integers modulo fixed integers. However, there was very little indication of a uniform procedure for generating the description. We may say that if we have an efficient pattern recognition procedure and a predefined knowledge of patterns, such as equivalences mod k, we can recognize these patterns through case studies, generating a theorem (like $((2p, 2q), 1) \in \bigcup_i K_i$) from the recognized patterns and proving them.

In some fortunate cases, the structures of sets like K_i and W_i become quite transparent; in others, techniques indicated by Theorems 3.16 and 3.17 become effective. The latter can be exemplified by the two last classes of games mentioned in Section 3.3.

We can see that both of these games (n is any finite number, and $\alpha \equiv \beta \equiv (\exists x_i)(j \neq i \to x_j = 0$ and $x_i > 0)$ in the first case and $\alpha \equiv \beta \equiv (\exists x_i)(j \neq i \to x_j = 0$ and $k \geq x_i > 0)$ for some specified k in the second case) can be described as sum compositions of n games. If we consider each separate heap as a separate game, then it follows from the definition of sum that the graph of the entire game is the sum of the games played on each heap, since moves are made only one heap at a time. In the first case ($x_i > 0$) the value of the Grundy function of the graph defined by each heap at each node equals the number of sticks in the heap (this fact can be gleaned from a very simple pattern recognition, at present nonmechanizable). In the second case, the value of the Grundy function at each node can be calculated by the same method as indicated for the case $n = 1$. Once these Grundy functions are known, the Grundy function of the entire game (considered on a sum graph) is calculated by the method indicated in Theorem 3.15.

A specific example will make the procedure clear. Let us take the case where there are 4 heaps of sticks and each move consists of removing not more than 3 sticks from one of the heaps. Then the value of the Grundy function for the situation $((i_1, i_2, i_3, i_4), p)$ is $M(i_1) \oplus M(i_2) \oplus M(i_3) \oplus M(i_4)$ where $M(i_k)$ is the remainder obtained by dividing i_k by 4. A winning strategy exists for all situations where a control is applicable and the value of the Grundy function is not zero. For example, for the situation $((7, 7, 6, 5), 0)$ the value of the Grundy function is $3 \oplus 3 \oplus 2 \oplus 1 = 3$. The value can be reduced to zero by removing 3 sticks from either the first or the second pile, reducing the situation in the first case to $((4, 7, 6, 5), 1)$. Any disturbance renders the value of the Grundy function nonzero. As an example, the disturbance $((0, 0, 0, 2), 1)$ reduces the situation to $((4, 7, 6, 3), 0)$ whose Grundy function is $0 \oplus 3 \oplus 2 \oplus 3 = 2$. The move $((0, 0, 0, 2), 0)$ reduces the situation to $((4, 7, 6, 1), 1)$ whose Grundy function is $0 \oplus 3 \oplus 2 \oplus 1 = 0$. A typical continuation to the end is shown in Figure 3.6.

The result of Theorem 3.15 is the strongest one known to the author regarding the calculation of kernels of game graphs. Other results pertinent to calculation of Grundy functions of graphs are known; however, the calculations are still prohibitively lengthy except in special cases. Results for parallel decomposition of graphs are available only for cases where the structures of the component graphs obey severe restrictions.

Many games do not have evident decompositions of the type exemplified above. However, it is believed that Theorem 3.17 and various weaker forms may permit the recognition of decomposability in games that are not evidently decomposable.

We can look for relaxation of these conditions by realizing that the

Figure 3.6.   Playing a 4-pile nim game.

relation R corresponding to the game may be partitioned into various classes of functions and we need not restrict ourselves to a unique set H of functions. We can try various partitions of R (as long as the elements of these partitions are easily describable) so that the conditions of Theorem 3.17 are satisfied by one of them.

Another way of relaxing the stringent conditions is to look for an analogous theorem involving covers rather than partitions in some manner analogous to the way Hartmanis and Stearns [24] develop their concept of set systems. Very little work has been done in these directions so far as is known to the author.

A large amount of work may have gone into the calculation of kernels of graphs composed by means other than summing: if that is so, then the paucity of the results indicate that methods for these may be difficult to come by. In the rest of the present chapter two other methods for recognizing $\bigcup_i W_i$ that have been used successfully in the literature are discussed.

3.9.   APPROXIMATION TO STRATEGIES IN TIC-TAC-TOE LIKE GAMES

Tic-tac-toe-like games have already been discussed in Section 3.5. In the present section certain subsets $\{W_i'\}$ of S (the set of situations) are discussed that contain the sets $\{W_i\}$ although they do not coincide with the sets $\{W_i\}$.

In what follows, the definitions for W_i' are introduced. It will be shown in Chapter 5 that descriptions of $\{W_i'\}$ are much easier to learn than those of $\{W_i\}$. The significance of this learning is clarified in Chapter 5.

It will be recalled that a tic-tac-toe-like game is completely specified by a set N of cells and two subsets, $\mathscr{A}$ and $\mathscr{B}$, of 2^N, called the winning and losing files. Given a game $\langle N, \mathscr{A}, \mathscr{B} \rangle$, we can define a reduced game $\langle N, \mathscr{A}, \varnothing \rangle$, with the same set of cells and winning files, but no losing files. The evaluations of $\langle N, \mathscr{A}, \mathscr{B} \rangle$ will be denoted by $\{W_i\}$ and those of $\langle N, \mathscr{A}, \varnothing \rangle$ by $\{W_i'\}$. Similarly, the situations to which (n, X) or (n, Y) are applicable will be denoted by $S_{(n, X)}$ and $S_{(n, Y)}$ as before for $\langle N, \mathscr{A}, \mathscr{B} \rangle$ and by $S'_{(n, X)}$ and $S'_{(n, Y)}$ for $\langle N, \mathscr{A}, \varnothing \rangle$.

The following theorem indicates how the sets $\{W_i'\}$ act as approximations to W_i.

THEOREM 3.18. *If* $s \in W_i$, *then* $s \in \bigcup_{j=1}^{i} W_i'$.

PROOF. If $s \in W_1$, then there is an $n \in N$ such that $s \in S_{(n, X)}$ and $s_1 = (n, X)(s) \in W$. However, $s \in S_{(n, X)}$ implies that $s \in S - L$, $|s^{-1}(X)| = |s^{-1}(Y)|$, and $s(n) = \Lambda$. Since L is empty in $\langle N, \mathscr{A}, \varnothing \rangle$, this also implies that $s \in S'_{(n, X)}$. Also, $s_1 = (n, X)(s) \in W$ implies that $s_1^{-1}(X) = A$ for some $A \in \mathscr{A}$ and if no $B \in \mathscr{B}$, $s_1^{-1}(Y) \supseteq \mathscr{B}$. Again, since $\mathscr{B}$ is empty in $\langle N, \mathscr{A}, \varnothing \rangle$, this implies $(n, X)(s) \in W$ for $\langle N, \mathscr{A}, \varnothing \rangle$ also. Hence, $W_1 \subseteq W_1'$. The theorem is thus true for $i = 1$.

Let the theorem be true for $i = k$. Let $s \in W_{k+1}$. If $s \in \bigcup_{j=1}^{k} W_j'$, there is nothing to prove. Otherwise, recall that there exists an $n \in N$ such that $s \in S_{(n, X)}$ and for each n' such that $(n, X)(s) \in S_{(n', Y)}$, $(n', Y)((n, X)(s)) \in \bigcup_{j=1}^{k} W_j \subseteq \bigcup_{j=1}^{k} W_j'$. Since $S'_{(n, X)} \supseteq S_{(n, X)}$, as proved before, and since $S'_{(n', Y)} \supseteq S'_{(n, Y)}$ can be proved similarly, this implies that $s \in W_{k+1}'$. This proves the theorem. ∎

In what follows, elements of $\bigcup W_i'$ are given an alternative description that is easier to test than the exhaustive trial, indicated by the definitions in Section 3.6, used so far. For this, the following ideas have to be introduced.

Let α and β be two arbitrary sets; let $C \subseteq \alpha \times \beta$ and let $\sharp$ be a function mapping the range of the relation C into integers. Then the pair $\langle C, \sharp \rangle$ will be called a *weighted graph* on α and β.

Given a situation s in a tic-tac-toe-like game, let $\langle C_s, \sharp_s \rangle$ be the weighted graph on N and $\mathscr{A}$ defined as

(i) $(n, A) \in C_s$ if and only if $s(n) = \Lambda$, $n \in A$ and $s^{-1}(Y) \cap A = \varnothing$;

(ii) $\sharp_s(A) = |A \cap s^{-1}(\Lambda)|$.

The ideas involved here are illustrated in Figure 3.7, showing some situations in a 3×3 tic-tac-toe game. If the cells are called 1 to 9 in the usual order, then the set of all files are $(1, 2, 3)$, $(4, 5, 6)$, $(7, 8, 9)$, $(1, 4, 7)$, $(2, 5, 8)$, $(3, 6, 9)$, $(1, 5, 9)$, and $(3, 5, 7)$. Calling these a to h, respectively, the weighted graph of the board shown in Figure 3.7a is

$$C = \{(7, c), (7, h), (2, e), (3, h), (3, f), (6, f), (8, e), (8, c)\},$$
$$\#(c) = 2, \quad \#(e) = 2, \quad \#(f) = 2, \quad \#(h) = 2;$$

C and $\#$ are represented in Figure 3.7b in a graphical form.

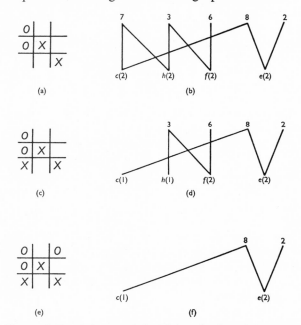

Figure 3.7.   Some weighted graphs for tic-tac-toe.

For an understanding of what follows it is worthwhile to indicate what happens to the graph $\langle C_s, \#_s \rangle$ as the situation changes as a result of applying controls and disturbances ("moves" and "countermoves"). Two steps of change are indicated in Figure 3.7(c, d, e, f). The effects indicated in these pictures can be formalized as follows.

For each element n of α, let X_n and Y_n be two functions from weighted graphs to weighted graphs defined as

$$X_n(\langle C, \# \rangle) = \langle C', \#' \rangle$$

where
$$C' = [(\alpha - \{n\}) \times \beta] \cap C$$
and
$$\sharp'(A) = \sharp(A) \qquad \text{if } (n, A) \notin C$$
$$= \sharp(A) - 1 \qquad \text{if } (n, A) \in C.$$
$$Y_n(\langle C, \sharp \rangle) = \langle C', \sharp' \rangle$$
where
$$C' = [(\alpha - \{n\}) \times (\beta - C(n))] \cap C,$$
$$\sharp'(A) = \sharp(A) \qquad \text{for all elements of the range of } C'.$$

THEOREM 3.19. *In any tic-tac-toe-like game and any situation s*

$$\langle C_{(n,X)(s)}, \sharp_{(n,X)(s)} \rangle = X_n(\langle C_s, \sharp_s \rangle),$$
$$\langle C_{(n,Y)(s)}, \sharp_{(n,Y)(s)} \rangle = Y_n(\langle C_s, \sharp_s \rangle)$$

whenever the left-hand sides are defined.

PROOF. Let $(n, X)(s)$ be defined; that is, let $s \in S_{(n,X)}$. Then $s(n) = \Lambda$. If $(n, X)(s) = s_1$, then $s_1(n) = X$ and for all $m \in N$, $m \neq n$ implies $s_1(n) = s(n)$. Hence, $(m, A) \in C_{s_1}$ if and only if $(m, A) \in C_s$ and $m \neq n$. Also, for any A is the domain of $C_{s'}, |A \cap s_1^{-1}(\Lambda)| = |A \cap s^{-1}(\Lambda)|$ unless $n \in A$; that is, if $(n, A) \in C$, in which case $|A \cap s_1^{-1}(\Lambda)| = |A \cap S^{-1}(\Lambda)| - 1$. This proves the first part of the theorem. The proof of the second part is left to the reader. ■

For an alternative description of the sets $\{W_i'\}$ we have to define the following class $\{J_i\}$ of sets of weighted graphs. A weighted graph $\langle C, \sharp \rangle$ belongs to J_1 if and only if there is an A in the range of C such that $\sharp(A) = 1$.

The set J_i is defined for $i > 1$ as follows. Let $\langle C', \sharp' \rangle$ be any graph that is a member of $\bigcup_{j=1}^{i} J_j$ and such that for all n it is true that $Y_n(C', \sharp') \in \bigcup_{j=1}^{i} J_j$. Let $\{C_1, C_2, \ldots, Cm\}$ be the set of all subgraphs of C' such that, for each p $(1 \leq p \leq m)$, $(C_p, \sharp_p)$ is a member of $\bigcup_{j=1}^{i} J_j$ ($\sharp_p$ is the restriction $\sharp'$ to the range of C_p). Let $(A_1, A_2, \ldots, A_m)$ be a set of elements in the range of C' such that there is at least one A_q $(1 \leq q \leq m)$ in the range of each C_p $(1 \leq p \leq m)$. Let n be any element of α not in the domain of C'. Let $\langle C'', \sharp'' \rangle$ be constructed as

$$C'' = C' \cup \{(n, A_1), (n, A_2), \ldots, (n, A_m)\},$$
$$\sharp''(A) = \sharp'(A) + 1 \qquad \text{if } A = A_q \ (1 \leq q \leq m)$$
$$\sharp'(A) \qquad \text{otherwise.}$$

A weighted graph belongs to J_{i+1} if and only if it does not belong to $\bigcup_{j=1}^{i} J_j$ but has $\langle C'', \sharp'' \rangle$ above as a subgraph.

THEOREM 3.20. *If a graph $\langle C, \sharp \rangle$ belongs to J_{i+1} there exists an n in the domain of C such that for all n'*

$$Y_{n'}(X_n(\langle C, \sharp \rangle)) \in \bigcup_{j=1}^{i} J_j.$$

PROOF. By definition of J_{i+1}, $\langle C, \sharp \rangle$ has no subgraph belonging to $\bigcup_{j=1}^{i} J$. Also, there is a graph $\langle C', \sharp' \rangle$ and a subgraph $\langle C'', \sharp'' \rangle$ of $\langle C, \sharp \rangle$ such that $\langle C'', \sharp'' \rangle$ is constructed from $\langle C', \sharp' \rangle$ as described in the definition of J_{i+1}. Let n be a member of α that occurs in C'' but not in C'. From construction of $\langle C'', \sharp'' \rangle$ it is evident that

$$X_n(C'', \sharp'') = \langle C', \sharp' \rangle.$$

Since $(C'', \sharp'')$ is a subgraph of $\langle C, \sharp \rangle$, $\langle C', \sharp' \rangle$ is a subgraph of $X_n(\langle C, \sharp \rangle)$. Since for all n', $Y_{n'}(\langle C', \sharp' \rangle) \in \bigcup_{i=1}^{i} J_i$, and $\langle C', \sharp' \rangle$ is a subgraph of $X_n(\langle C, \sharp \rangle)$, for all n'

$$Y_{n'}(X_n\langle C, \sharp \rangle) \in \bigcup_{j=1}^{i} J_j. \quad \blacksquare$$

THEOREM 3.21. *For any tic-tac-toe-like game, $s \in W'_k$ if and only if $|s^{-1}(X)| = |s^{-1}(Y)|$, $s^{-1}(X) \not\supseteq A$ for any $A \in \mathscr{A}$ and $\langle C_s, \sharp_s \rangle \in J_k$.*

PROOF. Let $k = 1$. If $\langle C_s, \sharp_s \rangle \in J_1$, then there exists an $A \in \mathscr{A}$ such that $|s^{-1}(\Lambda) \cap A| = 1$ and $s^{-1}(Y) \cap A = \varnothing$, that is, for all cells in A except one $s(m) = X$, and for one cell $n \in A$, $s(n) = \Lambda$. Since $|s^{-1}(X)| = |s^{-1}(Y)|$ and $s^{-1}(X) \not\supseteq A'$ for any $A' \in \mathscr{A}$, $s \in S_{(n, X)}$. Also, if $(n, X)(s) = s_1$, then $s_1(n) = X$ and $s_1(m) = s(m) = X$ for all cells of A. Thus $s_1^{-1}(X) \supseteq A$ and $(n, X)(s) = W$. Hence, $s \in W'_1$.

Let now $s \in W'_1$, so that there exists an $n \in N$ such that $(n, X)(s) \in W$. Let $(n, X)(s) = s_1$. Now $s_1^{-1}(X) = s^{-1}(X) \cup \{n\}$. Since $s_1 \in W$, there is an $A \in \mathscr{A}$ such that $s^{-1}(X) \cup \{n\} \supseteq A$. However, since $s \notin W$, $s^{-1}(X) \not\supseteq A$. Hence, $n \in A$ and for all $m \in A$ such that $m \neq n$, $s(m) = X$. Hence, $\sharp_s(A) = 1$ and $s \in J_1$.

Let now the theorem be true for $k \leq i$. Let $\langle C_s, \sharp_s \rangle \in J_{i+1}$. Then by Theorem 3.20 there exists an n such that for all n'

$$Y_{n'}(X_n(\langle C_s, \sharp_s \rangle)) \in \bigcup_{j=1}^{i} J_j.$$

However, since $s \notin W$ and $|s^{-1}(X)| = |s^{-1}(Y)|$, and from the proof of Theorem 3.21 of $\langle C_s, \sharp_s \rangle$ as a member of J_{i+1}, there is an $n \in N$ such that

$s(n) = \Lambda$, $s \in S_{(n,X)}$ and hence, $(n, X)(s)$ is defined. Also, whenever $(n', Y)((n, X)(s))$ is defined we have, by Theorem 3.20,

$$\langle C_{(n',Y)((n,X)(s))}, \#_{(n',Y)((n,X)(s))} \rangle = Y_{n'}(X_n(C_s, \#_s)) \in \bigcup_{j=1}^{i} J_j;$$

hence, there exists an n such that $s \in S_{(n,X)}$ and for all n' such that $(n, X)(s) \in S_{(n',Y)}$,

$$(n', Y)((n, X)(s)) \in \bigcup_{j=1}^{i} W_j.$$

Hence,

$$s \in W_{i+1}.$$

Let now $s \in W_{i+1}$. Then, there exists an n such that $s \in S_{(n,X)}$ and for all n' such that $(n, X)(s) \in S_{(n',Y)}$,

$$(n', Y)((n, X)(s)) \in \bigcup_{j=1}^{i} W_i$$

and hence,

$$Y_{n'}(X_n(\langle C_s, \#_s \rangle)) \in \bigcup_{j=1}^{i} J_i.$$

Since $Y_{n'}(X_n(\langle C_s, \#_s \rangle))$ is a subgraph of $X_n(\langle C_s, \#_s \rangle)$ by definition of $Y_{n'}$, $X_n(\langle C_s, \#_s \rangle)$ has subgraphs $\{\langle C_k, \#_k \rangle\} \in \bigcup_{j=1}^{i} J_i$. Also, none of $\{\langle C_k, \#_k \rangle\}$ are subgraphs of $\langle C_s, \#_s \rangle$, since $\langle C_s, \#_s \rangle \notin \bigcup_{j=1}^{i} J_i$ by induction hypotheses. Hence, n must occur in the domain of each of these subgraphs. So $\langle C_s, \#_s \rangle$ has a subgraph that is obtained from $\{\langle C_k, \#_k \rangle\}$ by the construction shown in the definition of J_{i+1}. Hence, $s \in J_{i+1}$. ∎

The reason for introducing the foregoing theorems is that the only predicates needed for the recognition of members of $\bigcup J_i$ are the values of $\#_s$ for the different files and (in view of the construction of J_{i+1} from $\bigcup_{j=1}^{i} J_j$) that $s(n) = \Lambda$ for some cell n common to a number of files. Given a situation $s \in \{X, Y, \Lambda\}^N$, that is, an assignment of X, Y, and Λ on the cells, the search for files with given values of $\#_s$ and having certain cells in $s^{-1}(\Lambda)$ in common among files is much more directed than the exhaustive mini-max searches indicated by the definition of $\{W_i\}$.

The difficulty with the description of W_i through the J_i, however, lies in the fact that the $\bigcup W_i'$ contains $\bigcup W_i$, but does not coincide with it. Hence, the J_i are only approximations to W_i. The reason for this is that the converse of Theorem 3.18 is not true. One reason for this, in turn, is that elements W_i' may be elements of L in $\langle N, \mathscr{A}, \mathscr{B} \rangle$, and are members of $\bigcup_{n \in N} S_{(n,X)}$ only because L' is empty in $\langle N, \mathscr{A}, \varnothing \rangle$. An example of this is given in Chapter 5, Section 5.6.

However, because the difference between $\{W_i\}$ and $\{W_i'\}$ consists mainly in the emptiness of L', a state in $\bigcup W_i'$ can be tested for membership in $\bigcup W_i$ by a somewhat well-directed search also. A method for doing this has been pointed out by Citrenbaum [64].

Another very important reason for using the $\{K_i\}$ as approximations to the $\{W_i\}$ is that the $\{J_i\}$, being obtainable from a specific mode of combination of statements of the form $\#_s(A) = i$ and $(\exists n)((n, A) \in C_s$ and $(n, B) \in C_s)$, leads to easy generalizations from examples. A learning program based on such generalization was developed by Koffman [65]. and is discussed in Section 5.6. The descriptions learned by this program are utilized by a game-playing program to make very deep forcing moves during the play of any tic-tac-toe-like game. In this sense, the program is game independent within this class of games. Given any game $\langle N, \mathcal{A}, \mathcal{B} \rangle$, it plays the game legally and, on the basis of its experience, improves its game, often to defeat its opponent.

3.10   RECOGNIZING FORCING STATES THROUGH LINEAR EVALUATION

We often try to recognize members of $\bigcup_i W_i$ by devising a language suitable to their description. This language may be constructed by a careful evaluation of its predicates with respect to the rules of the game (as shown in Section 3.9, one technique for doing this with respect to the tic-tac-toe-like games is particularly simple). Another way of constructing the language might be to use predicates that have been found useful (in some sense) in the game and try to combine them into statements whose denotations hopefully coincide with $\bigcup_i W_i$.

One mode of combination of predicates that has received a lot of attention in the literature can be given the general name "linear combination." In its most elementary form this coincides with the mode of combination called "combination by linear threshold gates." The predicates, in these cases, denote the equivalence classes of the kernels of functions mapping the universe of discourse into real numbers.

Let S be a set and $\varphi : S \to R$ be a function mapping S into real numbers. The kernel of this map, it will be recalled, is the equivalence relation $E = \varphi \circ \varphi^{-1}$ defined as

$$s_1 E s_2 \quad \text{if and only if} \quad \varphi(s_1) = \varphi(s_2).$$

This equivalence relation partitions S into disjoint sets called equivalence classes, yielding one equivalence class for each real number in the range of φ.

Each equivalence class is the denotation of a predicate of the form $\varphi(s) = r$. Let these predicates be represented by $P_{\varphi r}$.

Let $\Phi = \{\varphi_1, \varphi_2, \ldots, \varphi_n\}$ be a finite set of functions defined on S and let $\{P_{\varphi_i r} \mid \varphi_i \in \Phi, r \in \text{range of } \varphi_i\}$ be the set of predicates associated with them. Let $w_1, w_2, \ldots, w_n$ be a set of reals. We can define a new function on S as a linear combination of the φ_i.

$$\psi = w_1\varphi_1 + w_2\varphi_2 + \cdots + w_n\varphi_n$$

If the range of each function $\varphi_i \in \Phi$ is finite, the kernel of ψ defines a partition of S that is of finite index and whose equivalence classes are obtained from the equivalence classes of the kernels of φ_i by means of set operations.

Let each of the φ_i be a characteristic function of some subset of S. Also, let us define a subset T of S as

$$s \in T \quad \text{if} \quad \psi(s) \geq \theta$$

where θ is a specific real number. Clearly T is the union of a set of equivalence classes in the kernel of ψ. The set T defined this way by ψ is often called a "linearly separable function" of the subsets defined by the φ_i and their complements.

In what follows, attention is restricted to linear combinations of predicates in general; the discussion above is included to indicate that our understanding of linear combination of predicates extends no further than what is understood about linearly separable functions.

In what follows it is shown how a certain function ψ can be defined from the set of situations to reals in such a way that $\psi(s)$ exceeds a constant value for all members of $\bigcup_i W_i$. Remarks are then made regarding the feasibility of constructing $\psi(s)$ as a linear combination of the other functions.

Let $\langle S, F, G, W, L \rangle$ be a board game. Define a function:

$$\varphi : S - \bigcup_{f \in F} S_f - \bigcup_{g \in G} S_g \to R$$

having the following property.

L1 $s \in W$ and $\varphi(s') \geq \varphi(s)$ implies $s' \in W$.
L2 $s \in L$ and $\varphi(s') \leq \varphi(s)$ implies $s' \in L$.

It is clear that

LEMMA 3.9.

$$\underset{s \in W}{\text{glb}} \{\varphi(s)\} \geq \underset{s \in L}{\text{lub}} \{\varphi(s)\}.$$

PROOF.   Otherwise there exist real numbers y and y' such that

$$\text{glb}_{s \in W} \varphi(s) < y < y' < \text{lub}_{s \in L} \varphi(s).$$

and there exist $s \in W$ and $s' \in L$ such that $y = \varphi(s)$ and $y' = \varphi(s')$. But then by L1 and L2, both s and s' are members of L and W. Since L and W are disjoint, this is impossible.   ∎

It can also be seen easily that if $S - \bigcup_{f \in F} S_f - \bigcup_{g \in G} S_g \neq W \cup L$, then for any situation $s \in S - \bigcup_{f \in F} S_f - \bigcup_{g \in G} S_g - W - L$,

$$\text{glb}_{s \in W} \varphi(s) > \varphi(s) > \text{lub}_{s \in L} \varphi(s),$$

whence in this case $\text{glb}_{s \in W} \varphi(s) > \text{lub}_{s \in L} \varphi(s)$. However, it is always true that for any element $s \in S - \bigcup_{f \in F} S_f - \bigcup_{g \in G} S_g$, $\varphi(s) > \text{glb}_{s \in W} \varphi(s)$ implies $s \in W$. If F and G are finite, we can extend φ into ψ, defined over some elements of $(\bigcup_{f \in F} S_f) \cup (\bigcup_{g \in G} S_g)$ as follows.

$$\psi(s) = \varphi(s) \qquad \text{if } s \in S - \bigcup_{f \in F} S_f - \bigcup_{g \in G} S_g;$$

$$\psi(s) = \min\{\psi(g(s)) \mid s \in S_g\} \qquad \text{if } s \in \bigcup_{g \in G} S_g;$$

$$\psi(s) = \max\{\psi(f(s)) \mid s \in S_f\} \qquad \text{if } s \in \bigcup_{f \in F} S_f.$$

In the second and third equations above, if the right-hand side is not defined, then the left-hand side is not defined either. Hence, $\psi(s)$ may not have S as its domain. The following, however, is true.

THEOREM 3.22.   *In a progressively bounded board game let* $\varphi(s') = \text{glb}_{s \in W} \varphi(s)$ *for some* $s' \in W$, *and let* $s \in \bigcup_{f \in F} S_f$. *Then* $\psi(s) \geq \text{glb}_{s \in W} \varphi(s)$ *if and only if* $s \in \bigcup_i W_i$.

PROOF.   Define a control strategy Q_F as follows.

(i) If $\psi(s)$ is not defined, then $Q_F(s) = f$ where f is the first element of F (in some given ordering) such that $s \in S_f$.

(ii) If $\psi(s)$ is defined, then $Q_F(s)$ is the first element of F (in the given ordering) such that $\psi(Q_F(s)(s)) = \psi(s)$. By definition of ψ, such an element must exist.

Control strategy Q_F is a winning strategy for all elements $s_0 \in \bigcup_{f \in F} S_f$ such that $\psi(s_0) \geq \text{glb}_{s \in W} \varphi(s)$. To see this, let Q_G be an arbitrary disturbance strategy. Let $\psi(s_0) \geq \text{glb}_{s \in W} \varphi(s)$. Define a sequence of situations $s_0, s_1, \ldots$

as follows:

$$s_{i+1} = Q_F(s_i)(s_i) \quad \text{if } i \text{ is even;}$$
$$s_{i+1} = Q_G(s_i)(s_i) \quad \text{if } i \text{ is odd.}$$

We can see immediately that for all i, $\psi(s_i) \geq \psi(s_0)$. This is true for $s = 0$. Let it be true for $i \leq k$. If k is odd, then $s_{k+1} = g(s_k)$ for some $g \in G$. By definition of ψ, $\psi(g(s_k)) \geq \psi(s_k)$. If k is even, then by definition of Q_F, $\psi(s_{k+1}) = \psi(s_k)$.

Since the game is progressively bounded there is a last element s_m of the sequence $s_0, s_1, \ldots, s_m \in S - \bigcup_{f \in F} S_f - \bigcup_{g \in G} S_g$. Also, $\psi(s_m) = \varphi(s_m) \geq \psi(s_0) \geq \mathrm{glb}_{s \in W} \varphi(s)$. Hence, $s_m \in W$. Since Q_G is arbitrary, Q_F is a winning strategy for s_0. Since a winning strategy exists for s_0, $s_0 \in \bigcup_i W_i$.

Conversely, let $s_0 \in W_k \subseteq \bigcup_i W_i$. If $k = 1$, then there exists an $f \in F$ such that $f(s_0) \in W$ and hence, $\psi(f(s_0)) \geq \mathrm{glb}_{s \in W} \varphi(s)$. By definition of ψ, $\psi(s_i) \geq \varphi(f(s_0)) \geq \mathrm{glb}_{s \in W} \varphi(s)$. Hence, if $s_0 \in W_1$, $\psi(s_0) \geq \mathrm{glb}_{s \in W} \varphi(s)$.

Let it be true that if $s \in \bigcup_{i=1}^{k} W_i$, then $\psi(s) \geq \mathrm{glb}_{s \in W} \varphi(s)$. Let $s_0 \in W_{k+1}$. Then there exists an $f \in F$ such that for all $g \in G$ such that $f(s_0) \in S_g$, $g(f(s_0)) \in \bigcup_{k=1}^{k} W_i$ and hence, $\psi(g(f(s_0))) \geq \mathrm{glb}_{s \in W} \varphi(s)$. Hence,

$$\psi(f(s_0)) = \min\{\psi(g(f(s_0))) \mid (f(s_0)) \in S_g\} \geq \mathrm{glb}_{s \in W} \varphi(s).$$

But $\psi(s_0) \geq \psi(f(s_0))$ by definition. Hence, $\psi(s_0) \geq \mathrm{glb}_{s \in W} \varphi(s)$. ∎

Theorem 3.22 shows that if $\psi(s)$ could be calculated for all s for which ψ is defined, then a cautious strategy could be applied for the choice of controls. However, $\psi(s)$ cannot be calculated from the definition with any degree of efficiency.

In case we can easily calculate a set of functions $\varphi_1, \varphi_2, \ldots, \varphi_n$ mapping S into reals such that

$$\psi = w_1 \varphi_1 + w_2 \varphi_2 + \cdots + w_n \varphi_n,$$

then the predicate

$$\psi(s) \geq \theta$$

is a linear combination of the predicates corresponding to the equivalence classes of the kernels of the functions $\{\varphi_i\}$.

Given a set of functions $\varphi_1, \varphi_2, \ldots, \varphi_n$, a calculation of ψ would involve the search for a set of real numbers $w_1, w_2, \ldots, w_n$ with the two following properties. For all $s \in S - \bigcup_{f \in F} S_f - \bigcup_{g \in G} S_g$, $\sum w_i \varphi_i(s) \geq \theta$ if and only if $s \in W$, and for all $s \in \bigcup_{f \in F} S_f$,

$$\sum w_i \varphi_i(s) = \max_{f \in F} \min_{g \in G} \{\sum w_i \varphi_i(g(f(s))) \mid s \in S_f \text{ and } f(s) \in S_g\}.$$

In the case where φ_i are characteristic functions, methods are known for obtaining the φ_i by an adaptive procedure, when they exist [25], so that they satisfy the first of the two foregoing conditions. Some of the algorithms also indicate impossibility of fulfilling the conditions when no set w_1, w_2, ... exists that can fulfill it. Very little theoretical study has gone into methods when no set w_1, w_2, ... exists that can fulfil it. Very little theoretical study has gone into methods for fulfilling the second condition even when it can be fulfilled.

However, some excellent case studies have been done by Samuel [9] on the game of checkers, where certain adaptive techniques have been explored for the calculation of the w_i. The φ_i's were calculated by giving suitable mathematical interpretations to certain well-known important evaluations of checkerboard positions. The w_i's were calculated over the course of many games by adjusting them to fulfill the second condition above. The strategies resulting from the approximate descriptions of $\bigcup_i W_i$ so obtained have yielded an extremely powerful checker-playing program. There are indications that by the use of more than one "layer" of threshold logic, a stronger program can be obtained. However, the only method available for testing these strategies seems to be operational, to wit, accumulating statistics regarding the performance of the program against strong players.

Chapter 4

DESCRIBING PATTERNS

4.1. INTRODUCTION

The importance of pattern recognition to solutions of problems and games was discussed briefly in Section 1.3. In Chapters 2 and 3, as sets like T_i, T', S^0_{fX}, W_i, K_i, and blocks of E_i or of the kernels of functions like Q were discussed, it was implicitly or explicitly stated that the use of these sets in the construction of solution methods is practicable if and only if they can be described efficiently.

This chapter is devoted entirely to the discussion of descriptions, and of the way the efficiency of description depends on the set being described and the language used for describing it. Precise definitions are attempted for the ideas and terms involved. All the motivations for the formalisms introduced are not repeated here since some of them have already been discussed in Chapter 1. Specifically, the reader is reminded that a "pattern" is defined to be a subset of a predefined universe of discourse. However, it is worthwhile at this point to include an informal discussion of terms whose precise definition is not stressed in this chapter.

By the term "language" is meant a combination of two things: a set of syntactic expressions (generated, for instance, by some generative grammar [26]) and the interpretations of these expressions as denoting sets. For the latter to be possible, it is necessary that some of the syntactic entities be predicates defining certain "intuitively recognizable" sets of objects in the universe of discourse. In addition, the syntax has to have various ways of combining predicates to yield compound statements. These compound statements denote sets that are uniquely related to the intuitively recognizable sets in a way dictated by the structure of the compound statements.

The first few sections of this chapter are devoted to the development of some formal definitions and then to some specific languages that are meaningful in a wide variety of universes of discourse. The major emphasis is on the "efficiencies" of these languages.

By the efficiency of a language for the description of a given set is meant the "size" (in some sense) of the "shortest" expression that denotes that set.

This size depends on the set as well as the predicates of the language and the repertoire of combination modes available. It is taken for granted that new predicates can be defined for enriching the language. That is, some compound statements may be replaced by shorter expressions by defining new syntactic entities in the language.

The definition of the word "size" was kept purposely vague in the last paragraph because a precise definition (being heavily dependent on technology) is hard to give in absolute terms. In a very rough way we can say that the size of an expression is measured by the number of symbols in it. In the author's own thinking (for reasons that will be clarified in the proper context) certain symbols in the expression (like "or" of propositional calculus) seem to have greater size than others (like "and").

This discussion has been limited to the nature of statements that describe "given" sets. If by "given set" we mean a set for which a description is available, then the problem of obtaining a short description turns out to be a trivial one, or at least a problem of transliteration. However, if by a given set we mean a set whose elements are all available as a list, then we can consider the problem of generating a succinct statement in a language that will be satisfied by every element of the list and by none else. This, roughly, is the problem of "concept learning."

Since such lists are impossibly large in practical cases we may, instead, consider a case where only some members of a set are exhibited on a short list. This, however, can give no meaningful clue to a learning program. We can infer, without any contradiction from the presentation, that every object belongs to the set. It is essential that at least some members of the complement of the set also be exhibited in another short list. We can then consider the problem of generating a succinct statement that will denote some set that contains every element of the first list and none of the elements of the second list. Typically, such a statement will be satisfied by certain objects that do not appear on either list. Thus, the expression will have "generalized" on the examples given. The mode of this generalization will be dependent on the method used for generating the describing expressions and to a certain extent on the language, since the language determines the succinctness of the statements. However, the "correctness" of the resulting generalization—whether the description actually denotes the set we had in mind in constructing the lists—is not at all determinable from the method of description generation alone.

The next chapter describes certain algorithms for generalizations of the restricted ("not necessarily correct") variety. It also discusses the possible situations under which generalizations may turn out to be correct.

Rough definitions of a few more terms may be useful for the reduction of confusion. In the literature, the term "pattern recognition" is used in two implied senses. In one sense it stands for what has been called generalization above. In this book "pattern learning" and "concept learning," or simply "learning," are often meant to signify the same phenomenon. In the other sense the term "pattern recognition" means the recognition of an object as belonging to a pattern of known description. The terms "pattern recognition," "recognition," and "object recognition" are all used here in this sense. Another term, "concept formation," is often used for what has been called "concept learning" above. In the next chapter a much more complex phenomenon is called "concept formation."

The word "concept" is often used for the word "pattern" in this book. The reason for this is historical: the initial models and languages developed at Case [27, 28] were developed for understanding the psychological process of concept formation [14]. The relevance of the ideas to the field of pattern recognition was realized only later. This realization immediately led to the need for further developments of the formalisms. It is the author's belief that these further developments have made the theory even more relevant to psychology than they were before. The theory, in its present form, therefore, uses both terms.

4.2. SOME BASIC TERMS AND DISCUSSIONS

The present section formalizes some of the basic ideas referred to in Section 1.3, to initiate the discussion. A pattern recognition environment (called *environment* for short) is an ordered pair $\langle U, \mathscr{P} \rangle$ where U is an abstract set and $\mathscr{P}$ is a family of nontrivial partitions on U. In much of what follows, the family $\mathscr{P}$ and each of its elements are considered to be finite, although some of the definitions and results are meaningful even if some elements of $\mathscr{P}$ are infinite classes.

The set U is referred to as the universe of discourse (or *universe* for short). Each element of $\mathscr{P}$ is called a *property*. If P is a property, then each element of $p \in P$ (where p, clearly, is a subset of U) is called a *value* of P.

The reader will notice that the word "value" is used for certain predefined subsets of the universe of discourse, whereas in most mathematical literature the word "property" is used in this sense. However, it is worthwhile to recall that the property "redness" and the property "color" are two distinct things. "Redness" is a property in the usual mathematical sense. But "color" is also referred to as property in common parlance: a fact we would like to recognize in the theory. Psychologists use the words "characteristic" or "dimension" instead of "property" [29].

A *concept* (or a *pattern*) is defined recursively as follows:

C1.   A value of a property is a concept.
C2.   If A and B are concepts, then $A \cup B$ is a concept.
C3.   If A is a concept, then the complement $\bar{A}$ of A is a concept.
C4.   Nothing is a concept unless its being so follows from C1, C2, and C3.

In most of the previous work at Case, C3 was replaced by "If A and B are concepts, then $A \cap B$ is a concept." In such cases, however, the class of concepts does not form a Boolean algebra except for the cases where each element of $\mathscr{P}$ is a finite partition. This is because complements of concepts may not always be concepts if partitions have an infinite number of blocks. The difficulty is removed by the foregoing definitions. It could also have been removed by allowing infinite unions and intersections: however, since the description languages presupposed in this book begin to have practical difficulties any time infinite operations are used (difficulties shared by any pattern recognition scheme using infinite processes) it was considered more meaningful to have the definitions as above. We can motivate the foregoing definition of a concept by saying "A concept is a set of things whose elements are recognizable as belonging to it by virtue of their properties."

For convenience of later discussion, we define an environment to be *finite* if $\mathscr{P}$ is a finite family and each element of $\mathscr{P}$ is a finite partition. Given a subfamily $\mathscr{P}'$ of $\mathscr{P}$, we define a subclass $\mathscr{C}_{\mathscr{P}'}$ of the class of all concepts as follows.

(i)   Any value of any element of $\mathscr{P}'$ is a member of $\mathscr{C}_{\mathscr{P}'}$.
(ii)   If A and B are members of $\mathscr{C}_{\mathscr{P}'}$, then $A \cup B$ and $\bar{A}$ are members of $\mathscr{C}_{\mathscr{P}'}$.
(iii)   Nothing is a member of $\mathscr{C}_{\mathscr{P}'}$ unless its being so follows from (i) and (ii).

By this definition, the class $\mathscr{C}_{\mathscr{P}}$ is the class of all concepts.

A subfamily $\mathscr{P}'$ of $\mathscr{P}$ is called a *fine structure* family if and only if $\mathscr{C}_{\mathscr{P}'} = \mathscr{C}_{\mathscr{P}}$.

A finite fine structure family $\mathscr{P}' = \{P_1, P_2, \ldots, P_n\}$ is said to be *full* if

$$p_{1i_1} \cap p_{2i_2} \cap \cdots \cap p_{ni_n} \neq \varnothing \qquad (4.1)$$

for each $p_{ri_r} \in p_r$.

A fine structure family of properties in any environment sets the limit to the distinguishability of members of the universe, as will be shown presently. If the fine structure family is much smaller than the set $\mathscr{P}$, then the properties outside the fine structure family merely affect the efficiency of description and not the ultimate capability of description. Nevertheless, since efficiency of description is crucial, the distinction between $\mathscr{P}$ and $\mathscr{P}'$ is essential to the considerations of this chapter. To keep this basic role of the fine structure family clear, we define as follows.

A *real environment* is a triple $\langle U, \mathscr{P}, \mathscr{P}' \rangle$ where $\langle U, \mathscr{P} \rangle$ is an environment and $\mathscr{P}'$ is a fine structure subfamily of $\mathscr{P}$. ($\mathscr{P}'$ is not necessarily a proper subfamily of $\mathscr{P}$, although in all interesting cases it would be.) Subfamily $\mathscr{P}'$ is called the *input properties* of the environment.

In the next few sections only finite real environments are considered. In the work described in the next section, real environments with a full fine structure family of input properties are assumed.

All description languages discussed in this chapter have as their motivation the Boolean algebraic structure of the class of concepts as just defined. Although these languages differ in the mode of describing concepts, one aspect of them remains the same: any concept of the form shown in expression (4.1) is, in one sense, very basic. That is, two members of U both of which belong to the set

$$p_{1i_1} \cap p_{2i_2} \cap \cdots \cap p_{ni_n}$$

are indistinguishable; if one of them belongs to any concept C, then the other must also belong to it. This can be readily shown by induction over the least number of set-theoretical operators needed to exhibit the concept to be one according to C1, C2, and C3. In fact, an even stronger version of this statement can be offered.

THEOREM 4.1. *Let $\mathscr{P}'$ be indexed by the (not necessarily finite) set I so that $\mathscr{P}' = \{P_i\}_{i \in I}$. For each $i \in I$, let $p_i \in P_i$. Let a and b be two elements of U such that for each $i \in I$, both a and b are members of p_i. Let C be any concept. Then $a \in C$ if and only if $b \in C$.*

PROOF. Let C be a concept according to C1 in the definition. Then there is a $P_i \in \mathscr{P}'$ and $p_{i'} \in P_i$ such that $C = p_{i'}$. Since $a \in P_i$ and $a \in C = p_{i'}$, we have $p_i \cap p_{i'} \neq \varnothing$. But since P_i is a partition, $p_i \cap p_{i'} \neq \varnothing$ implies $i = i'$. Since by hypothesis $b \in p_i$, we also have $b \in C$. The converse follows. Let now the theorem be true for any concept that can be constructed with n or less set-theoretical connectives. Let C be constructed by $n + 1$ set-theoretical connectives. If $C = A \cup B$, then either $a \in A$ or $a \in B$. Let $a \in A$. Since A is constructible with less than n connectives, $b \in A$ by induction hypothesis, so that $b \in A \cup B$; similarly if $a \in B$. The converse follows also. If $C = \bar{A}$, then if b is not in C, it is in A. But A has less than n connectives. Hence, since $b \in A$ and by the symmetry of the theorem, $a \in A$, which is impossible since $a \in \bar{A}$, hence, $b \in C$. ∎

Any object in U, then, can be completely specified (so far as its membership in all concepts is concerned) by indicating its membership in one element of each of the properties in $\mathscr{P}'$. On the basis of this fact we can make the following definitions.

Given a finite real environment $\langle U, \mathscr{P}, \mathscr{P}' \rangle$, a *generalized object* is a string of characters of the form $(P_{i_1}, p_{i_1}, P_{i_2}, p_{i_2}, \ldots, P_{i_n}, p_{i_n})$ where n is a finite integer such that for each k, $P_{i_k} \in \mathscr{P}'$, $p_{i_k} \in P_{i_k}$, and $p_{i_1} \cap p_{i_2} \cap \cdots \cap p_{i_k} \cap \cdots \cap p_{i_n} \neq \varnothing$.

A generalized object is an *object* if for all $P \in \mathscr{P}$ and $p \in P$, $p_{i_1} \cap \cdots \cap p_{i_n}$ is either contained in or disjoint from p.

For any finite environment (or even an environment where $\mathscr{P}'$ is finite) n in an object may be considered to be equal to the cardinality of $\mathscr{P}'$ even where the environment is not full. In a full environment, of course, it is necessary to have n equal to the cardinality of $\mathscr{P}'$ in any object. It may be noticed that an object defines a concept, to wit, the concept $p_{i_1} \cap p_{i_2} \cap \cdots \cap p_{i_n}$. The use of the symbols P_{i_k} may, therefore, seem unnecessary in the definition of objects. However, retaining the properties, together with the values, has some important uses that will become clear toward the end of this chapter. Meanwhile, we refer to the concept defined by an object also as the object. Very little confusion arises from this double use; when it does occur, it can be resolved from the context. On the other hand, the double use of the term often considerably reduces the complexity of the discussion and introduces stronger motivation.

The basic predicates out of which the descriptions of concepts will be built consist of statements of the form $P(x) = p$ where P is some property, p a value of P, and x a variable. The predicate will be true for all members of the value p of the property P. Any member of the object $(P_{i_1}, p_{i_1}; \ldots; P_{i_n}, p_{i_n})$ then satisfies the statement $S(x)$, where $S(x)$ denotes the statement

$$(P_{i_1}(x) = p_{i_1}) \wedge (P_{i_2}(x) = p_{i_2}) \wedge \cdots \wedge (P_{i_n}(x) = p_{i_n}).$$

This statement may be considered to "describe" the object $(P_{i_1}, p_{i_1}; \ldots; P_{i_n}, p_{i_n})$ in the sense that the sentence $S(a)$ will be true for all elements a of the object.

Obviously, concepts other than objects can be similarly "described" by statements involving the basic predicates $P(x) = p$ where $P \in \mathscr{P}$, $p \in P$, and the usual logical connectives. Given any object and the description of any concept in such a language, we can readily determine whether the object is contained in the concept or not. Algorithms and formats used for such recognition processes will be described presently. Meanwhile, certain important aspects of this elementary language bear discussion.

The central questions regarding descriptions are the following.

1.   Given a concept, how should its description be stored so as to use as small an amount of memory as possible?

2.   How should the description of a concept be stored and processed so that, given an object and a concept, we can determine as efficiently as possible whether the object is contained in the concept?

3.   Given two sets of objects, how should we construct a short description of a concept that contains all elements of the first set and no element of the second?

In this and the next chapter some of the earlier alternative attempts at answering these questions are described. They are included here because they compare favorably with some published work by others [30, 31] and, in the author's opinion, shed some light on the nature of the problem.

4.3.   CONCEPTIONS—A DESCRIPTION LANGUAGE

The discussions in this section are based on the work of the author [28] and Pennypacker [32]. The formalism developed here grew out of some of the author's previous thoughts [27], which led to a more primitive description language that was later abandoned as inefficient. However, some of the basic ideas relevant to that work have been retained; these were discussed in the preceding section.

Given an environment $\langle U, \mathscr{P} \rangle$ and a concept C, a property is called *directly relevant* to a nonempty concept if and only if it has at least one value whose intersection with the concept is empty.

A property P is called *relevant to a nonempty concept C with respect to a family $\mathscr{F}$ of properties* if and only if either it is directly relevant to C or there exists a property Q ($\neq P$) in $\mathscr{F}$ with a value q such that $q \cap C$ is nonempty and P is relevant to $q \cap C$ with respect to $\mathscr{F}$.

In short, a property is not relevant to a concept when knowing about the value of this property for an object does not (either by itself or in conjunction with other properties) help in the recognition of the object as belonging in the concept. This statement will be formalized presently; the following definitions and theorem are needed for this formalization.

Given an environment $\langle U, \mathscr{P} \rangle$ and a concept C, a finite subfamily $\{P_1, P_2, \ldots, P_n\}$ of $\mathscr{P}$ is called *sufficient* for C if and only if either

S1 $n = 1$ and C has nonempty intersections with more than one value of P_1

or

S2 $C = \bigcap_{k=1}^{n} p_{ij_i}$ where $p_{ij_i} \in P_i$ and there is no subset of $\{P_i \mid 1 \leq i \leq n\}$ with this property. (Note: n can be 1 in this case also.)

A set of properties $\mathscr{F}$ is called a *sufficiency family* for a concept C if either $\mathscr{F}$ is sufficient for C according to S2 or there is a member $P \in \mathscr{F}$ that is sufficient for C by S1 and $\mathscr{F}$ is the union of P with some sufficiency family of each of the nonempty intersections of C with the values of P.

THEOREM 4.2. *Let* $\{P_i \mid (1 \leq i \leq n)\}$ *be a sufficiency family for* C. *Let* $p_i \in P_i$ *for each* i. *Then either* $p_1 \cap p_2 \cap \cdots \cap p_n \subseteq C$ *or* $p_1 \cap p_2 \cap \cdots \cap p_n \cap C = \varnothing$.

PROOF. If there is no property P_k in $\{P_i\}$ such that P_k has more than one value with nonempty intersections with C, then $C = p_1 \cap p_2 \cap \cdots \cap p_n$ and the theorem is evident. Let the theorem be true if there are k properties in $\{P_i\}$ with more than one value with nonempty intersections with C. The theorem is true for $k = 0$. If it is true for $k = m$, let $k = m + 1$. Assume (without loss of generality) that P_1 has more than one value with nonempty intersections with C and for any $p' \in P_1$ such that $C \cap p' \neq \varnothing$, $C \cap p'$ has a sufficiency family that is a subset of $\{P_i\}$. If $C \cap p_1 = \varnothing$, then the theorem follows immediately. Otherwise, the sufficiency family for $C \cap p_1$ that is a subset of $\{P_i\}$ contains less than or equal to m properties that have more than one value with nonempty intersections with $C \cap p_1$. Hence, $p_1 \cap p_2 \cap \cdots \cap p_n \subseteq C \cap p_1 \subseteq C$ by induction hypothesis. ∎

This theorem leads to the following explication of the significance of relevant properties.

THEOREM 4.3. *Let* $\mathscr{F} = \{P_1, P_2, \ldots, P_n\}$ *be a sufficiency family for the concept* C. *Let* $P_1 \in \mathscr{F}$ *be not relevant to* C *with respect to* $\mathscr{F}$. *Let* $P_1 = \{p_{11}, p_{12}, \ldots, p_{1m}\}$. *For any set* $\{p_i \mid p_i \in P_i, 2 \leq i \leq n\}$ *if* $\varnothing \neq p_{11} \cap p_2 \cap \cdots \cap p_n \cap C$, *then for all* k $(1 \leq k \leq m)$, $p_{1k} \cap p_2 \cap \cdots \cap p_n \cap C \neq \varnothing$.

PROOF. By Theorem 4.2 the hypothesis $p_{11} \cap p_2 \cap \cdots \cap p_n \cap C \neq \varnothing$ implies $p_{11} \cap p_2 \cap \cdots \cap p_n \subseteq C$, or

$$p_{11} \cap p_2 \cap \cdots \cap p_n \cap C = p_{11} \cap p_2 \cap \cdots \cap p_n \neq \varnothing.$$

If $p_{1k} \cap p_2 \cap \cdots \cap p_n = \varnothing$, then P_1 is directly relevant to $p_2 \cap \cdots \cap p_n \cap C$ $(\neq \varnothing)$ and hence, relevant to C, leading to contradiction. ∎

This theorem indicates that when testing an object for inclusion in a concept, irrelevant properties need not be tested.

Let C be a concept with sufficiency family $\{P_1, P_2, \ldots, P_n\}$ and let each property P_i be relevant to C with respect to $\{P_1, P_2, \ldots, P_n\}$. Then a list of k lists, headed by the name "C," is called a *conception list of* C if either

C1. $k = 1$, the unique list is headed by the name "P_i" where $1 \leq i \leq n$ and P_i has more than one value with a nonempty intersection with

P_i; it is a list of ordered pairs consisting of the names of the values of P_i with nonempty intersections with C together with the names for these intersections;

or

C2. $n = k$ and each list is headed by a name "P_i" and contains a single ordered pair consisting of the name of the unique value $p_i \in P_i$ that has nonempty intersection with C and of the name "C."

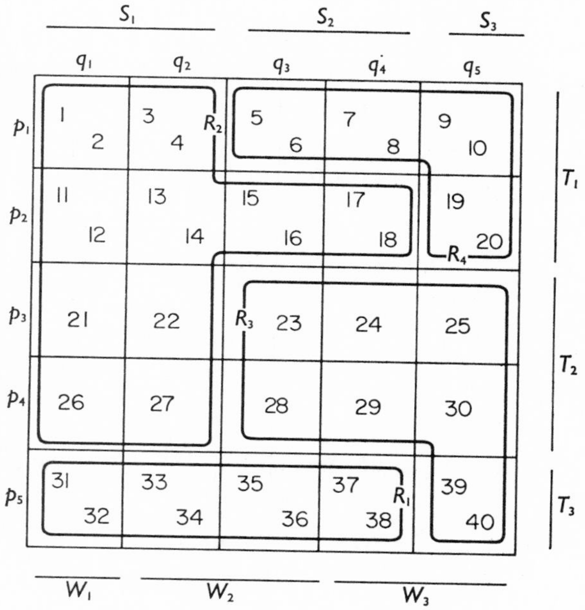

Figure 4.1. Illustration of noninput properties.

A set of conception lists forms a *conception* of a concept C if and only if it contains a conception list of C and a conception of every concept whose name occurs in the conception list. It is clear that a conception list of C satisfying C2 is a conception in itself.

Some of the ideas associated with the foregoing definitions and assertions can be exemplified by considering a specific universe. Consider a universe of discourse consisting of 40 elements as described in the following and exhibited in Figure 4.1. (This same basic universe will also be used in exemplifying the ideas introduced in Section 4.5.)

The 40 elements are denoted by the consecutive positive integers. The following subsets of the universe are taken to form the elements of the basic partitions.

$$p_1 = \{1, 2, \ldots, 10\},$$
$$p_2 = \{11, 12, \ldots, 20\},$$
$$p_3 = \{21, 22, 23, 24, 25\},$$
$$p_4 = \{26, 27, 28, 29, 30\},$$
$$p_5 = \{31, 32, \ldots, 40\},$$
$$q_1 = \{1, 2, 11, 12, 21, 26, 31, 32\},$$
$$q_2 = \{3, 4, 13, 14, 22, 27, 33, 34\},$$
$$q_3 = \{5, 6, 15, 16, 23, 28, 35, 36\},$$
$$q_4 = \{7, 8, 17, 18, 24, 29, 37, 38\},$$
$$q_5 = \{9, 10, 19, 20, 25, 30, 39, 40\};$$
$$R_1 = p_5 - q_5, \quad R_2 = q_1 \cup q_2 - p_5 \cup (p_2 \cap (q_3 \cup q_4)),$$
$$R_3 = q_5 \cup \{(q_3 \cup q_4) \cap (p_3 \cup p_4)\} - p_1 - p_2,$$
$$R_4 = U - R_1 - R_2 - R_3;$$
$$S_1 = q_1 \cup q_2, \quad S_2 = q_3 \cup q_4, \quad S_3 = q_5;$$
$$T_1 = p_1 \cup p_2, \quad T_2 = p_3 \cup p_4, \quad T_3 = p_5;$$
$$W_1 = q_1, \quad W_2 = q_2 \cup q_3, \quad W_3 = q_4 \cup q_5.$$

Figure 4.1 identifies the basic sets and the elements of the universe. There are five properties in this environment.

$$S = \{S_1, S_2, S_3\}, \quad T = \{T_1, T_2, T_3\},$$
$$W = \{W_1, W_2, W_3\}, \quad R = \{R_1, R_2, R_3, R_4\},$$
$$p = \{p_1, p_2, p_3, p_4, p_5\},$$
$$q = \{q_1, q_2, q_3, q_4, q_5\};$$

$\{p, q\}$ is a fine structure family for this environment; so is $\{p, W, S\}$. The family $\{p, q\}$ is a full fine structure family, while $\{p, W, S\}$ is not full. In the present discussion, p and q are taken to be input properties, yielding the real environment $\langle U, \{S, T, W, p, q, R\}, \{p, q\}\rangle$. In this environment $\{11, 13\}$ is not a concept, for example.

If we consider the concept T_1, it can be seen that q is not relevant to it with respect to $\{p, q, T\}$. However, q is relevant to T_1 with respect to $\{q, W, p\}$; R is not directly relevant to q_3, although it is relevant to q_3 with respect to $\{p, R\}$.

The conception of the concept $A = W_2 \cap R_2$ (i.e., the set $\{3, 4, 13, 14, 15, 16, 22, 27\}$) can be written variously.

$$
\begin{array}{c}
A \\
| \\
W - (W_2, A) \\
| \\
R - (R_2, A)
\end{array}
$$

would be a possible (and the shortest possible) conception. One other would be

$$
\begin{array}{ll}
A & B \\
| & | \\
p - (p_2, B) - (p_3, C) - (p_4, D) - (p_1, G) & q - (q_2, E) - (q_3, F)
\end{array}
$$

$$
\begin{array}{lllll}
C & D & E & F & G \\
| & | & | & | & | \\
p - (p_3, C) & p - (p_4, D) & p - (p_2, E) & p - (p_2, F) & p - (p_1, G) \\
| & | & | & | & | \\
q - (q_2, C) & q - (q_2, D) & q - (q_2, E) & q - (q_3, F) & q - (q_2, G)
\end{array}
$$

using $\{p, q\}$ as a sufficiency family. Another, somewhat shorter, would be the following.

$$
\begin{array}{ll}
A & B \\
| & | \\
p - (p_2, B) - (p_1, G) - (p_4, D) - (p_3, C) & p - (p_2, B) \\
& | \\
& W - (W_2, B)
\end{array}
$$

$$
\begin{array}{lll}
C & D & G \\
| & | & | \\
p - (p_3, C) & p - (p_4, D) & p - (p_1, G) \\
| & | & | \\
q - (q_2, C) & S - (S_1, D) & q - (q_2, G) \\
& | & \\
& W - (W_2, D) &
\end{array}
$$

which uses (p, q, S, W) as sufficiency family. It can be seen easily that (p, q, W) or (p, S, W) could be used as sufficiency families also. It can also be seen that the size of the sufficiency family used has no strong effect on the size of the conception. While (R, W) is a very effective sufficiency set for A, (p, q) is not. The size of the conception gets smaller when we augment this last sufficiency set to (p, q, S, W). Changing (p, q, S, W) to (p, q, W) actually decreases the size of the conception.

It should also be noted that when we use a full fine structure sufficiency family, the conception of any concepts other than values of fine structure properties and their intersections end up containing the conception of every object contained in the concept. This is the consideration that leads to the need for properties other than input properties for purposes of description. This point will be discussed again in later sections.

4.4. A RECOGNITION ALGORITHM USING CONCEPTIONS

The importance of conceptions arises because there exists an algorithm that can recognize a given object in a real environment as belonging to a concept whose conception is given. This algorithm is given later, after some other ideas associated with recognition have been discussed; however, the basic idea involved in it can be indicated here quite easily.

Let there be given an object $(P_1, p_1; P_2, p_2; \ldots ; P_n, p_n)$ and the conception of a concept C. We can determine whether the object belongs to the concept as follows. If the conception list of C includes only one relevant property (according to C1) P, then C has nonempty intersections with more than one value of P. Assume for simplicity that P is an input property. Then the object indicates the value of P in which it is contained. If this value does not occur in the conception list of C, then the object is not contained in C. (See Lemma 4.4.) On the other hand, if the object is contained in a value p_1 of P, then we do not know for certain that the object is contained in C. (A red bull is not a red ball!) We then interrogate the conception of $C \cap p_1$, whose name appears in the conception list C. The program then recursively determines if the object is contained in $C \cap p_1$. The adequacy of this procedure is indicated in Lemma 4.1.

We have to be careful, however, of one thing: that the recursive determination of the containment of the object in $C \cap p_1$ does not involve us in an infinite loop. That this does not occur is indicated by Lemma 4.3, which indicates that if a property occurs alone in the conception list of C, then further tests are unnecessary.

We also have to discuss the case where a set of properties $P, P', P'', \ldots$ occurs in the conception of C according to C2. If this is a unit set, then the procedure is as indicated above, except that the name of $C \cap p_1$ is C and by Lemma 4.3 the object is known to be contained in C. Otherwise, C has the form $p_1 \cap p' \cap p'' \cap \cdots$ and we merely test successively to see if the object is contained in p', p'', and so on till the list is exhausted. The validity of this process is brought out by Lemma 4.2.

The following four lemmata, although quite trivial, are included here for completeness and to establish that the structure "conception" is designed with the care that should go into the design of every complicated data structure, no matter how complicated.

LEMMA 4.1. *If $p_1 \in P_1$ has nonempty intersection with C and if X is an object with nonempty intersection with p_1, then $X \subseteq C$ if and only if $X \subseteq C \cap p_1$.*

PROOF. The "if" part is obvious. For the "only if" part, we note that if $X \cap p_1 \neq \varnothing$, then $X \subseteq p_1$ by Theorem 4.1 and by the fact that p_1 is a concept. (Note that if $X \nsubseteq p_1$, then $X \cap \bar{p}_1$ is nonempty and hence, some objects of X are elements of p_1 and others are not, contradicting Theorem 4.1.) Hence, if $X \subseteq C$, then $X = X \cap p_1 \subseteq C \cap p_1$. ■

LEMMA 4.2. *If $C = p_{1i_1} \cap p_{2i_2} \cap \cdots \cap p_{ni_n}$ and $X \cap p_{1i_1} \neq \varnothing$, then $X \subseteq C$ if and only if $X \subseteq p_{2i_2} \cap \cdots \cap p_{ni_n}$.*

PROOF. If $n = 1$, the set $\{p_{2i_2}, \ldots, p_{ni_n}\}$ is empty and their intersection is the universe. Also, $X \subseteq p_{1i_1}$ and $C = p_{1i_1}$. Hence, $X \subseteq C$. The converse follows trivially since $X \subseteq C \subseteq U$.

Let $n > 1$. If $X \subseteq p_{1i_1}$ and $X \subseteq p_{2i_2} \cap \cdots \cap p_{ni_n}$, then $X \subseteq p_{1i_1} \cap \cdots \cap p_{ni_n} = C$. Again, if $X \subseteq C = p_{1i_1} \cap \cdots \cap p_{ni_n}$, then $X \subseteq p_{2i_2} \cap \cdots \cap p_{ni_n}$.

LEMMA 4.3. *If $\{P\}$ is sufficient for C, and p_1 is a value of P such that $C \cap p_1 \neq \varnothing$, then $\{P\}$ is sufficient for $C \cap p_1$ only if $C = p_1$.*

PROOF. Only one value of P has nonempty intersection with $C \cap p_1$. Hence, $\{P\}$ can be sufficient for $C \cap p_1$ only by virtue of S2 above. Hence, if $\{P\}$ is sufficient for $C \cap p_1$, then $C = p_1$. ■

LEMMA 4.4. *If $p_1 \cap C = \varnothing$ and $X \subseteq p_1$, then $X \cap \varnothing$.* ■

The proof is evident.

It was assumed in our qualitative discussion that the properties mentioned in the conceptions are all input properties and hence are listed in the object. In this case, determination of the truth of statements like $X \subseteq p_1$ above is a trivial matter of searching through a list.

However, the test to be performed to find whether $X \subseteq p_1$ is not always such a straightforward process. If P is not a member of $\mathscr{P}'$, we need extra information to know if $X \subseteq p_1$. This information will be codified in the present recognition scheme by stipulating that conceptions for the values of

P are available in an acceptable form. The following definitions clarify what is meant by "acceptable" here.

The *description list of the universe* is a list of lists headed by the name "U." Each list in the list of lists is headed by the name of a property in $\mathscr{P}$ relevant to U with respect to $\mathscr{P}'$ and there is a list headed by the name of each relevant property in $\mathscr{P}$. The list headed by P is a list of ordered pairs containing the names of the values of P and the name of their intersections with U.

A set of lists is a *description list structure of the universe* if it contains the description list of the universe and a conception for all concepts whose name occurs in the description list of the universe.

It is to be noted that given a real environment $\langle U, \mathscr{P}, \mathscr{P}' \rangle$, the description list of the universe is unique. However, the conception list of any other concept is not necessarily unique: nor is a description list structure of the universe unique. However, the following theorem is true.

THEOREM 4.4.   *In an environment $\langle U, \mathscr{P}, \mathscr{P}' \rangle$, each element of $\mathscr{P} - \mathscr{P}'$ is relevant to the universe with respect to $\mathscr{P}'$.*

PROOF.   Since $\mathscr{P}'$ is a fine structure family of properties, any concept is a Boolean function of values of elements of $\mathscr{P}'$. Also, since each element P of $\mathscr{P}$ is a nontrivial partition, any value p of P is a proper subset of the universe. Hence, there is an object X that is not contained in p. Let $X = p_1 \cap p_2 \cap \cdots \cap p_n$ where n is the cardinality of $\mathscr{P}'$. Then, since $p \cap p_1 \cap p_2 \cap \cdots \cap p_n = \varnothing$, P is directly relevant to $p_1 \cap p_2 \cap \cdots \cap p_n$ and hence relevant to the universe.   ∎

Thus the name of every element of $\mathscr{P} - \mathscr{P}'$ heads some list in the description list of the universe. However, this does not necessarily make a description list structure of the universe "acceptable" information for finding whether an object X is contained in some value p of a noninput property. Some further definitions are needed.

Given a description list structure of the universe, a property $P \in \mathscr{P}$ is called *predefined* if and only if either

D1 $P \in \mathscr{P}'$

or

D2   all properties whose names occur in the conceptions of all values of P are predefined properties.

A description list structure of the universe is called *valid* is every element of $\mathscr{P}$ is predefined. To exemplify validity, the following is a description list of the universe shown in Figure 4.1. The description list of U is

$$
\begin{array}{l}
U \\
| \\
R - (R_1, R_1) - (R_2, R_2) - (R_3, R_3) - (R_4, R_4) \\
| \\
S - (S_1, S_1) - (S_2, S_2) - (S_3, S_3) \\
| \\
T - (T_1, T_1) - (T_2, T_2) - (T_3, T_3) \\
| \\
W - (W_1, W_1) - (W_2, W_2) - (W_3, W_3)
\end{array}
$$

A possible description list structure of U might contain, in addition to the foregoing, the following conceptions.

$$
\begin{array}{ll}
R_1 & \quad\quad\quad \alpha \\
| & \quad\quad\quad | \\
q - (q_1, \alpha) - (q_2, \beta) - (q_3, \gamma) - (q_4, \delta) \quad p - (p_5, \alpha) \\
& \quad\quad\quad\quad\quad\quad\quad\quad\quad\quad | \\
& \quad\quad\quad\quad\quad\quad\quad\quad\quad\quad q - (q_1, \alpha)
\end{array}
$$

$$
\begin{array}{lll}
\beta & \gamma & \delta \\
| & | & | \\
p - (p_5, \beta) & p - (p_5, \gamma) & p - (p_5, \delta) \\
| & | & | \\
q - (q_2, \beta) & q - (q_3, \gamma) & q - (q_4, \delta)
\end{array}
$$

$$
\begin{array}{ll}
R_2 & M \\
| & | \\
S - (S_1, M) - (S_2, N) & T - (T_1, J) - T_2(K)
\end{array}
$$

$$
\begin{array}{lll}
N & F & H \\
| & | & | \\
q - (q_3, F) - (q_4, H) & p - (p_2, F) & p - (p_2, H) \\
& | & | \\
& q - (q_3, F) & q - (q_4, H)
\end{array}
$$

$$
\begin{array}{lll}
J & K & R_3 \\
| & | & | \\
T - (T_1, J) & T - (T_2, K) & S - (S_2, L) - (S_3, Z) \\
| & | & \\
S - (S_1, J) & S - (S_1, K) &
\end{array}
$$

$$L$$
$$|$$
$$S - (S_2, L)$$
$$|$$
$$T - (T_2, L)$$

$$Z \qquad\qquad\qquad \varepsilon \qquad\qquad I$$
$$| \qquad\qquad\qquad\qquad | \qquad\qquad\quad |$$
$$T - (T_2, \varepsilon) - (T_3, I) \quad T - (T_2, \varepsilon) \quad T - (T_3, I)$$
$$| \qquad\qquad\qquad\quad |$$
$$q - (q_5, \varepsilon) \quad S - (S_3, I)$$

$$R_4 \qquad\qquad\qquad\qquad \psi \qquad\qquad\qquad \varphi$$
$$| \qquad\qquad\qquad\qquad\qquad | \qquad\qquad\qquad |$$
$$p - (p_1, \varphi) - (p_2, \psi) \quad p - (p_2, \psi) \quad S - (S_2, \xi) - (S_3, \eta)$$
$$| $$
$$q - (q_5, \psi)$$

$$\xi \qquad\qquad\qquad \eta$$
$$| \qquad\qquad\qquad |$$
$$S - (S_2, \xi) \quad q - (q_5, \eta)$$
$$| \qquad\qquad\qquad |$$
$$p - (p_1, \xi) \quad p - (p_1, \eta)$$

$$S_1 \qquad\qquad\qquad\qquad S_2 \qquad\qquad\qquad\qquad S_3$$
$$| \qquad\qquad\qquad\qquad\quad | \qquad\qquad\qquad\qquad |$$
$$q - (q_1, W_1) - (q_2, q_2) \quad q - (q_2, q_3) - (q_4, q_4) \quad q - (q_5, S_3)$$

$$W_1 \qquad\qquad\qquad W_2 \qquad\qquad\qquad\qquad W_3$$
$$| \qquad\qquad\qquad\quad | \qquad\qquad\qquad\qquad\quad |$$
$$q - (q_1, W_1) \quad q - (q_2, q_2) - (q_3, q_3) \quad q - (q_4, q_4) - (q_5, S_3)$$

$$T_1 \qquad\qquad\qquad T_2 \qquad\qquad\qquad T_3$$
$$| \qquad\qquad\qquad | \qquad\qquad\qquad |$$
$$T - (T_1, T_1) \quad T - (T_2, T_2) \quad T - (T_3, T_3)$$

This description list structure would not be valid, since the concept T_1 is described in terms of T, which is not a predefined property; also, descriptions of the concepts q_2, q_3, q_4, whose names occur in the descriptions of values of S, do not occur in the list. In the list above, if we replaced the conceptions of T_1, T_2, and T_3 by

$$T_1 \qquad\qquad\qquad T_2 \qquad\qquad\qquad T_3$$
$$| \qquad\qquad\qquad\qquad | \qquad\qquad\qquad\qquad |$$
$$p - (p_1, p_1) - (p_2, p_2) \quad p - (p_3, p_3) - (p_4, p_4) \quad p - (p_5, T_3)$$

and added the conceptions

$$q_2 \qquad\qquad\qquad q_3 \qquad\qquad\qquad q_4$$
$$| \qquad\qquad\qquad | \qquad\qquad\qquad |$$
$$q - (q_2, q_2) \quad q - (q_3, q_3) \quad q - (q_4, q_4)$$

$$p_1 \qquad\qquad p_2 \qquad\qquad p_3 \qquad\qquad p_4$$
$$| \qquad\qquad | \qquad\qquad | \qquad\qquad |$$
$$p - (p_1, p_1) \quad p - (p_2, p_2) \quad p - (p_3, p_3) \quad p - (p_4, p_4)$$

the description list structure would be valid.

THEOREM 4.5. *Given any object X, a property P, $p \in P$, and a valid description list structure of a finite universe, it can be determined by a finite process whether $X \subseteq p$.*

PROOF. We first associate an integer with every property as follows. With each element of $\mathscr{P}'$ we associate the integer 1. With any other property P, we associate an integer n_P defined as

$$n_P = 1 + \max\{n_{p'} \mid P' \text{ occurs in the conception of some value of } P\}.$$

With a valid conception of the universe, n_P is uniquely defined for every property. The proof is by induction over n_P.

If $n_P = 1$, then $P \in \mathscr{P}'$ and the name of a value of P occurs in X. The object $X \subseteq p$ if and only if this name is identical with p. Hence, the theorem is true for P if $n_P = 1$.

Let the theorem be true if $n_P \leq k$. If $n_P = k + 1$, then in the conception of p, only such properties Q occur that $n_Q \leq k$.

If the conception list of p contains the name of more than one value of a property Q, then $X \subseteq p$ only if $X \cap q \neq \varnothing$ for exactly one $q \in Q$. (Otherwise X is properly contained in two disjoint sets.) Since there are only a finite number of such values, the containment of X in one of them can be determined by a finite process.

If the conception list of p has one value from a finite number of properties, then, since for each property Q in this list $n_Q \leq k$, the containment of X in p can be determined by a finite process. ∎

To understand the way the integers $\{n_P\}$ are associated with the properties in the foregoing proof, we can once more invoke the valid description list structure of the universe exemplified in Figure 4.1. The integers associated with the various properties according to the scheme described in Theorem 4.5 are shown in Table 4.1. It will be also noticed that conceptions for q_5, p_5, and q_1 did not have to be included in the valid description list structure since their names never occurred in the right-hand side of any ordered pair in any of the conceptions.

In view of the discussions of this section and the last, the reader should be able to convince himself that the process indicated by the recursive flow chart shown in Figure 4.2 can effectively determine whether an object X belongs to a concept C, if the conception of C and a valid description list

Table 4.1

P	1
q	1
R	3
S	2
T	2
W	2

structure of the universe are available. In this flow chart three push-down stacks are used: j, P, and C. The list L is a list of ordered pairs that is to be empty at the first entry to the program. The name of the concept is to be entered in stack C before starting the program. In the flow chart, all variables are to be interpreted in the normal manner as denoting the content of the address named. In the case of stacks, also, the same convention is followed except that the content of the latest call is denoted by the stack name. When the stacks (rather than their contents) are referred to, quotes are used.

We can recall at this point the different conceptions for the concept A in the previous example. It can be seen that the second conception (having (p, q) as a sufficiency set), although the most space consuming, could be used most efficiently, because the route marked 2 in Figure 4.2 (necessitating the use of the description list structure of the universe) is never used. On the other hand, the first conception shown (using W and R) needs a description list structure of the universe.

It may be of some interest to indicate by an example the way the valid description list structure is used in the operation of the flow chart in Figure 4.2 for recognition of an object being a subset of the concept A.

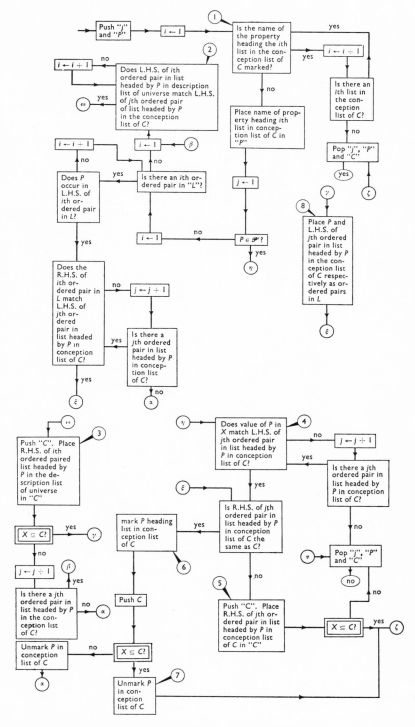

Figure 4.2.   Detailed structure of "$X \subseteq C$?"

The assumption is made that the conception of A being used happens to be

$$A$$
$$|$$
$$W - (W_2, A)$$
$$|$$
$$R - (R_2, A)$$

and the object involved is $(p, p_3; q, q_2)$.

Initially, the list L is empty and "C" contains the name "A." The test in box 1 finds W unmarked in the conception list of A and the name W is entered into "P." Since $W \notin \mathscr{P}'$, the list headed by W in the description list of the universe is searched by box 2 for the name W_2, which matches the value of W in the conception list of A. Then box 3 reenters the program recursively to test if the object is in W_2 (the intersection of W_2 with the universe). The value q is unmarked in the conception list of W_2 and hence is entered in "P." Since $q \in \mathscr{P}'$, box 4 matches the value q_2 in the object to q_2, the left-hand side of the first ordered pair in the conception list of W_2. The intersection of q_2 with W_2 being distinct from W_2, box 5 enters the program recursively, to test if the object is in q_2. The list headed by q in description of q_2 being unmarked and since $q \in \mathscr{P}'$, box 4 matches the value q_2 (left-hand side of first ordered pair in the list headed by q in the conception list of q_2) to the value of q in the object. The right-hand side of this ordered pair being q_2, box 6 marks q in the conception list of q_2 and reenters the program, testing for X being contained in q_2. On this entry, box 1 fails to find any unmarked property of q_2; on the resulting "yes" exit, box 7 unmarks q (which has popped back in P following the recursive entry). As a result, there is a "yes" exit into box 8, which places (W, W_2) into the list L. The intersection of W_2 with A_2 being A again, box 6 marks W in the conception list of A and reenters the program, testing X as subset of A, but with W marked. Box 1 isolates R, the next unmarked property in conception list A, and places it in P. Since $R \notin \mathscr{P}'$ and no ordered pair with R at the left-hand side exists in L, box 2 isolates R_2 in the list headed by R in the description list of the universe matching R_2 in the conception list of A. As a result, box 3 reenters the program, testing the object as a subset of R_2. Since the property S occurring in the conception list of R_2 is unmarked, not a member of $\mathscr{P}$, and not occurring in L, box 2 matches S_1 in the description list of the universe with S_1 occurring in the conception list of R_2. Hence, box 3 reenters the program, testing the object as a subset of S_1. The value q is unmarked, not in L, and occurs in $\mathscr{P}$. So box 4 matches q_2 in the conception list of S_1

with the value of q in the object. Hence, box 5 tests the object as a subset of q_2 (as it did testing for W_2) and on success, box 8 places (S, S_1) in the list L, following which box 5 reenters the program testing the object as a subset of M (the intersection of S_1 with R_2). The value T is not marked in the conception list of M; nor is it in P; hence, box 2 isolates the value T_1 in the description list of the universe and box 3 tests the object as a subset of T_1. The value p, being unmarked in the conception list of T_1, not occurring in L, and not being a member of $\mathscr{P}'$, an attempt is made in box 4 to match the value of p in the object (p_3) with the values p_1 and p_2 occurring in the conception list of T_1. This results in a failure exit and box 3 tests the object as a subset of T_2. This succeeds (in the same way that $X \subseteq W_2$ succeeded). Hence, (T, T_2) is placed in L by box 8 and box 5 tests the object as a subset of K. The first unmarked property in the conception list of K (T), occurs in L (saving the trouble of a reevaluation), its value (T_2) matches the value of T in K. Box 6 marks T in the conception list of K, tests for the object as subset of K with T marked, finds S, the next unmarked property of K in L; matches its value (S_1) in L with that in the conception list of K; hence, S is marked in the conception list of K and the next reentry exits, unmarking properties of K, then recognizing M and hence, box 8 places (R, R_2) in L. The intersection of R_2 with A being A, R is marked in the conception list of A and the next recursive entry exits with success, finding the object as a subset of A and unmarking the conception list of A.

4.5. CONJUNCTIVE AND SIMPLE CONCEPTS

As has been pointed out before, every description language is constructed out of a set of predicates and a mode of combination of predicates to yield compound statements with only one free variable so that in its interpretation it denotes a subset of the universe of discourse. In the languages discussed in this section, the basic predicates are also unary (containing a single variable). In the language discussed so far (whose sentences are conceptions) each set is described either as the union of a class of disjoint sets or as the intersection of a class of property values. The basic building blocks of the concepts, then, are the class of concepts each of which are intersections of a class of property values. The building blocks are called "conjunctive concepts" for the purposes of the present discussion.

The size of a conception describing a conjunctive concept certainly depends on the number of property values to be intersected to obtain the concept. The size of a conception describing concepts other than conjunctive concepts is larger than the sum of the sizes of the conceptions describing the disjoint conjunctive concepts of which the given concept is the union. If there is more than one conception for the same concept, then it is quite difficult to decide without careful study which of the given conceptions has the minimum size. It can be surmised that in a real environment where $\mathscr{P} = \mathscr{P}'$ and is full, the conception of a concept will be smaller, the fewer the number of conjunctive concepts used as building blocks for the concept. In what follows the supposition is made that if a conception describes a concept as a conjunctive concept, then this is the smallest conception for the concept. Whether such a conception exists or not for a concept certainly depends on the environment, that is, on the structure of the properties available.

Given a certain real environment and a certain conception, it may be of interest to find a shorter conception that denotes the same concept. A method for doing this has been developed by J. C. Pennypacker [32]. Other related methods developed by him are discussed later.

Given a universe (for instance, the set of all occurrences of bit configurations on a square grid of photo cells) whose elements can be coded into computer inputs, we can generally come up with some fine structure family of properties for that universe. In the case of the square grid of photo cells, for instance, the excitation value of a particular photo cell divides the set of all bit configurations on the grid into two disjoint subsets. The family of properties defined by the class of all photo cells forms a full fine structure family. The universe of all configurations on a chessboard has as fine structure family, the occupancy of each square on the board. (As an aside, this fine structure family, of course, is not full: not more than one white square can be occupied by a black bishop, for instance.) We can surmise with some confidence that finding a fine structure family of properties for a universe is a problem that can be safely relegated to the intuition of the experimenter.

However, in most universes (except those specially designed by psychologists for specific tests) we are specially interested in having descriptions for certain given concepts (the set of all B's on a photo cell grid; the set of all forcing situations on a chessboard; etc.). Generally these concepts are not conjunctive concepts if we restrict ourselves to the input properties alone. In the interest of practicable brevity, it is essential to have properties in the environments such that the conceptions for these concepts be short and (if practicable) conjunctive. A large part of the effort in the field of pattern recognition is directed toward the search for suitable properties (the values of these properties are called "features" in the field). Often, acceptable-looking features are assumed to exist and statistical methods are developed to reduce the probability of incorrect classification by choosing the least harmful conjunctive concept to approximate the concept at hand. Concepts other than conjunctive ones are often succinctly expressed by invoking modes of combination other than the ones used in logic. These will be discussed where appropriate later. Meanwhile, we pose the general problem, "Given a class of concepts in a given real environment $\langle U, \mathscr{P}, \mathscr{P}' \rangle$, to enlarge the class of properties such that each concept in the class is conjunctive." In this form, the problem has a trivial solution: "Use each concept in the class together with its complement as a property." This, of course, does not reduce the memory size in any way. For a more realistic posing of the problem, we need to take into account the size increase involved in incorporating these new properties into the description list structure of the universe. The problem called "feature extraction" is closely related to this problem. To the best of the author's knowledge, such a problem has not been taken up in the literature in this form. Also, since the measure of size is highly language dependent, the development of more powerful description languages is a prerequisite.

The major point considered in this section is a mode of combining unary predicates that renders it easy to have short descriptions, not only for conjunctive concepts, but for a much larger class of concepts, which we will call "simple" concepts. The theory developed for the purpose also indicates methods for describing a nonsimple concept by the use of simple concepts that approximate it. Also, in a later chapter it will be shown how we can use this language for "generalization" or concept learning.

At the present level of development of this theory, no distinction is made between input and noninput properties. Since given an environment $\langle U, \mathscr{P} \rangle$, $\mathscr{P}$ itself is a fine structure family, we can say that the theory deals with a real environment $\langle U, \mathscr{P}, \mathscr{P} \rangle$. At the present stage of thought it is not clear whether the extension of the theory to the case where $\mathscr{P}' \neq \mathscr{P}$ in any but the most trivial way will be of use or not. A large amount of theoretical development also is needed because the class of simple concepts indicates close relationships to topologies on the one hand and decomposition of games on the other. This will be indicated in detail later.

As before, finite environments will be considered. Let $\mathscr{P} = \{P_1, P_2, \ldots, P_n\}$ and let for each i ($1 \leq i \leq n$), $P_i = \{p_{i1}, p_{i2}, \ldots, p_{ir_i}\}$. Given a concept X, define a set X^s, called the *superconcept of X*, as follows.

$$X^s = \bigcap_{i=1}^{n} \bigcup \{p_{ij} \mid p_{ij} \cap X \neq \varnothing\}.$$

That is, for each i, we define the set X_i, which is the union of those values of P_i that have nonempty intersection with X. The set X^s is obtained by taking the intersection of X_i for all values of i. As an example, in the environment indicated in Figure 4.1, the superconcept of the concept $\alpha = \{5, 6, 7, 8,$

9, 10, 13, 14, 15, 16, 19, 20} would be the concept $T_1 \cap (W_2 \cup W_3) \cap (p_1 \cup p_2) \cap (q_2 \cup q_3 \cup q_4 \cup q_5) \cap (R_2 \cup R_4) \cap (S_1 \cup S_2 \cup S_3)$; that is,

$$\alpha^s = \{3, 4, 5, 6, 7, 8, 9, 10, 13, 14, 15, 16, 17, 18, 19, 20\}.$$

The concept α^s has α as its subset. This is true in general. That is

THEOREM 4.6.   *For any concept X, $X \subseteq X^s$.*

PROOF.

$$X = X \cap U = X \cap \bigcup_{j=1}^{r_i} p_{ij} = \bigcup_{j=1}^{r_i} \{X \cap p_{ij}\}$$

for each i ($1 \leq i \leq n$). However,

$$\bigcup_{j=1}^{r_i} \{X \cap p_{ij}\} = \bigcup \{X \cap p_{ij} \mid X \cap p_{ij} \neq \varnothing\}.$$

Hence,

$$X = \bigcup \{X \cap p_{ij} \mid X \cap p_{ij} \neq \varnothing\}.$$

But

$$X \cap p_{ij} \subseteq p_{ij};$$

hence,

$$X \subseteq \bigcup \{p_{ij} \mid X \cap p_{ij} \neq \varnothing\} \qquad \text{for each } i \ (1 \leq i \leq n).$$

Hence,

$$X \subseteq \bigcap_{i=1}^{n} \bigcup \{p_{ij} \mid X \cap p_{ij} \neq \varnothing\} = X^s. \qquad \blacksquare$$

From this theorem it follows that X^s can be taken as an approximation for X in the sense that any element that is not a member of X^s is certainly not a member of X. As a matter of fact, a much stronger statement can be made regarding the approximating ability of superconcepts. It can be noticed, for instance, that $\bar{\alpha}^s = (R_1 \cup R_2 \cup R_3) \cap (W_1 \cup W_2 \cup W_3) \cap (S_1 \cup S_2 \cup S_3) \cap (T_1 \cup T_2 \cup T_3) \cap (p_1 \cup p_2 \cup p_3 \cup p_4 \cup p_5) \cap q_1 (\cup q_2 \cup q_3 \cup q_4 \cup q_5)$, whose complement is the set $\neg(\neg\alpha)^s = \{5, 6, 7, 8, 9, 10, 19, 20\}$, which is a subset of α. This also is true in general: that is

COROLLARY 4.1.   *For any concept X, $\neg(\neg X)^s \subseteq X$.*

PROOF. $(\neg X)^s \supseteq \neg X$. Hence, $X \supseteq \neg(\neg X)^s$.

Thus, $\neg(\neg X)^s$ and X^s can be looked upon as lower and upper bounds of X. Hence, if we store descriptions of X^s and $\neg(\neg X)^s$, we can recognize various objects as being definitely contained in X, others as definitely not being contained in X.

In addition to the fact that the superconcepts of a concept and its complement yield good approximations to a concept, it is to be noted that they also have rather simple descriptions in a specific language. This is brought out by the following theorem.

THEOREM 4.7. *For any concept*

$$X^s = \neg \bigcup \{p_{ij} \mid p_{ij} \in P_i, P_i \in \mathscr{P}, p_{ij} \cap X = \varnothing\}.$$

PROOF.

$$X^s = \bigcap_{i=1}^{n} \bigcup \{p_{ij} \mid p_{ij} \in P_i, p_{ij} \cap X \neq \varnothing\}$$

$$= \bigcap_{i=1}^{n} \neg \bigcup \{p_{ij} \mid p_{ij} \in P_i, p_{ij} \cap X = \varnothing\}$$

$$= \neg \bigcup_{i=1}^{n} \bigcup \{p_{ij} \mid p_{ij} \in P_i, p_{ij} \cap X = \varnothing\}$$

$$= \neg \bigcup \{p_{ij} \mid p_{ij} \in P_i, p_i \in \mathscr{P}, p_{ij} \cap X = \varnothing\}. \quad \blacksquare$$

Hence, the superconcept of any concept X can be described by storing the list of those property values that have empty intersections with X. Thus, the description of α^s could be stored as

$$\alpha^s = \neg \bigcup (\{p_3, p_4, p_5, q_1, R_1, R_3, T_2, T_3, W_1\}).$$

Clearly, this new mode of description of concepts makes it necessary to have a new algorithm for determining whether a given object is contained in a superconcept or not. Such a program will be discussed later. Meanwhile, it is worthwhile pointing out that the present language of description (describing the superconcept of a concept and its complement) does not restrict us to storing approximations alone. At some extra cost, all concepts can be described exactly if we allow in the language the capability of expressing the union of described sets. To see how this can be done the following are introduced.

THEOREM 4.8. *For all concepts* $X^s = (X^s)^s$.

PROOF.

$$X^s = \neg \bigcup \{p_{ij} \mid p_{ij} \in P_i\, P_i \in \mathscr{P}, p_{ij} \cap X = \varnothing\};$$

hence, for any $p_{ij} \in P_i$ such that $P_i \in \mathscr{P}$, $p_{ij} \cap X = \varnothing$ implies $p_{ij} \subseteq \neg X^s$; that is, $p_{ij} \subseteq \neg X$ implies $p_{ij} \subseteq \neg X^s$; replacing X by X^s, we obtain $p_{ij} \subseteq \neg X^s$ implies $p_{ij} \subseteq \neg (X^s)^s$. That is, $p_{ij} \subseteq \neg X$ implies $p_{ij} \subseteq \neg (X^s)^s$. Hence,

$$\neg X^s = \bigcup \{p_{ij} \mid p_{ij} \in P_i, P_i \in \mathscr{P}, p_{ij} \cap X = \varnothing\}$$

$$\subseteq \bigcup \{p_{ij} \mid p_{ij} \in P_i, P_i \in \mathscr{P}, p_{ij} \subseteq \neg (X^s)^s\} \subseteq \neg (X^s)^s$$

or

$$X^s \supseteq (X^s)^s.$$

However, by Theorem 4.6,

$$(X^s)^s \supseteq X^s$$

and the theorem follows. ∎

Concepts that are equal to their superconcepts will be called *simple concepts*. The superconcept of any concept is simple.

THEOREM 4.9.   *All conjunctive concepts are simple.*

PROOF.   Let X be conjunctive; that is, there exists a subset $\mathscr{P}' = \{P_{i_1}, P_{i_2}, \ldots, P_{i_m}\}$ of $\mathscr{P}$ and a value $p_{i_k j_k} \in P_{i_k}$ for each k $(1 \leq k \leq m)$ such that

$$X = \bigcap_{k=1}^{m} p_{i_k j_k}.$$

We have

$$X^s = \bigcap_{i=1}^{n} \bigcup \{p_{ij} \mid p_{ij} \cap X \neq \varnothing\} \subseteq \bigcup \{p_{i_k j} \mid p_{i_k j} \cap \neq \varnothing\} = p_{i_k j_k}$$

$$(1 \leq k \leq m).$$

Hence,

$$X^s \subseteq \bigcup_{k=1}^{m} p_{i_k j_k} = X.$$

The reverse inequality, follows from Theorem 4.6. Hence $X = X^s$, showing that X is simple. ∎

Since it has been indicated in the previous section that any concept can be described as an union of conjunctive concepts, any concept may be described as the union of simple concepts. However, the number of simple concepts involved in the union may be much smaller than the number of conjunctive concepts needed. All simple concepts that are not conjunctive (the concept α^s in the previous example, for instance) can be stored as a single description.

A very straightforward algorithm exists for testing whether an object is contained in a simple concept or not. More generally, given two simple concepts (it is to be noted that an object, being a conjunctive concept, is simple), it is extremely easy to determine if one is contained in the other. This is established through the following definitions and theorems.

Let K denote the set of the names of all property values, that is, the set

$$\{p_{11}, p_{12}, \ldots, p_{1r_1}, p_{21}, \ldots, p_{2r_2}, \ldots, p_{nr_n}\}.$$

With each subset of K, $\{t_1, t_2, \ldots, t_r\}$ we can associate the simple concept

$$X = \neg \bigcup \{t_1, t_2, \ldots, t_r\} = \neg(t_1 \cup t_2 \cup \cdots \cup t_r.)$$

Let $H(\{t_1, t_2, \ldots, t_r\})$ denote this concept X. Thus, H is a mapping from the set of all subsets of K to the set of all simple concepts. It has been shown by Windeknecht that a sublattice of the set of all subsets of K, considered as a lattice under inclusion, is antihomomorphic to the lattice of all simple concepts under inclusion [33]. For the purpose of this section it is only necessary to show that the set of all subsets of K, partially ordered by inclusion, is antihomomorphic to the set of all simple concepts, partially ordered by inclusion. The mapping H described above is the antihomomorphism involved. This is shown in the following theorem.

THEOREM 4.10.   *Let α and β be subsets of K and let $H(\alpha)$ and $H(\beta)$ be the corresponding simple concepts. Then $\alpha \subseteq \beta$ implies $H(\beta) \subseteq H(\alpha)$.*

PROOF.   If $\alpha \subseteq \beta$, then $p_{ij} \in \alpha$ implies $p_{ij} \in \beta$ for each $p_{ij} \in P_i$, $P_i \in \mathscr{P}$. Hence,

$$\bigcup \{p_{ij} \mid p_{ij} \in \alpha\} \subseteq \bigcup \{p_{ij} \mid p_{ij} \in \beta\}.$$

Hence,

$$H(\beta) = \neg \bigcup \{p_{ij} \mid p_{ij} \in \beta\} \subseteq \neg \bigcup \{p_{ij} \mid p_{ij} \in \alpha\} = H(\alpha). \quad \blacksquare$$

The converse of this theorem is not necessarily true: there may be more than one α with the same value for $H(\alpha)$. However, from among all α having the same value for $H(\alpha)$ a unique one can be chosen.

THEOREM 4.11.   *If $H(\alpha) = H(\beta) = A$, then $H(\alpha \cup \beta) = A$.*

PROOF.   Let α and β be two arbitrary subsets of K,

$$p_{ij} \in \alpha \quad \text{implies} \quad p_{ij} \cap H(\alpha) = \varnothing \, ;$$

whence

$$p_{ij} \subseteq \neg H(\alpha).$$

Similarly,

$$p_{ij} \in \beta \quad \text{implies} \quad p_{ij} \subseteq \neg H(\beta);$$

hence

$$p_{ij} \in \alpha \cup \beta \quad \text{implies} \quad p_{ij} \subseteq \neg H(\alpha) \cup \neg H(\beta)$$

or

$$p_{ij} \subseteq \neg(H(\alpha) \cap H(\beta)),$$

whence

$$\bigcup \{p_{ij} \mid p_{ij} \in \alpha \cup \beta\} \subseteq \neg(H(\alpha) \cap H(\beta))$$

or

$$H(\alpha \cup \beta) \supseteq H(\alpha) \cap H(\beta).$$

However, by Theorem 4.10

$$H(\alpha) \supseteq H(\alpha \cup \beta), \quad H(\beta) \supseteq H(\alpha \cup \beta),$$

so that

$$H(\alpha) \cap H(\beta) \supseteq H(\alpha \cup \beta) ,$$

which, with the previous inequality, shows

$$H(\alpha) \cap H(\beta) = H(\alpha \cup \beta).$$

If

$$H(\alpha) = H(\beta) = A,$$

as given by the hypothesis,

$$A = H(\alpha) = H(\alpha) \cap H(\beta) = H(\alpha \cup \beta). \quad \blacksquare$$

Since the set of all subsets of K is finite, the set of all subsets α of K such that $H(\alpha) = A$ is a finite class of sets. If $M(A)$ is the union of all subsets α of K such that $H(\alpha) = A$, then this $M(A)$ is a unique set such that $H(M(A)) = A$. In the following theorem, discussion is limited to those subsets of K that are $M(A)$ for some simple concept A.

THEOREM 4.12. *If A and B are simple concepts, then $A \subseteq B$ implies $M(B) \subseteq M(A)$.*

PROOF.

$$A \subseteq B;$$

hence,

$$A \cap B = A$$

since

$$A = H(M(A)) \quad \text{and} \quad B = H(M(B)),$$

$$H(M(A) \cup M(B)) = A \cap B = A,$$

as indicated in proof of Theorem 4.11.

But by definition of the function M,

$$H(M(A) \cup M(B)) = A \quad \text{implies} \quad M(A) \cup M(B) \subseteq M(A),$$

whence

$$M(B) \subseteq M(A). \quad \blacksquare$$

Given any simple concept A, $M(A)$ can be found effectively. It will be shown in the next chapter, on concept learning, that a rather straightforward algorithm exists that can find the value of M for the smallest simple concept containing a given set of exemplars. James Snediker has written a program, based on Windeknecht's work, which learns superconcepts of concepts from examples and stores them as values of the M function [34]. For the purposes of this chapter, it is assumed that the descriptions of simple concepts A are stored as the lists $M(A)$. According to the last two theorems, given two concepts A and B, we can find, by merely comparing the lists $M(A)$ and $M(B)$, whether A is a subset of B or not.

If now we have the values of $M(A^s)$ and $M((\neg A)^s)$ stored in a computer memory, we can deduce if a certain object X is a member of A in an approximate manner. If $M(X) \nsupseteq M((\neg A)^s)$, then $X \nsubseteq (\neg A)^s$. However, X, being an object, is either contained in $(\neg A)^s$ or is disjoint from it, according to Theorem 4.1. Hence, $X \subseteq \neg((\neg A)^s) \subseteq A$. If, on the other hand, $M(X) \nsupseteq M(A^s)$, then $X \nsubseteq A^s$. In this case, $X \subseteq \neg A^s$, and since $A \subseteq A^s$, $X \nsubseteq A$. If neither of these cases hold, then no conclusion can be drawn regarding the inclusion of X in A.

This approximate procedure is an analog of the Pennypacker recognition procedure described in the preceding section. However, it is done by very simple programs based on very simple data structures.

If we can find simple methods for calculating the M-functions $\{\alpha\}$ whose corresponding simple concepts $\{H(\alpha)\}$ yield a given concept by union, then the approximate recognition method above can be improved quite easily. In that case, the problem reduces more to assuring ourselves that the number of simple concepts needed to describe a concept not be excessively large, even though we already have the assurance that it would not be larger than the number of conjunctive concepts needed to describe a concept.

Before this last aspect of efficiency of description is discussed (and it is discussed in a more generalized case in the next section), we must also note that for the list comparison algorithm to be effective, the description M for the concepts involved has to contain every property in the environment, not merely a fine structure family of properties. Hence, it is required to introduce some further algorithms for deducing property values from the input properties, as was done in the previous section. This would require the storing of certain property values as described concepts. Efficient methods for this have not been developed yet.

4.6. A GENERALIZED DESCRIPTION LANGUAGE: SYNTACTIC AXIOMATIZATIONS

In this section the ideas introduced previously are generalized and given a syntactic form similar to that of a formal logic. This enables generalizations to description languages of greater flexibility and descriptive strength than were heretofore available. Several stages of development of such a language are exhibited and their use exemplified. Indications will be given later of how far these uses have been implemented on a computer.

It probably need not be established in any great detail to the discerning reader that what have been called conceptions and subsets of K in the previous sections are merely different ways of putting together atomic formulas to yield statement forms. These statement forms are characterized by the fact that they have only a single free variable. The component predicate letters are all unary (have only one argument) and give rise to predicates with one free variable. When these are put together to form statements, they all have the same free variable so that the resulting statement form has one free variable only.

What have been called objects in the previous sections are also examples of compound statement forms with a single free variable. These statements with a single free variable define sets of elements for which the statements are true. On the basis of this, tests have been described so far that test the inclusion of one set in another. However, it has been tacitly implied that these tests are used more often (and in the case of Pennypacker and the author's work, exclusively) when the included set is denoted by an object.

In the cases treated so far, where the environments have been finite, it has been possible to construct objects such that the name of every input property occurred in it. As a result, the sets indicated in Theorem 4.1 could actually be denoted by a finite statement corresponding to an object. Since two elements in such a set cannot be distinguished by any concept, we might consider each object as denoting a single element. As a result, the objects themselves could be considered the elements of the universe. This point of view is pursued in the rest of this section even though some of the discussions of this paragraph are invalid in cases where the universe is not finite.

When an object k is an element of the value p_{ij} of the property P_i, this fact can be expressed by a statement of the form $k \in p_{ij}$. This would necessitate that values of different properties have different names; there are, however, certain advantages to using the same symbols for the names of values of different properties. (Some of these advantages were indicated in Section 1.3.) If such similarities of names are allowed, then a statement of the form $k \in p_{ij}$ becomes ambiguous since p_{ij} and $p_{i'j'}$ may be the same symbol. It is more advantageous to express the fact that the object k is an element of the value p_{ij} of property P_i by a statement of the form $P_i(k) = p_{ij}$.

In the past, names of concepts have been attached to the conceptions or the lists $M(A)$. In effect, the descriptions have stood for statements $S(x)$ with a single free variable x, and the names C of the concepts attached to the descriptions have indicated in effect that an object k is an element of the concept C if and only if the sentence $S(k)$ is true; in effect, these have stood for statements of the form $x \in C \equiv S(x)$.

So far it has been assumed that names of properties, their values, and concepts are symbols. However, it has already been indicated in Chapter 1 that various concepts can be given short descriptions if we allow the processing of the names of properties and values. It is therefore advantageous to allow these to be objects, so that set-theoretical processes can be carried out on them. This would allow the same programs that process objects to process the names also and a large amount of descriptive power would be obtained without vitiating the flexibility of the processing and without unduly increasing the size of the programs that do the processing.

We must, of course, take cognizance of the fact that the set-theoretical processes discussed so far are merely capable of working on sets defined by unary predicates, while most of the time the processing of names that goes on in pattern recognition activities involves the calculation of functions and the ascertainment of relations. This, however, presents no problems, since functions and relations, being sets of ordered n-tuples, may themselves be considered concepts in a universe of ordered n-tuples. Also, n-tuples have the obvious n properties defined by each of their components. This fact is made use of repeatedly in the examples that follow. It may be pointed out, of course, that this point of view indicates that some objects under discussion are constructed out of property names that are entirely different from the property names used for constructing other objects. This may be looked upon as indicating the existence of a set of environments rather than a single one. Alternatively, we can consider that each object is constructed out of only a subset of properties. This certainly would preclude the objects' being unit sets. Since such a possibility has to be admitted in any infinite environment (and, as will be seen presently, this is a very natural requirement), we need not disregard this interpretation of an object. There is, moreover, a philosophical justification to it when we consider that the description of an "object" (in common parlance) often depends on the context. When we talk about a person, for instance, we may be talking about every appearance of the person on every occasion ("He expresses himself well") or about a specific appearance of a specific trait ("He was angry today"). When we say, "The letter 'X'," we may be talking of a class of letters or a single mark on paper viewed from five directions or the same single mark seen in a certain illumination at a certain time.

In any case, the complete set-theoretical interpretation of the syntactic structure has not been investigated yet. Especially in its fully developed form, discussed at the end of this section, this lack of interpretation raises several questions regarding the formal properties of the logic involved. For the present, attention is directed toward the syntactic properties of the language only and its interpretation is taken informally to be as motivated by the discussion above.

The major syntactic features of the language have already been discussed. Initially, we assume a set of symbols, which are taken to be countably infinite. To give syntactic meaning to such a set, they are identified with words on a finite alphabet. The set of symbols, together with the special symbols (,), ,, ;, =, $\in$, $\lor$, &, $\rightarrow$, $\equiv$, and $\sim$ and a specific string IN (standing for a single variable "*Input*"), will construct all valid phrases of the language. The most obvious interpretations will be on the set of all "objects" as defined before. In what follows the basic definitions of the syntactic entities are given and later exemplified by some examples to bring out the power of the language under some interpretations.

1.   A finite sequence of lowercase Latin letters is a *symbol*.

2.   A symbol is a *term*.

3.   If α is a term and β is a term, then α, β is an *ordered pair;* α is the *left-hand element* of the ordered pair and β is the *right-hand element* of the ordered pair α, β.

4.   An ordered pair is an *ordered pair string;* if α and β are ordered pair strings, then a; β is an *ordered pair string*.

5.   If α is an ordered pair string, then (α) is an *object*.

6.   An object is a *term*.

An example of the syntactic appearance of an object is apt here:

$$\text{(name, harry; house, (number, five; street, luther))}$$

denotes (under interpretation) a person called harry whose house is distinguished from others by an address. The value of the property "house" itself is an object here.

7.   The string IN is a *term*.

8.   If α is a term and β is a term, then $\alpha(\beta)$ is a *term*.

9.   If α is a term and β is a term, then $(\alpha = \beta)$ is a *statement*.

10.   If α is a statement and β is a statement, then $\sim\alpha$, $(\alpha \lor \beta)$, $(\alpha \& \beta)$, $(\alpha \rightarrow \beta)$ are *statements*.

11.   If α is a term and β is a symbol, then $(\alpha \in \beta)$ is a *statement*.

12.   If α is a symbol and β is a statement, then IN $\in \alpha \equiv \beta$ is a *concept;* α is the *name* of the concept and β the *intention* of the concept.

It is worth remarking at this point that the syntactic entity "concept" as defined here is at variance with the meaning attached to the word in previous discussions. In the parlance of the earlier discussions, a concept would be the set of all elements of the universe that satisfies the intention of a syntactic entity "concept." The intention is what has previously been alluded to as the "description" of the concept.

Among the set of statements defined above, a subset is now defined to be the set of "true statements." For this some auxiliary definitions are needed. This involves a mapping (called "value") from a subset of the set of all terms and ordered pair strings into the set of all terms and ordered pair strings, defined as follows.

13. The value of a symbol is itself.

14. The value of IN is not defined.

15. The value of a term of the form $\alpha(\beta)$ is defined if and only if the values of α and β are defined, the value of β is an object, and the value of α is the left-hand element of some unique ordered pair in the value of β. In this case, the value of $\alpha(\beta)$ is the right-hand element of the ordered pair of which the value of α is the left-hand element.

As examples, the value of color((shape, square; color, blue)) is blue while the values of color((color, red; color, blue)) and color((shape, square; size, big)) are undefined.

16. The value of an ordered pair α, β is defined if and only if the values of α and β are defined. In that case its value is α', β' where α' and β' are the values of α and β, respectively.

17. The value of an ordered pair string α; β is defined if and only if the values of α and β are defined. In that case its value is α'; β' where α' and β' are the values of α and β, respectively.

18. The value of (α) is defined if and only if the value of α is defined. In that case the value of (α) is (α') where α' is the value of α.

19. An object is an *exemplar* if its value is itself.

20. Two symbols are *identical* if they constitute the same string of characters.

21. Two ordered pairs are *identical* if their left-hand elements and their right-hand elements are identical.

22. Two exemplars are *identical* if each ordered pair of one is identical to some ordered pair of the other and vice versa.

23. A statement ($\alpha = \beta$) is *true* if and only if the values of α and β are defined and the value of α is identical to the value of β.

24.   Given a set D of concepts, a statement is *D-true* if and only if it is true or if the statement is of the form $(\alpha \in \beta)$, β is the name of some concept K in D and the statement obtained by replacing every occurrence of IN in the intention of K by α, a D-true statement results.

25.   Statement $(\alpha \vee \beta)$ is *D-true* if and only if either α or β is D-true; $(\alpha\ \&\ \beta)$ is *D-true* if and only if both α and β are D-true. $(\alpha \rightarrow \beta)$ is *D-true* if and only if $(\sim\alpha \vee \beta)$ is D-true; $\sim\alpha$ is *D-true* if and only if α is not true and does not contain the term IN.

It is worthwhile at this point to exemplify the utility of this system in terms of the example used at the end of Section 1.3. Let D consist of the single concept

$$\text{IN} \in a \equiv ((\text{head}(\text{borders}(\text{IN})) = t)\ \&\ ((\text{head}(\text{crosses}(\text{IN})) = f)$$

$$\vee ((\text{tail}(\text{borders}(\text{IN})) = t)\ \&\ (\text{tail}(\text{crosses}(\text{IN})) = f)))).$$

Then the statement $((\text{crosses}, (\text{head}, f; \text{tail}, t); \text{borders}(\text{head}, t, \text{tail}, f)) \in a)$ is a D-true statement. This can be seen as follows. Since the statement is of the form $\alpha \in \beta$, we obtain, by definition 24 above, that the statement is true if and only if the statement obtained by replacing all occurrences of IN in the statement to the right of $\equiv$ in the concept above by $(\text{crosses}, (\text{head}, f;$ $\text{tail}, t); \text{borders}, (\text{head}, t; \text{tail}, f))$ is D-true. This statement is of the form $\alpha\ \&\ \beta$. The right-hand conjunct of this statement is $(\text{head}(\text{border}((\text{crosses},$ $(\text{head}, f; \text{tail}, t); \text{borders}, (\text{head}, t; \text{tail}, f)))) = t)$. By definition 23 this is true if the values of the terms on the left and right of the $=$ be identical. The value of the term t is t by definition 13. The value of the left-hand term is defined by rule 15 to be the value of $\text{head}((\text{head}, t; \text{tail}; f))$, which is t again. So one of the conjuncts of the intention of the concept named "a" is true. The other conjunct is of the form $\alpha \vee \beta$ and is true by rule 25 if either of the two disjuncts is true. The first disjunct is

$$(\text{head}(\text{crosses}((\text{crosses}, (\text{head}, f; \text{tail}, t); \text{borders}, (\text{head}, t; \text{tail}, f)))) = f),$$

which is again true by definitions 23 and 15 and 13. One disjunct being true, the statement is true.

Before exhibiting by some more examples the extent of the power of the language, it is worthwhile to point out that any statement in this language that does not contain IN can be tested for truth by carrying out on the statement an algorithm that is closely related to definitions 1–25. This algorithm is shown in Figures 4.3 and 4.4 in flow chart form.

In the flow chart it has been assumed that the tests indicated in the control boxes of the chart can indeed be performed. The assumption can be justified on the basis of what is known about syntax-directed parsing today [66]. The point will not be belabored here.

Since the programs are recursive, some of the variables used are actually stacks. To distinguish them from other variables, their names have been written in uppercase letters while other variables are named in lowercase letters. As before, names are written in quotes and their content without quotes.

It would be useful if we could derive conditions that have to be satisfied by concepts such that the algorithm exhibited in Figure 4.3 would terminate. This would lead to statements regarding the "decidability" of the language, that is, whether given any statements in the language it can be decided with a finite number of operations whether the statement is true. Such considerations, and in particular considerations of consistency and completeness, would be even more important when, later in this section, the

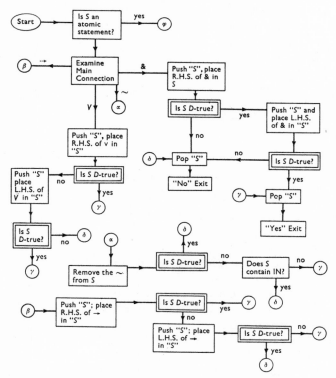

Figure 4.3. Detailed algorithm for "Is S D-true?"

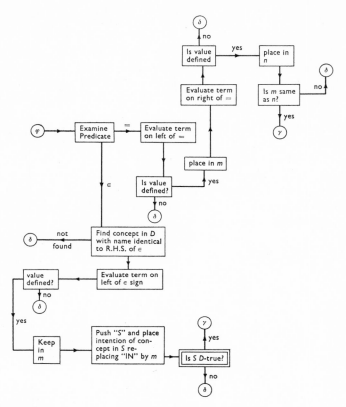

Figure 4.3   (contd.)

language is extended into a deductive system of logic. Such considerations have not yet been taken up and will not be discussed further. Meanwhile, the following examples show that the language, even in its present form, has considerable strength.

The first example indicates how representations of integers and operations on integers can be described within the machinery of the language described so far. The integers are considered to be expressed by binary numerals. Each numeral is considered to have two properties, "head" and "tail." The values of "tail" are "0" and "1," and stand for the least significant digit of the numeral. The values of "head" are either "null" or an integer, representing the more significant digits of the numeral. To make sure that confusion does not result from leading zeros, they are disallowed in the description. In what follows, a set of concepts is introduced that will define positive integers, the relation of natural ordering among integers, and sums of integers. From these, the reader will convince himself, the arithmetic of positive integers can also be defined with some work.

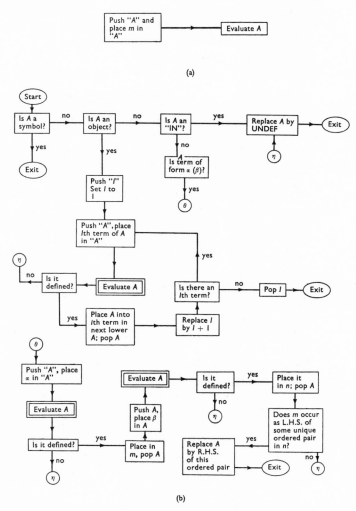

Figure 4.4 (a) Skeleton of "Evaluate term *m*." (b) Details of "Evaluate *A*."

IN ∈ digit ≡ ((IN = 0) ∨ (IN = 1))

IN ∈ lessd ≡ ((first(IN) = 1) & (second(IN) = 0))

IN ∈ numer ≡ (((head(IN) = null) & (tail(IN) = 1)) ∨ ((head(IN)
  ∈ numer) & (tail(IN) ∈ digit)))

IN ∈ less ≡ (((head(first(IN)) = null) & ∼(head(second(IN))
  = null))) ∨ ((first, head(first(IN)); second, head
  (second(IN))) ∈ less)
  ∨ ((head(first(IN)) = head(second(IN)))
  & ((first, tail(first(IN)); second, tail(second(IN)))
  ∈ lessd))

IN ∈ sumd ≡ ((second(IN) = 0) & (first(IN) = third(IN)))
  ∨ ((second(IN) = 1) & ∼(first(IN) = third(IN)))

IN ∈ carry ≡ ((first(IN) = 1) & (second(IN) = 1))

IN ∈ sum ≡ (((first, tail(first(IN)); second, tail(second(IN));
  third, tail(third(IN))) ∈ sumd) & ((∼((first, tail
  (first(IN)); second, tail(second(IN))) ∈ carry) &
  ((first, head(first(IN)); second, head(second(IN));
  third, head(third(IN))) ∈ sum))
  ∨ (((first, tail(first(IN)); second, tail(second(IN)))
  ∈ carry) & ((first, head(first(IN)); second, head
  (second(IN)); third, head(third(IN))) ∈ ripple))))
  ∨ ((first(IN) = null) & (second(IN) = third(IN)))
  ∨ ((second(IN) = null) & (first(IN) = third(IN)))

IN ∈ ripplecar ≡ ((first(IN) = 1) ∨ (second(IN) = 1))

IN ∈ ripple ≡ (∼((first, tail(first(IN)); second, tail(second(IN));
  third, tail(third(IN))) ∈ sumd) & ((∼((first, tail
  (first(IN)); second, tail(second(IN))) ∈ ripplecar)
  & ((first, head(first(IN)); second, head(second(IN));
  third, head(third(IN))) ∈ sum)) ∨ (((first, tail(first
  (IN)); second, tail(second(IN))) ∈ ripplecar) &
  ((first, head(first(IN)); second, head(second(IN));
  third, head(third(IN))) ∈ ripple)))) ∨ ((first(IN)
  = null) & ((first, second(IN); second, (head, null; tail, 1);
  third, third(IN)) ∈ sum)) ∨ ((second(IN)
  = null) & ((first, first(IN); second, (head, null;
  tail, 1); third, third(IN)) ∈ sum)).

Some explanation is probably necessary for the last three concepts. The elements of "sum" are ordered triples of numerals such that the third is the sum of the first two in the usual sense. The universe of triples has three properties, "first," "second," and "third." The description of "sum" essentially says "The tail of the third is the sum of the tails of the first and second. If there is no carry, then the head of the third is the sum of the heads of the first and second. If there is a carry, then the heads of the first, second, and third are related by ripple." The description of ripple is the same as the description of sum, except for the addition of a bit in the least significant digit, which is allowed to "ripple through."

An example, representing the binary sum $1 + 11 = 100$, will probably clarify matters further. The element of sum of concern here is

(first, (head, null; tail, 1); second, (head, (head, null; tail, 1);

tail, 1); third, (head(head(head, null; tail, 1); tail, 0); tail, 0)).

Initially, tail(first(IN)) = 1; tail (second(IN)) = 1; and tail(third(IN)) = 0, satisfying the first conjunct of the first disjunct in the intention of the concept named "sum." Hence, since (first, 1; second, 1) is an element of "carry" the object (first, null; second, (head, null, tail, 1); third, (head, (head, null; tail, 1); tail, 0)) is to be a member of "ripple" by the second disjunct of the second conjunct of the first disjunct in intention of "sum." Since "first(IN)" for this new object is "null" the third disjunct of "ripple" has to be satisfied, that is, the object (first, (head, null; tail, 1); second, (head, null; tail, 1); third, (head(head, null; tail, 1); tail 0)) has to belong to "sum." Again, the tails satisfy the first conjunct in the first disjunct. Also, there is a carry so that the object (first, null; second, null; third, (head, null; tail, 1)) must be a member of ripple. Hence, again by the third disjunct of ripple, (first, null; second, (head, null; tail, 1); third(head, null; tail, 1)) must belong to sum. By third disjunct of sum we must have ((head, null; tail, 1) = (head, null; tail, 1)), which is true.

We might object to the rather cumbersome nature of the concepts. However, any statement describing a complicated operation like arithmetic sum is bound to be somewhat cumbersome. The present statements are certainly less cumbersome than, say, the Boolean expression describing a parallel 36-bit adder and yet is expressing operations on strings of arbitrary length.

However, the expression (head, (head, (head, null; tail, 1); tail, 0); tail, 0) is certainly a more cumbersome expression than 100 or even $(x = 1)$ & $(y = 0)$ & $(z = 0)$. Later on in this section methods are considered that reduce the unwieldiness of objects in the language and also permit the attachment of names to objects. This way, it is easier to express operations by means other than through relations.

The importance of the last sentence above becomes clear when we want to express facts like $1 + 1 + 1 = 11$ and $11 + 101 = 100 + 100$. Unless some concept other than sum is to be introduced anew (a wasteful procedure), we have to introduce existential and universal quantifiers into the language, so the facts above can be expressed, respectively, by saying "for any z such that $1 + 1 = z$ it is true that $z + 1 = 11$" and "for any z such that $11 + 101 = z$ it is true that $100 + 100 = z$." This, of course, renders the recognition process of Figure 4.3 inadequate. Before these facts are discussed, one more example will be given, which brings out some further strengths and weaknesses of the language.

We can imagine classifying the residents of a street by their name, house of residence, age range (small, big), and sex. The house of residence may be described by its size, color, and level of beauty (and perhaps even number, which would render the environment for houses nonfull, which it is anyway). A typical person might be an object like

(name, lucy; age, small; house, (size, small; color, white; look, pretty);

sex, girl).

In such a universe, a relation like fatherhood can be expressed as

IN ∈ father ≡ ((house(first(IN)) = house(second(IN))) & (age(first

(IN)) = big) & (sex(first(IN)) = man));

that is, "of two people in the same house, the adult male is the other one's father." The description is certainly incomplete, but can be improved upon.

The difficulty here again is our inability to make such simple statements as "Harry is Susan's father." We can try to get around this by including the father's name in the object, but then we have to make a decision whether to include the father's name only or to include the entire object describing the father. The second gives rise to an infinite recursion; the first leads to the obvious problem of finding the father's father. Any cross-indexing needs the attachment of names to objects, as are needed in the case of numerals.

These and related difficulties can be resolved (as far as the descriptive strength of the language is concerned) by introducing variables other than IN into the language and allowing logical quantifiers. Also, capabilities have to be established for naming objects by strings of symbols. However, strings of symbols, unlike symbols, should be processable. To make this possible, we introduce a new syntactic entity. In this new notation, the object (head, (head(head, null; tail, 1); tail, 0); tail, 0) could have the representative STRING $(1, 0, 0,$ numer) and if (first, α; second, β) were an element of "fatherhood," then α could be represented by STRING (father, of, β). Such naming processes, of course, should be describable within the language. Also, we should have the freedom of introducing axioms in D other than concepts. To do this, the symbol ≡, which so far has no logical significance, has to be a part of the theory. The concept of "proof" has to be introduced, as in any logic. This renders recognition of objects as belonging to concepts more difficult. However, Milliken has shown that a suitable modification of the algorithm shown in Figure 4.3 can be made that permits recognition of some concepts even in this extended language [35]. Since the extended language permits its own description and can describe integers, it is clear that a mechanical recognition procedure for all objects is impossible [36].

The extended language is introduced and exemplified in what follows. A large part of the language is similar to the one discussed before.

A. THE SYNTAX

1. Any string of lowercase Latin letters and Arabic numerals is a *symbol*. A symbol is a *term*. Any string of greek letters is a *variable*. A variable is a *term*.

2. If A and B are terms, then A, B is an *ordered pair*. An ordered pair is an *ordered pair string*. If A and B are ordered pair strings, then $A; B$ is an *ordered pair string*. If A is an ordered pair string, then (A) is an *object*. An object is a *term*.

The important thing added to the syntax at this point is the variable. The discerning reader probably noticed before this that IN was playing a role similar to a variable in the previous discussion. However, a larger repertoire of variables is necessary for full flexibility of use.

3. If A is a term and B is a term, then $A(B)$ is a *term*. The term

$$\text{color}(a)$$

stands for the English phrase "the color of a." Generally, such a term is meaningful only when a stands for some object like

$$(\text{color}, \text{red}; \text{size}, \text{big}; \text{number}, 135);$$

in this case color(a) would stand for

$$\text{red.}$$

However, this interpretation, unlike the previous case, is part of our axiom set now.

4. If A and B are terms, then $(A = B)$ and $(A \in B)$ are *statements*. If A and B are statements, then $(A \lor B)$, $(A \,\&\, B)$, $(A \to B)$, $(A \equiv B)$, and $\sim A$ are *statements*.

5.   If A is a statement and B is a variable, then $(\forall B)A$ and $(\exists B)A$ are *statements*.

Rule 5 is one of the major reasons for introducing variables as parts of the syntax. Also, the use of $\equiv$ now has a logical interpretation as a propositional connective, rather than merely as a cue for recognition, as in the previous discussion.

It has already been pointed out that in this description language we have the freedom of giving names to sets of objects and using these names to define new sets of objects. These names, however, are arbitrarily given symbols and have no syntactic relationship to the set of objects being defined. Hence, if we had to define a class of sets that had similar structures, this similarity would not be reflected in the given names. Thus, the set of all numbers greater than 3 and the set of all numbers greater than 50 would be given two different names and the fact that each set has a lower bound would be lost. Nor would calling them things like "greater than 3" help, since the language deals with symbols as a single entity.

A part of what follows is directed toward giving a number of string-processing abilities to any automaton using the language. It is also aimed at making these abilities usable for tying in the names of sets and objects with their respective structures. In line with procedures used earlier, however, the mapping that defines the process is included only in the axioms of the system. What follows, then, is only the syntactical part.

6.   A symbol is a *train*. If A and B are trains, then A, B is a *train*. If A is a train, then STRING(A) is a *string*. A string is a *train*.

7.   A term is an *operand*. If A and B are operands, then A, B is an *operand*. If A is an operand, then TIE(A) is a *representative*. A string is a *representative*. A representative is an *operand*.

8.   EMPTY is an *operand*. If A is a representative, then STRIP(A), END(A), and REST(A) are *operands*.

9.   If A is a representative, then REPINV(A) is a *term*. If A is a term, then REP(A) is a *representative*.

Examples of strings and representatives are

        STRING(2, 0, 1 num)
        STRING(STRING(1, 0, num), STRING(2, 1, num), sum)
        TIE(STRIP(REP(α)), end(β))
        TIE(brother, of, name(first(α)))

10.   If A and B are representatives, then $(A = B)$ is a *statement*.

The following examples indicate the usefulness of strings in obviating the difficulties mentioned earlier. Although the concept of "truth" has not been introduced in this formalism, the reader should be able to follow the examples from an intuitive understanding of the meaning of truth.

Let there be a concept in D as given before

$$a \in \text{father} \equiv (\text{age(first}(\alpha)) = \text{big}) \;\&\; (\text{sex(first}(\alpha))) = \text{man})$$
$$\&\; (\text{house(first}(\alpha)) = \text{house(second}(\alpha))).$$

A typical object in "father" might be

> (first, (name, frank; sex, man; house, (size, small;
> color, blue; look, pretty); age, big); second, (name,
> susan; sex, girl; house, (size, small; color, blue;
> look, pretty); age, small)).

We can call Frank "Susan's father"—a rather generalized naming operation that was impossible in the language so far. For this, we can now define an axiom as

$$\alpha \in \text{father} \rightarrow (\text{REP(first}(\alpha)) = \text{TIE(father, of, name(second}(\alpha)))),$$

which, by the rules described later, would yield the statement

> REP((name, frank; sex, man; house of residence
> (size, small; color, blue; look, pretty); age, big)) =
> STRING(father, of, susan).

The exact way in which the truth of this statement is derived in the language will be shown after the axiom system has been discussed.

B. The Axiom Schemata

1. A statement $(A = B)$ is an *axiom* if and only if
    (i) A and B are each the same (identical) term. Two objects are identical if every ordered pair appearing in A is identical to some ordered pair appearing in B and vice versa. Two ordered pairs are identical if their first elements are identical and their second elements are identical.
    (ii) A and B are identical trains.
    (iii) If A is a term of the form $C(D)$ where D is an object, C the first element of some unique ordered pair of D, and B the second element of the same ordered pair.

(iv) If A is of the form TIE(C) or TIE(C, EMPTY) or TIE(EMPTY, C), C is a train, and B is the string STRING(C).

(v) If A is of the form END(C) where C is a string of the form STRING(D, B) and B is either a symbol or a string.

(vi) If A is of the form REST(C) and C is a string of the form STRING (B, D) where D is a symbol or a string; or if C is a symbol and A is EMPTY.

(vii) If A is of the form STRIP(STRING(B)).

2. Every statement $\sim(A = B)$ is an *axiom* if and only if

(i) If A and B are symbols but not identical or if A (alternatively B) is a symbol and B (alternatively A) is an object.

(ii) If A and B are both objects that do not contain terms of the form $C(D)$ and A and B are not identical.

(iii) If A and B are both trains and not identical.

3. Every statement $\sim(A \in B)$ is an *axiom* if B is an object.

4. If A and B are statements and X is a variable, then the following are *axioms*.

(i) $(A \rightarrow (B \rightarrow A))$.

(ii) $((A \rightarrow (B \rightarrow C)) \rightarrow ((A \rightarrow B) \rightarrow (A \rightarrow C)))$.

(iii) $((\sim A \rightarrow \sim B) \rightarrow (B \rightarrow A))$.

(iv) $((\forall X)(A \rightarrow B) \rightarrow (A \rightarrow (\forall X)B))$.

(v) $((\forall X)A \rightarrow S_{\cdot Y}^{X} A/)$.

In (iv) X must not occur free in A. In (v) Y is either a variable or a term; however, no free occurrence of X in A must be in a substatement B of A in the form $(\forall Y)C$ where X is a free variable in C.

An occurrence of a variable X in a statement A is said to be bound if it occurs in some substatement of A in the form $(\forall X)C$. An occurrence that is not bound is called free.

The symbol $S_{\cdot Y}^{X} A/$ stands for the statement A' obtained by replacing all free occurrences of X in A by Y.

5. If A and B are statements and X is a variable, then the following are axioms.

(i) $((\exists X)A \equiv \sim(\forall X)\sim A)$.

(ii) $((A \lor B) \equiv ((A \rightarrow B) \rightarrow B))$.

(iii) $((A \mathbin{\&} B) \equiv \sim(\sim A \lor \sim B))$.

(iv) $((A \equiv B) \equiv ((A \rightarrow B) \mathbin{\&} (B \rightarrow A)))$.

It will be noticed that some statements that were true in the previous system are now axioms. For instance, (color((size, big; color, red)) = red) is an axiom. However, since the recursive function "value" is not defined in the new system, some other statements, like (color(first((first, (color, red; size, big); second, hand))) = red), are not axioms, because first(first(color, red; size, big); second, hand) is not an object but a general term that is not covered by rule 1(iii) of Section 4.6,B. The truth of the statement above will only follow from the definition of the rules of inference as given in Section 4.6,C. Meanwhile, note that although the statement is not an axiom, its negation is not one either. Truth and falsity of statements are much more difficult to test in the new system, a price we pay for flexibility.

C. RULES OF INFERENCE

Given a set D of statements and a statement A, we say A is derivable from D if there exists a sequence $S_1, S_2, \ldots, S_n$ of statement such that S_n is the same as A and for every i $(1 \leq i \leq n)$ either S_i is an axiom, or S_i is a member of D or is inferred from previous statements S_j, S_k $(j, k < i)$ by one of the following 5 rules of inference.

1. From A to infer $(\forall X)A$ where X is a variable.
2. From A and $(A \rightarrow B)$ to infer B.
3. From A and $(X = Y)$, to infer A' where A' is obtained from A by replacing some occurrences of X by Y and some occurrences of Y by X.
4. From $(REP(X) = Y)$ (where X is a term and Y is a representative), to infer $(REPINV(Y) = X)$.
5. From $(A = B)$ to infer $(B = A)$.

It is worth pointing out here how some of the previously discussed statements are derivable from certain axioms. The statement

color(first((first, (color, red; size, big); second, hand))) = red)

is derivable ("true") since

(first((first, (color, red; size, big); second, hand)) = (color, red; size, big))

is an axiom by above.

Also, (color(color, red; size, big) = red) is an axiom. Since both of the foregoing are derivable, we can replace (according to rule 3 of this subsection "(color, red; size, big)" in the second by "first((first, (color, red; size, big); second, hand))," the left-hand side of the first statement; deriving the initial statement.

Again, we can derive REP(name, frank; sex, man; house of residence, (size, small; color, blue; look, pretty); age, big) = STRING(father, of, susan) from the concept named "father" and the statement

$$(\alpha \in \text{father}) \rightarrow (\text{REP}(\text{first}(\alpha)) = \text{TIE}(\text{father, of, name}(\text{second}(\alpha))))$$

in a similar manner, in view of some of the axioms discussed earlier.

Before closing this section it is worthwhile to indicate how the REP (representation) of the object named "frank" does not have to be unique. If locations of houses in cities and professions of people were included in the universe, this object might also have STRING(frank, the, barber, of, seville) as a representation and we could have statements like

REPINV(STRING(father, of, susan))

= REPINV(STRING(frank, the, barber, of, seville)).

An example from the field of character recognition may motivate some readers more. Assume that the universe consists of the different configurations of excitations on a square array of photo cells and suppose we are interested in all configurations in which all excited photo cells lie on a straight line inclined to the horizontal edge of the photo cell at −45°. Call it "negative-diag."

In this universe each photo cell determines a property whose values are called 0 and 1. Each photo cell is determined by its coordinates. Hence, the universe of photo cells has two properties, corresponding to the X and Y coordinates, which will be called "first" and "second" here. The values of both these properties are integers, which have been discussed before in connection with the description language. The reader will verify that a typical configuration on a 2 × 2 array may be denoted by the object

((first, (head, null; tail, 1); second, (head, null;
tail, 1)), 1; (first, (head, (head, null; tail, 1);
tail, 0); second, (head, null; tail, 1)), 0; (first,
(head, null; tail, 1); second, (head, (head, null;
tail, 1); tail, 0)), 1; (first, (head, (head, null;
tail, 1); tail, 0); second, (head, (head, null, tail,
1); tail, 0)), 0)

representing the configuration

1   0
1   0

We can now write a statement that defines the set "negativediag."

$$\alpha \in \text{negativediag} \equiv (\exists\beta)(\exists\gamma)((\beta(\alpha) = 1) \ \& \ (\gamma(\alpha) = 1) \ \& \sim(\beta = \gamma))$$
$$\& \ (\exists\beta)(\forall\gamma)((\gamma(\alpha) = 1) \rightarrow ((\text{first, first}(\gamma);$$
$$\text{second, second}(\gamma); \text{third, } \beta) \in \text{sum})).$$

The language, while describing concepts, has usefulness in other information retrieval systems. Its use in such systems has not been investigated but
it may be safe to say that its capability, even if somewhat curtailed, may be
greater than any conjunctive system of descriptors or association strength
networks discussed in the field [37].

4.7. OTHER DESCRIPTION LANGUAGES

Set-theoretical descriptions have been used for concepts mostly by workers
interested in simulating human cognitive activity. However, the entire basis
of pattern recognition as a phenomenon is set theoretical or, more precisely,
logical. The motivation behind the different methods used in synthesizing
concept-learning algorithms often lie in fields like statistics [38] or linear
algebra [39]; in every case, however, the final algorithm for recognizing an
object as belonging to a concept or pattern (after the "learning phase") can
be looked upon as using a compound statement as the description of the
concept. This will be clear if we consider the case of a set of binary vectors
whose components satisfy a linear inequality. The set $\{000, 001, 011, 100,$
$101, 111\}$ of binary vectors, for instance, can be represented by the linear
inequality $\frac{1}{2} - y + z > 0$ or the Boolean expression $(\sim y + z)$ or the statement $(y = 0) \vee (z = 1)$. Similar statements can be constructed for cases
where the discriminating functions are nonlinear or even when the components of the vectors come from a continuum. Each component of the
vector is a property whose values isolate subsets of the universe. In the
latter case, however, the logical expressions representing these functions
need quantifiers to take care of infinite set-theoretical connectives.

The modes of combination available to pattern recognition schemes based
on statistics or linear algebra are richer than those available to Boolean
algebra. However, very often the effectiveness of the various modes of combination dealt with in the literature are strongly dependent on the initial
measurements (i.e., the input properties or "features"), and dependent in an
extremely ill-understood way; also, there is no uniform method for changing
one set of algebraic operations into another to yield new "features" from
old ones. It is to achieve such flexibility and to tie down the description with

the basic set-theoretical structure of the problem that the language of Section 4.6 was developed.

Very little can be said regarding the ultimate effectiveness of the various algebraic or statistically oriented languages available for description of patterns. Some of them (like linear separation) essentially restrict the capability of description for the sake of simplicity of description and "training." Others, like Braverman's potential functions [40], are essentially "open ended" and can be used (like Boolean functions) to describe any concept whatever. However, the latter lead to problems of confidence limits and "generalization." It may be well to defer discussions of these to the next chapter, when learning is discussed.

Returning to the discussion of the use of simple Boolean expressions (or expressions in propositional calculus) as a description language, it was shown in Section 4.5 how the class of describable concepts can be restricted for parsimony, yielding, say, the class of conjunctive and simple concepts. Although the class of simple concepts properly contains the class of conjunctive concepts, all concepts are not simple and modes of description have to be available for describing every concept. The language of the property lists is not adequate for this. A suitable extension of it has been suggested that is capable of describing any concept. Conceptions can describe any concept also. The efficiency of both the property list and the conception list is severely restricted for a large class of concepts. However, the ultimate capability for description is not limited, as they are for perceptronlike devices, which use hyperplanes as discriminating surfaces.

Two other languages, the CLS by Hunt [41] and EPAM by Feigenbaum [42], are restricted in their ability to the same extent as the conceptions. The relationship between the two has been discussed by Hunt. It is relevant to discuss here the salient points of difference between the conceptions on the one hand and the CLS and the EPAM on the other.

That the systems used by Hunt and Feigenbaum are binary trees, whereas the conceptions allow more than two branches to emanate from the nodes, is not a crucial difference. All three are essentially tree structures; the fact that only one of the trees is nonbinary is easily attributable to the strong influence that the word "bit" has had on psychologists since 1948.

There are two crucial differences between the CLS and EPAM tree and the conceptions, however. One is that the name of the concept described by the tree is placed at the root of the tree in the conceptions, whereas it is placed in the leaves in the other two languages. This looks like an essentially wasteful feature of the conceptions, since there has to be a different tree for every concept. There are, however, some essential reasons for doing this, as an analysis of the basic sets involved shows.

For one thing, a property that is relevant to a concept A may not be relevant to a concept B. This fact can be used advantageously in the conceptions. But when the EPAM processor, say, is testing an object for membership of B, it still has to go through a test for this nonrelevant property, just because it was worth testing in testing for A.

There is another, much stronger reason for attaching concept names to roots of trees. Very often the same concept turns out to be the subconcept of two different concepts, in the sense that there is a concept C, two property values $p \in P$ and $q \in Q$, and two concepts A and B such that $C = p \cap A = q \cap B$. Then, the name C can be placed on the conceptions of A and B instead of placing the entire C tree twice in the conceptions of A and B, as would be necessary in the CLS or the EPAM. (These remarks do not pertain to CEPAM, developed by Ernst and Sherman [50], which will be discussed later.)

These differences occur essentially since it is overlooked in the other languages that a specific object can be a member of more than one concept; hence, more than one name has to be attached to every leaf if the names of the concepts are to be attached to leaves. Also, some of the intermediate nodes of a tree may contain enough information to identify an object in a concept, whereas to recognize the same object in one of its subconcepts would necessitate going deeper into the tree.

The need for attaching concept names to nodes becomes even more clear when we need to define a new test in terms of old tests in the interest of simplicity of description. In the conceptions, it is a matter of adding a new list into the conception of the universe, whereas it is impossible in the other two structures. No flexible language has appeared in the pattern recognition or cognitive process research as a counterpart of the description language discussed in Section 4.6. Various languages, like the ones developed by Narasimhan [43] and Kirsch [44], carry out operations on names of properties, but the procedures do not have the same flexibility and uniformity. However, the SIR system of Raphael [45] has certain similarities to the language of Section 4.6 that ought to be discussed.

One of the greatest similarities between SIR and the language described in Section 4.6 is in the structure of objects. The same property value pairs are strung together, and values of properties may be objects themselves; it is not clear whether names of properties can be objects in SIR.

In SIR, a list of symbols is also allowed to names of values of properties. Thus, (name, harry; brothers, (tom, dick, don); age, 15) would be a valid object. The advantage of this arrangement, of course, is that the object, in a sense, has greater efficiency of processing. For instance, let the question be asked "Is Tom Harry's brother?" (i.e., let tom $\in$ brother(harry) be posed as a theorem). A special processor could answer this "yes." However, if the question is asked "Does Harry have a brother aged 20?" the processor will have to know that there are objects whose property "name" has values "tom," "dick," and "don," a fact that is not clear from the format; a separate processor would be needed to incorporate such extra assumptions.

In fact, SIR as originally conceived and implemented consisted mostly of a series of processors capable of handling a special class of objects. The syntactic restrictions the objects were to satisfy were defined more in terms of the structures of the processors. As a result, certain facts about objects were easy to describe whereas others were impossible, unlike the language described in Section 4.6, where certain parts are easy to describe and others merely more difficult to describe. Also, in the language of Section 4.6, facts that were originally difficult to describe can be made easy to describe by adding new concepts. Most present-day description languages lack this flexibility through expansion.

SIR I [46], which was suggested by Raphael as the improved and flexible version of SIR, would basically be much more similar to the language discussed in Section 4.6.

In its generality, the language of Section 4.6 (as well as SIR I) is a first-order theory in the sense of symbolic logic. Hence, the testing of the truth of certain statements turns out, in most general cases, to be a search for appropriate steps of the proof. This is at present extremely difficult [47, 48]. On the other hand, many theorems in the system can be proved by simple processes, as was shown in the first part of Section 4.6. Even the addition of certain flexibilities of the language appearing in the second part of Section 4.6 does not vitiate the facility.

The present chapter has discussed the role played by languages in the description of patterns. It has neglected the discussion of languages where the basic predicates involve arithmetic operations, although it is clear, from both metamathematics and the discussion in Section 4.6, that such operations can be included in the languages discussed in this chapter. However, these arithmetic (and "statistical") languages are best discussed in terms of their "generalizing" ability. This will be done in the next chapter.

Chapter 5

LEARNING AND GENERALIZATION

5.1. INTRODUCTION

In Chapter 4, our major concern was to develop languages in which sets of objects could be described in such a way that a specific object could be tested for membership in a set in terms of the object's properties. Associated with any technique of concept learning, whether by discriminant functions [40], probability estimation [49], or whatever, there must be a language in which expressions can be written to define a set. The major points of difference between the ones described in Chapter 4 and the more popular ones in the field are the following. Initially, the languages described in Chapter 4 are essentially nonnumerical, so that the objects do not have to be preprocessed to yield numerical values of the properties. In the field of pattern recognition, this preprocessing is essentially a phenomenon left out of the learning and recognition techniques analyzed. It is the author's belief that this separation of preprocessing from recognition places great difficulties in the way of answering the most important question in the field today, "How does one determine the most effective preprocessors in a pattern recognition problem?" It is to be noted that in the languages described in Chapter 4, the noninput properties stand for the results of preprocessing the input properties. Thus the preprocessing is described in the same format as the patterns. Therefore, the "effectiveness" of preprocessors can be discussed in a uniform way. It was indicated while discussing the language of Section 4.6 that this does not necessarily remove the advantages inherent in numerical processing.

This chapter describes certain algorithms for pattern learning, using two of the languages described in the preceding chapter. It is indicated how the resulting descriptions are "succinct" when the pattern being learned fulfills certain conditions. Although one of the algorithms presented is strong enough to learn any concept (rather than only those that satisfy the given conditions), the description learned in the general case ceases to be succinct. How this lack of succinctness affects the statistical degree of confidence in the learned description is indicated.

The arguments used in these discussions are shown to have direct analogs to cases where the description is written in terms of discriminant function or maximum likelihood ratios, as is often done in the literature. It is indicated how these arguments bring out the great need for a meaningful discussion of feature extraction or "concept formation."

Since the flexible languages discussed in Chapter 4 can describe preprocessing in the same format as descriptions, we can discuss the modification of $\mathscr{P}$ in an environment to render descriptions succinct.

5.2. LEARNING CONJUNCTIVE CONCEPTS

The algorithm described in this section was developed by Pennypacker [32] for developing conceptions (see Section 4.3) for patterns on the basis of examples of objects belonging to the patterns. Unlike most experiments conducted in the field (except those conducted with psychological interest by Bruner and his followers [14, 30]), the algorithm is given the freedom of choosing examples on the basis of past examples shown by the trainer; also, it is given the freedom of asking two other questions: "Is the pattern described by the following conception completely contained in the pattern under consideration?" and "Is this a correct conception for the pattern under consideration?" Both these questions can be replaced by statistical tests and this may be necessary in real circumstances. However, the purpose of the investigation was to establish the logical structure of the algorithm.

The basis of the algorithm lies in the isolation of a set of property values $G = \{p_{1i_1}, p_{2i_2}, \dots, p_{si_s}\}$ such that $p_{1i_1} \cap p_{2i_2} \cap \cdots \cap p_{si_s} \subseteq X$ where X is the pattern being learned and such that there is no subset of G whose intersection is contained in X. If X is a conjunctive pattern, this basic algorithm converges to yield a short conception for X. Otherwise, it yields a conjunctive pattern that is a proper subset of X. Examples outside the pattern and inside X are then interrogated to yield other conjunctive patterns. The process continues till a set of conjunctive patterns is obtained whose union covers X.

The operation of the algorithm needs the ability to obtain conceptions of Boolean functions of patterns having known conceptions and to test for identity of concepts and containment of one concept in another. It must also be capable of evaluating properties of objects, given the values of its input properties. Algorithms for doing these have been developed by Pennypacker: some were discussed briefly in the preceding chapter. The operation of the algorithm depends on the following lemmata.

LEMMA 5.1.   *Let $\langle U, \mathscr{P} \rangle$ be an environment and let*

$$p_{1i_1} \cap p_{2i_2} \cap \cdots \cap p_{ni_n} \subseteq p_{k_1j_1} \cap p_{k_2j_2} \cap \cdots \cap p_{k_sj_s}$$

where for all t $(1 \leq t \leq n)$, $p_{ti_t} \in P_t \in \mathscr{P}$ *and for all* r $(1 \leq r \leq s)$, $p_{k_r j_r} \in P_{k_r} \in$ $\mathscr{P}$. *Also, let* $p_{2i_2} \cap \cdots \cap p_{ni_n} \neq p_{1i_1} \cap \cdots \cap p_{ni_n}$ *and* $p_{2i_2} \cap \cdots \cap p_{ni} \subseteq$ $p_{k_1 j_1} \cap \cdots \cap p_{k_s j_s}$. *Then for no* r $(1 \leq r \leq s)$, $p_{k_r j_r} = p_{1i_1}$.

PROOF.   Assume to the contrary; then

$$p_{2i_2} \cap \cdots \cap p_{ni_n} \subseteq p_{k_1 j_1} \cap \cdots \cap p_{k_s j_s} \subseteq p_{k_r j_r} = p_{1i_1},$$

whence

$$p_{2i_2} \cap \cdots \cap p_{ni_n} = p_{1i_1} \cap p_{2i_2} \cap \cdots \cap p_{ni_n},$$

contrary to hypothesis.   ∎

LEMMA 5.2.   *Let* $\langle U, \mathscr{P} \rangle$ *be an environment and* $\{P_1, P_2, \ldots, P_n\} \subseteq \mathscr{P}$. *Let*

$$\varnothing \neq p_{1i_1} \cap p_{2i_2} \cap \cdots \cap p_{ni_n} \subseteq p_{k_1 j_1} \cap p_{k_2 j_2} \cap \cdots \cap p_{k_s j_s}$$

where for each r $(1 \leq r \leq s)$, $1 \leq k_r \leq n$ *and for all* m, $p_{mi_m} \in P_m$ $(1 \leq m \leq n)$. *Then for each* r $(1 \leq r \leq s)$

$$j_r = i_{k_r}.$$

PROOF.   Let $k_r = t$. Then

$$p_{1i_1} \cap p_{2i_2} \cap \cdots \cap p_{ni_n} \subseteq p_{ti_t} = p_{k_r i_{k_r}}$$

and

$$p_{k_1 j_1} \cap p_{k_2 j_2} \cap \cdots \cap p_{k_s j_s} \subseteq p_{k_r j_r}.$$

The theorem follows since P_{k_r} is a partition and $p_{k_r j_r} \cap p_{k_r i_{k_r}} \neq \varnothing$.   ∎

LEMMA 5.3.   *Under the hypothesis of Lemma 5.2 if*

$$p_{2i_2} \cap \cdots \cap p_{ni_n} \nsubseteq p_{k_1 j_1} \cap \cdots \cap p_{k_s j_s},$$

then for some r $(1 \leq r \leq s)$

$$k_r = 1.$$

PROOF.

$$1 \leq k_r \leq n \qquad \text{for all } r \ (1 \leq r \leq s)$$

and

$$k_r \neq 1 \qquad \text{for all } r \ (1 \leq r \leq s)$$

indicates

$$2 \leq k_r \leq n \qquad \text{for all } r,$$

contradicting the hypothesis.   ∎

LEMMA 5.4.   *Under the hypothesis of Lemma 5.2 let*

$$p_{1i_1} \cap \cdots \cap p_{ni_n} \neq p_{k_1 j_1} \cap \cdots \cap p_{k_s j_s}$$

and let $\{p_{1i_1}, p_{2i_2}, \ldots, p_{ti_t}\}$ be the set of all terms on the left-hand side such that $p_{mi_m} \neq p_{k_r j_r}$ for any r $(1 \leq r \leq s)$. Then,

$$p_{(t+i)i_{t+1}} \cap \cdots \cap p_{ni_n} \neq p_{1i_1} \cap \cdots \cap p_{ni_n}.$$

PROOF.   By construction of the set $\{p_{1i_1}, \ldots, p_{ti_t}\}$, the left-hand side is equal to $p_{k_1 j_1} \cap \cdots \cap p_{k_2 j_2}$, which directly contradicts the hypothesis.   ∎

The algorithm can now be justified rigorously. Any object is an intersection of a set $\{p_{ij_i}\}$ of property values. If this object is properly contained in a conjunctive concept that is to be learned, then the hypothesis of Lemma 5.2 is fulfilled. If we now remove from the set $\{p_{ij_i}\}$ one value $p_{i_0 j_0}$, then one of four things may occur:

1. The new concept obtained by intersecting the elements of $\{p_{ij_i}\} - p_{i_0 j_0}$ is the same as the object.

2. The new concept as obtained above contains the object properly and is properly contained in the conjunctive concept being learned. This fulfills the condition of Lemma 5.1; hence, $p_{i_0 j_0}$ does not occur in the expression for the conjunctive concept to be learned and hence, can be removed from the set $\{p_{ij_i}\}$ without violating the hypothesis of Lemma 5.2.

3. The new concept coincides with the concept to be learned. This terminates the learning process.

4. The new concept is not contained in the concept being learned. Then Lemma 5.3 holds and $p_{i_0 j_0}$ occurs in the expression for the conjunctive concept being learned.

If case 2 holds, we can start the process over again by removing a new property value $p_{i'_0 j'_0}$ from the set $\{p_{ij_i}\} - p_{i_0 j_0}$. If case 4 holds, then $p_{i_0 j_0}$ is left in the set $\{p_{ij_i}\}$ and never removed again. In either case, the test to be performed on the set $\{p_{ij_i}\}$ is constrained to be performed on a smaller set. Hence, if on each removal of a $p_{i_0 j_0}$ only case 2, 3, or 4 holds, the successive removal comes to an end. If it does not come to an end at (3), then the concept to be learned is not conjunctive.

Note that the foregoing discussion provides the rationale for Bruner's conservative focusing strategy. Case 1 never occurs in his experiments since his input properties are all the properties in the environment and the input properties form a full fine structure family (see Chapter 4). In the present case, where the environment contains many noninput properties, so that the entire property set is not full, the algorithm needs the modification discussed below.

If (1) is the case, then other property values have to be removed from the set $\{p_{ij_i}\}$. If (1) holds for all values so removed, then a combination of two values is removed from $\{p_{ij_i}\}$ and the process is repeated. At this point fulfillment of (4) does not yield any result, since the condition of Lemma 5.2 is not necessarily fulfilled any more. However, the fulfillment of condition 2 is still significant, since the hypothesis of Lemma 5.2 was not involved in the proof of Lemma 5.1.

By Lemma 5.4, as long as there is any property value left in $\{p_{ij_i}\}$, there will be some combination of property values whose removal will result in fulfillment of condition 2. This way, all property values not occurring in the expression of the conjunctive concept are removed in a finite number of operations and condition 3 occurs. If, however, the concept being learned is not conjunctive, then condition 4 occurs on the removal of any property value. In this case a new object is chosen which is contained in the concept being learned but not in the conjunctive concepts learned so far and the process is repeated. Since in a finite environment any concept is the union of a finite number of conjunctive concepts (see discussion following Theorem 4.9), the process terminates with the recognition of the concept.

The discussion above constitutes an informal proof of the following theorem.

THEOREM 5.1. *In a finite environment the algorithm shown in the flow chart, Figure 5.1, terminates in a finite number of steps with the recognition of a concept.* ■

It may be pointed out that the finiteness of the algorithm does not in any way assure a short description of the concept learned, because a short description may not exist at all. Also, the process, though finite, may be inordinately long. This also has some extremely adverse effects on the "generalization" of the concept. The generalization is discussed in a later section. In the next section an algorithm that learns simple concepts in a finite number of steps is discussed. It utilizes the language discussed in Section 4.5, and hence, can construct simple descriptions for a much richer class of concepts than the conjunctive. However, in many realistic cases (for instance, in environments where properties are two valued) even this excludes many concepts.

5.3. LEARNING SIMPLE CONCEPTS

This section presents an algorithm that, given a set of objects $\{X_1, X_2, \ldots, X_p\}$, generates a subset T of K (see Chapter 4, Section 4.5), such that $H(T) = \{X_1 \cup X_2 \cup \cdots \cup X_p\}^s$. This algorithm is then used as a basic component of a method for generalization and learning.

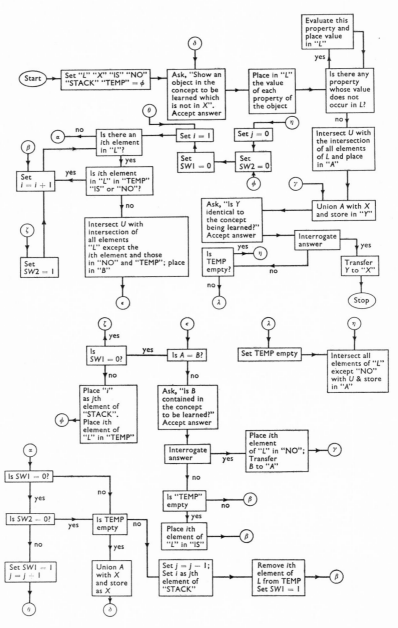

Figure 5.1. Pennypacker's learning algorithm.

158

Given a concept X, we define a set G_X of property values $(G_X \subseteq K)$

$$G_X = \{p_{ij} \mid p_{ij} \in P_i, P_i \in \mathscr{P}, p_{ij} \subseteq \neg X\}.$$

From Theorem 4.8 and the fact that $p_{ij} \subseteq \neg X$ if and only if $p_{ij} \cap X = \varnothing$, we see right away that an alternative method for writing an expression for X^s is

$$X^s = \neg\bigcup \{p_{ij} \mid p_{ij} \in G_X\} = H(G_X).$$

Also

LEMMA 5.5. *If $H(T) = X^s$, then $T \subseteq G_X$.*

PROOF. Since $\neg X^s \subseteq \neg X$.

$$\neg H(T) = \bigcup \{p_{ij} \mid p_{ij} \in T\} = \neg X^s \subseteq \neg X.$$

Hence, $p_{ij} \in T$ implies $p_{ij} \subseteq \neg X$ or $p_{ij} \in G_X$. ∎

This lemma indicates that G_X is the largest subset of K such that $H(G_X) = X^s$. That is, G_X is identical to $M(X)$ as defined in Chapter 4.

Let now $\{X_1, X_2, \ldots, X_p\}$ be a sequence of objects. Associate with this sequence a sequence of subsets $\{K_0, K_1, \ldots, K_p\}$ of K as

$$K_0 = K.$$

If $K_i = \{t_i, t_2, \ldots, t_m\}$ and $X_i = p_{1i_1} \cap p_{2i_2} \cap \cdots \cap p_{ni_n}$, then $K_{i+1} = \{t \mid t = t_i$ from some i $(1 \le i \le m)$ and $t \ne p_{ki_k}$ for any k $(1 \le k \le n)\}$.

The following lemma is important.

LEMMA 5.6. $K_p = M(X_1 \cup \cdots \cup X_p)$.

PROOF. Let $p_{ms} \notin K_p$. Then there is some X_t $(1 \le t \le p)$ such that $X_t \subseteq p_{ms}$.

But $p_{ms} \in M(X_1 \cup \cdots \cup X_p)$ implies $p_{ms} \subseteq \neg X_1 \cap \neg X_2 \cap \cdots \cap X_p \subseteq \neg X_t$, which leads to a contradiction. Hence, $p_{ms} \notin M(X_1 \cup \cdots \cup X_p)$. Hence, $\neg K_p \subseteq \neg M(X_1 \cup \cdots X_p)$ or $K_p \supseteq M(X_1 \cup \cdots X_p)$.

Now let $X_t = p_{1i_1} \cap \cdots \cap p_{ni_n}$. Then $p_{mi_m} \notin K_p$ for any m $(1 \le m \le n)$. Hence, $X_t \subseteq p_{mk}$ implies $p_{mk} \notin K_p$ or $K_p \subseteq \{p_{mn} \mid X_t \not\subseteq p_{mn}\} = \{p_{mn} \mid X_t \cap p_{mn} = \varnothing\} = \{p_{mn} \mid p_{mn} \subseteq \overline{X}_t\} = M(X_t)$ (since X_t, being an object, is either wholly contained in or disjoint from any property value: see Theorem 4.1).

So $K_p \subseteq M(X_t)$ for all t $(1 \le t \le p)$ or $K_p \subseteq \bigcap_{t=1}^p M(X_t) = M(X_1 \cup \cdots \cup X_t)$ (Theorem 4.11). This with the previous inequality yields the lemma. ∎

We can thus construct the following algorithm for learning a concept. The algorithm starts with two copies of K (K_0^1 and K_0^2) in memory. Every time an object $p_{1i_1} \cap \cdots \cap p_{ni_n}$ is presented as belonging to a concept X, the values p_{mi_m} ($1 \leq m \leq n$) are removed from K_i^1 to yield K_{i+1}^1. Similarly, any time the object is presented as belonging to $\neg X$, K_i^2 is similarly modified to K_{i+1}^2. At any stage of learning, if m positive and n negative instances are presented, then $H(K_m^1) \subseteq X^s$ and $H(K_n^2) \subseteq \neg X^s$.

If X and $\neg X$ are both simple concepts, then the algorithm converges at some value of m and n such that $H(K_m^1) = X$ and $H(K_n^2) = \neg X$. However, if either X or $\neg X$ is not simple, then we have to remain satisfied with the approximation to X given by X^s and $\neg((\neg X)^s)$.

A test has been developed by Windeknecht and Snediker [33, 34] to find out if a concept and its complement are both simple. The test depends on the following lemma.

LEMMA 5.7. $X^s = X$ and $(\neg X)^s = \neg X$ if and only if $X^s \cap (\neg X)^s = \varnothing$.

PROOF.   The "only if" part is immediate. For the "if" part we note that $X \cup \neg X \subseteq X^s \cup (\neg X)^s$. But $X \cup \neg X = U$. Hence, $X^s \cup (\neg X)^s \supseteq U$, yielding $X^s \cup (\neg X)^s = U$. Hence, $(\neg X)^s = \neg X^s$ from hypothesis or $X^s = \neg((\neg X)^s)$. But by cor. 4.1, $X \supseteq \neg((\neg X)^s) = X^s$, and $X \subseteq X^s$ whence $X = X^s$; $\neg X = (\neg X)^s$ follows similarly.

The application of this test depends on a test for $H(K_m^1) \cap H(K_m^2)$ being empty or, according to Theorem 4.11, for $H(K_m^1 \cup K_m^2) = \varnothing$. The test for this is not straightforward; given a subset $T \subseteq K$, it may not be easy to find out if $H(T) = \varnothing$. Clearly for any $P \in \mathscr{P}$, $H(P) = \varnothing$. Also, if $T' \supseteq P$, then $H(T') \subseteq H(P) = \varnothing$. There may, however, be some T that does not contain any $P \in \mathscr{P}$ as a subset and yet $H(T) = \varnothing$. The set $\{R_2, R_3, R_4, T_3\}$ in the example of Chapter 4 is an instance.

A rather involved procedure has been developed by Snediker for the test. Rather than describing the test in detail here, it may be more worthwhile to discuss the effectiveness of the procedures discussed here and in the previous sections in realistic situations and compare them with other well-known pattern recognition techniques.

5.4. PROBLEMS OF LEARNING AND FEATURE EXTRACTION

A study of either of the methods of learning in the two previous sections is very illuminating in that it brings to the attention of the reader some of the major difficulties in the way of pattern learning and points out some of the important requirements for an effective pattern-learning technique.

It will be noticed in the case of both the methods that they are most effective in learning patterns (or concepts) in certain classes. The Pennypacker technique, although an effective procedure for all concepts, ensures rapid convergence only for conjunctive concepts. The Windeknecht–Snediker technique converges to the correct concept only if the concept is simple. In the Pennypacker technique, however, there is a technique for finding out when a concept is not conjunctive and modifying the algorithm to take account of this fact. In the Windeknecht–Snediker algorithm, the corresponding test indicates, not whether the concept being learned is simple, but whether both it and its complement are simple. No algorithm has been developed that would learn any concept as a union of simple concepts in a way analogous to the Pennypacker algorithm.

However, the Pennypacker algorithm takes certain liberties that are not used by any other algorithm known to us. It asks the experimenter questions about the inclusion relationship between the concept being learned and concepts described by the algorithm. The Bruner conservative focusing strategy, on which the Pennypacker algorithm is based, did not allow these liberties, although it did envisage questions from the subject regarding memberships of specific objects in the concept being learned. The extra liberties were necessitated by the fact that unlike in Bruner's case (and the case of most psychological work after him), it was not assumed that the input properties of the real environment are full. This invalidates some of the methods used in the psychological experiments for obtaining new objects from a focus object.

It is difficult to say how many of the advantages of the Pennypacker algorithm over the Windeknecht–Snediker algorithm would remain if the extra liberties were taken away. Just as we need to develop methods for asking Bruner-type questions ("membership rather than inclusion") in the environment envisaged by Pennypacker, methods need to be developed also for modifying the Windeknecht–Snediker algorithm to the cases where the concepts learned are nonsimple. In any case, since there are more simple concepts in an environment than there are conjunctive ones, the Windeknecht–Snediker method ought to be more effective in general. However, in environments where all properties have only two values, all simple concepts are conjunctive. In this case the relative advantages disappear.

The weaknesses and strong points of the learning methods discussed in this chapter may be used to develop a set of criteria for the evaluation of concept-learning methods in general. In the previous paragraphs the methods of this chapter have been discussed on the basis of the following questions.

1. How rich is the class of concepts any one of whose members can be learned by this method?

2. How rich is the class of concepts any one of whose members can be learned efficiently by this method?

3. How rich is the class of concepts whose descriptions are succinct when expressed in the language envisaged by the algorithm?

4. Given the interpretation of an environment as a real pattern-learning situation, how many patterns to be learned can be expected to be members of the classes described in questions 1, 2, and 3?

It can be seen that the class described in question 1 contains the class described in question 2. (Nothing can be learned efficiently unless it is learned!) In the case of many methods, the latter class coincides with the class described in question 3. However, this may not be true for all methods and languages. A mathematical study of this point cannot be attempted unless precise and acceptable definitions of the words "succinct" and "efficient" be given. This will not be attempted.

Question 4, perhaps, needs some clarification, since it refers not to an abstract entity called the "environment" in the discussion, but to the un-formalizable thing called "real life," and the way we abstract it to an "environment" in the technical sense. In question 4, the phrase "patterns to be learned" refers to real life, as for example, the class of "all roman letters projected on a grid of photo cells" while the "classes described in questions 1, 2, and 3" refer to the describable classes after a class of properties have been abstracted and used in a mathematical system. If in real life we were called upon to learn all concepts possible (for instance, if learning the class containing "all lowercase a's, uppercase Q's, and all symmetrical figures" was as necessary as learning the class of all uppercase B's), the answers to question 4 would coincide with the answers to questions 1, 2, and 3, respectively. However, this is often not true.

It has already been seen that in the case of the Pennypacker technique the class described by question 1 is "the class of all concepts." The class described by questions 2 and 3 is "the class of all conjunctive concepts." Of course, how rich the latter class is depends on the richness of the family of properties in the environment. This point will be discussed presently. Meanwhile, it is worth pointing out that if we restrict ourselves to a family of input properties (like, say, "the excitation level of each photo cell in the grid"), the class of conjunctive concepts is not very rich, especially with respect to real life.

It ought to be pointed out, however, that the flexibility of the languages described in Chapter 4 is such that the definition of new properties is extremely easy to incorporate into the language. This can be done, moreover, with respect to the class of patterns described in question 4. No efficient algorithm exists for introducing such new properties, but certain heuristics can be considered. This is done below with respect to the universe exemplified in Chapter 4, Section 4.3.

If the environment consists of the two properties p and q, then the only conjunctive concepts are the ten values of p and q and the twenty-five objects. Let us now assume that the concept $A = \{3, 4, 13, 14, 15, 16, 17, 18, 1, 2, 11, 12\}$ has to be learned. The only way the Pennypacker algorithm could learn the concept would be as a union of exemplars. This would render the learning process extremely inefficient; also, the conception of the pattern learned would be unwieldy. The same would be the case with respect to learning the concepts $B = \{5, 6, 7, 8, 9, 10, 19, 20\}$, $C = \{21, 22, 26, 27\}$, and $D = \{23, 24, 25, 28, 29, 30\}$. At this point, however, it could be realized (if we had an algorithm strong enough to do it) that $A \cup B$ (or T_1, so far unknown), $C \cup D$ (or T_2), and $U - T_1 - T_2$ could be used as a property of the environment and so could $A \cup C = R_2$, $B = R_4$, and $U - R_2 - R_4$. This would yield $A = R_2 \cap T_1$ and $C = R_2 \cap T_2$ at a considerable increase in succinctness of description. However, this succinctness would be purchased at the expense of storing T_1, T_2, R_2, R_4, T_3, and $R_3 \cup R_1$ in the description list of the universe. Such property generation, then, can only be justified if it yields succinct descriptions of many concepts. This leads to efficient learning of concepts encountered later. Also, it has profound significance with respect to the "generalizing ability" of the learning algorithm, as will be shown in the next section.

The reader will have noted that the concepts T_1, T_2, R_2, and R_4 as defined above led to the descriptions of concepts that would not have been learned from examples. They would have been internally generated to facilitate the storage of concepts that have been learned from examples. Such concepts are generally called "features" in the literature, and processes that isolate them are called "feature extraction." In this book, the term "concept formation" has also been reserved for this phenomenon.

It is worthwhile at this point to consider some of the other learning algorithms in the literature and how they stand with respect to the presently described methods. Because of the similarity of the description languages, the first methods that come to mind are the EPAM [31] and the CSL-I [30]. The comparative advantages of the languages have already been discussed. The major point to be made about EPAM concerns the limitations of its tree. Because the name of the concept occurs at the root of the tree, two non-disjoint concepts cannot be very well described in an EPAM tree. This puts essential restrictions on EPAM as a learning algorithm; however, a recognizer using the EPAM tree as the description makes an extremely efficient property evaluator.

Some of the drawbacks of the EPAM net have been removed by Ernst and Sherman [50]. It has enabled the building of a description language incorporating some of the highly desirable characteristics of the predicate calculus language described in Section 4.6. Since the exact form of the Ernst and Sherman language is not completely formalized, a detailed description of the language will not be given here. We will, however, point out a few important characteristics.

The universe of discourse of the language has two properties, "Ex" and "Na." The values of "Ex" (short for "exemplar") are objects in the sense discussed in Section 4.6. The values of "Na" are concept names. The EPAM-like tree describes a single concept consisting of exemplar–name pairs such that each exemplar belongs to the concept having the paired name. Thus, if an object X belongs to both the concepts A and B, then in the Ernst–Sherman language the objects (Ex, X; Na, A) and (Ex, X; Na, B) would both belong to the concept described by the tree.

The other major departure of the Ernst–Sherman tree from EPAM lies in the fact that the test nodes of the tree may contain statements of the form "term $\in$ term" as well as "term $=$ term," whereas the conventional EPAM test nodes consist of the latter types only. This enables the language to have some of the advantages of the language of Section 4.6. As a result, the Ernst–Sherman learning algorithm can make use of previously learned concepts in describing new concepts, and thus shows an important aspect of truly adaptive behavior.

Like most learning techniques based on Boolean algebraic methods (the Windeknecht–Snediker technique being a notable exception), the learning algorithm is most effective in learning conjunctive concepts; like the Pennypacker algorithm, however, it can learn any concept. Moreover, it can learn concepts whose descriptions involve statements of the form "term $\in$ term."

The CSL-I technique of Hunt, learning with the description tree developed by him, has one capability that the Pennypacker algorithm lacks: it can learn succinct descriptions of concepts whose complements are conjunctive. To do this, it has to store in memory all the objects shown in the concept and its complement, instead of modifying the description with each new presentation of an exemplar, as do the Pennypacker algorithm and its parent, Bruner's conservative focusing strategy. Unlike the Pennypacker method, there is no method in CSL-I for using noninput properties in the description. As a matter of fact, the advantages of having noninput properties (an advantage that is used by all human beings) seems to have been completely neglected in all psychologically oriented structures of pattern recognition that the present author has come across.

On a superficial study, it might appear that the numerical techniques of pattern recognition discussed often in the literature are far stronger than the ones discussed here. As a matter of fact, there is a tendency to include in the field of pattern recognition only techniques based on the theory of vector spaces and probability. The importance of the study and development of flexible description languages as done here often seems to be outside the pale of the field of pattern recognition. This is extremely hard to understand in view of the constant bemoanings in the pattern recognition field regarding the elusive nature of the feature extraction problem, which is intimately associated with the basic predicates of description languages. A short discussion of the present author's interpretation of the methods and results in the field of numerical pattern recognition follows.

As has been pointed out before, for these methods to be effective, we have to have properties whose values can be represented as real numbers. Thus, in any environment with a finite number of input properties (and no distinction has yet been attempted between input and noninput properties), each object (many authors prefer to call the objects "patterns" but it will be safer here to hold to a uniform terminology) is represented by a vector in the space of n-tuples of reals. The learning algorithms, on the basis of a list of objects, tagged by their membership in a given concept C, construct a real function f of n variables (the "discriminant function") such that for a large number of objects x encountered or expected to be encountered, $f(x)$ would be positive if and only if the object belonged to C. In symbols,

$$f(x) > 0 \equiv x \in C.$$

Just as in the case of the algorithms described previously, the form of the function f is restricted to a class, at least by the efficiency of recognition. That is, for some of the algorithms the class of concepts described in question 1 is restricted and in others this specific class is unrestricted, while the class described in questions 2 and 3 are restricted and, in most cases, identical. The class described in question 4 can only be considered on the basis of experimentation and the results of the experimenters. Different methods have varied, both with respect to their quality of the results and conclusiveness of the experiments.

Comparisons of these different learning techniques are generally made on the basis of the operational mode of the learning algorithm. One criterion for this is whether a technique is adaptive, that is, whether the algorithm stores all the tagged objects and constructs the function f on the basis of the entire set of tagged objects or whether the function f, starting from an arbitrary initial value, is modified by each tagged object in succession, so they do not have to be stored for processing en masse.

Another important criterion for distinction may be on the basis of "motivation," that is, the basis of choosing the class of functions to be constructed.

In some cases this function is generated on the basis of the estimation of the parameters in a set of probability distributions [51, 52]. That is, it is assumed that the concept C and its complement $\bar{C}$ are such that there exist two distributions p and q, characterized by a vector of parameters $\bar{\theta}$ such that the function f has the form

$$f(x) = \frac{p(x; \bar{\theta})}{q(x; \bar{\theta})} - 1$$

for some parameter vector $\bar{\theta}$. The class f is determined by the forms of p and q and the allowed range of choice of the vector θ. The forms for p and q are chosen either on the basis of the worker's belief (on the basis of empirical data, hopefully) that the distributions p and q are adequate or because the estimation of the parameters is computationally feasible for a large set of tagged objects if p and q are assumed to have some given form. Unfortunately, reality does not often conform to the conveniences or limitations of the theoretician.

Another basis for the choice of the class of functions f may be dictated by certain "distance functions" [39]. That is, we start with the axiom that there is a metric ρ on the space of n-tuples such that if A is the set of all objects tagged as belonging to C and B the set of all objects tagged as belonging to $\bar{C}$, then f is often defined by

$$f(x) = \min_{y \in A}\{\rho(x, y)\} - \min_{y \in B}\{\rho(x, y)\}$$

or

$$f(x) = \bar{\rho}(x, y)\big|_{y \in A} - \bar{\rho}(x, y)\big|_{y \in B},$$

$\bar{\rho}$ denoting average value. Again, the class f is determined on the basis of the investigator's choice of ρ, hopefully on some rational or empirical basis. Often the classes of f chosen by different methods turn out to be the same.

A large number of authors restrict the class f directly without reference to any statistical or metric criteria, which to the present author's mind is no less justifiable than choosing the class on the basis of the faiths discussed above. The most popular form, of course, is the linear one, where

$$f(x) = \bar{a} \cdot x + b$$

where $\bar{a}$ is a vector and b a real number [53]. It appears that although the class of concepts describable by these linear functions (the "linearly separable patterns") is much richer than the class of functions discussed in the previous sections, it is still a very small fraction of the class of all possible concepts, even where the vector space under consideration is the finite space of all possible binary sequences. What is worse, even the class of concepts described by question 4 turns out to be inadequate on the basis of experimental evidence, unless the set of properties defined by the components of the vector is "adequately chosen"—and there is no uniform way of choosing the "adequate" representation.

The class f has been enriched by many workers by including nonlinear functions, especially polynomials of large degree. The only major difficulty with respect to such choice lies with the very large number of coefficients needed for an adequate description of the concepts. This difficulty is analogous to the cases where the Pennypacker technique learns a concept as the union of an inordinately large number of conjunctive concepts. Another analogous case arises where the description is taken to be "piecewise linear"; that is, where the description of C takes the form

$$x \in C \equiv B((f_1(x) > 0), \quad (f_2(x) > 0), \ldots, (f_p(x) > 0))$$

where B is a logical combination of the statements $\{(f_i(x) > 0 \mid 1 \leq i \leq p\}$ and $f_i(x)$ is a linear function. A subclass of the class of functions so describable are those describable by the so-called two-layer nets, that is, where B yields a linearly separable function, so that the statement above can be rewritten

$$x \in C \equiv \sum_{i=1}^{p} a_i \, \text{sgn}[f_i(x)] + a_0 > 0$$

where $\text{sgn}[t] = 1$ if $t > 0$ and 0 otherwise. "Multilayer nets" can be similarly constructed, yielding richer classes of describable concepts.

When we consider adaptive techniques for the evaluation of coefficients appearing in the representations in any of the schemes described above, an important question arises regarding the "convergence" of the training scheme. Convergence proofs are known only for some of the algorithms based on statistical estimation [52] as also algorithms on the basis of linear separability [54]. The earlier algorithms were proven to converge only in cases where the tagged objects were from a linearly separable concept and its compliment. Algorithms have been suggested recently where the algorithms also indicate failure when the concept is not linearly separable [55]. In many cases algorithms are introduced on the basis of empirical evidence that they converge "in many cases." Nothing is known regarding the convergence of algorithms for multilayer nets, although empirical algorithms have been used for designing these in the literature, both for pattern recognition and game playing.

As has been indicated above, another major difficulty with nonlinear or piecewise linear discriminant functions (and to the author's mind these are the only functions that have any promise of success) lies with the extremely large number of coefficients to be stored. An equally important consideration closely connected with this is the generalizing ability of the discriminant functions formed from these coefficients. As was said in the beginning of Chapter 4, our discussion has been limited to learning, and describing concepts without any reference to the phenomenon of generalization. Some attempts at discussing generalization are made in the next section. The discussion attempts to bring out the importance of appropriate description languages and "features."

5.5. GENERALIZATION—CONCEPT FORMATION AND LANGUAGES

It was shown in the preceding section that concept formation or feature extraction plays a very important role in simplifying the expressions that describe a concept. There has also been a belief that, somehow, extracting the "correct" features makes subsequent learning easier, and that once we are in possession of a correct set of features (i.e., have formed the right concepts), we can generalize from the encountered tagged objects well enough to recognize latter objects with a high degree of confidence based on the descriptions formed by a learning program. In the absence of good features, "rote learning" seems to be the only possible learning method and we cannot generalize well from a description learned "by rote." In what follows, a preliminary effort will be made to give a rough mathematical framework to give meaning to the terms used above and justification for the beliefs indicated.

The very existence of a possibility of generalization indicates that the class of all concepts to be recognized (the class described by question 4 in Section 5.4) is restricted to a subset of the class of all concepts. To make this point clear, it may not be necessary to take the most general environment. It suffices as an example, to take a universe having a full fine structure family of input properties having n properties in the family and m values of each property. The main concern here is the richness of the class of concepts rather than the simplicity of their description: hence, noninput properties need not be considered.

There are m^n objects in this environment and hence, 2^{m^n} possible concepts. Any time a specific object, $p_{1i_1} \cap \cdots \cap p_{ni_n} = X$, is known to belong to a specific (unknown) concept, those concepts to which X does not belong are eliminated from those under consideration, and the concept to be learned is known to belong to one of 2^{n^m-1} possible concepts. In general, when k_1 objects are presented to a learning algorithm as belonging to a concept and k_2 objects are presented as belonging to the complement of a concept, then there are $2^{n^m - k_1 - k_2}$ possible choices for the concept. This number, it will be noticed, does not reduce to 1 (to "correct" learning) till $k_1 + k_2 = n^m$ (i.e., till every object in the universe has been presented).

A restriction of the class of concepts to be learned, then, seems essential. Such restriction leads to extremely fast convergence (exemplified, for instance, by the Pennypacker algorithm in the case of conjunctive concepts). However, results of experiments (on the perceptron, e.g., or even what we can foresee in the future for the CSL or the Pennypacker–Snediker algorithms, indiscriminately applied) indicate that *ad hoc* restrictions have very little chance of "standing up to reality." The restriction has to be learned, just as the concepts themselves have to be learned.

The last sentence has to be pursued with some care. It will be noticed that the learning of a concept consists of the learning of the *union* of a class of objects. The learning of a restriction, on the other hand, consists of the learning of a *class* of concepts. Although the language of Section 4.6 is adequate for describing both sets and classes of sets (so glibly, in fact, that unless $\alpha \notin \alpha$ is introduced as an axiom, contradiction will result!), it is probably premature to suggest that both the learnings go on in the same language! Much better understanding of the "second-level" learning (learning of classes) will be needed before that.

For the present, it is assumed that there exist certain concepts that (even though we are not called upon to learn them through tagged objects) may be used in constructing simple descriptions of concepts that are learned by tagged objects. Second-level learning (or feature extraction or concept formation) can be thought of as consisting in the recognition of the former concepts. In Section 5.4, an example was given to indicate how this phenomenon may possibly be made into an algorithm. Very little research has gone on in this area (extraction of masks, as done by Uhr [56] and Nilsson [57], are efforts in this direction, although they are strongly biased in the direction of character recognition and can fail (see, e.g., BOGART [58]), when tried on more ambitious projects.

It may be somewhat easier to express the thoughts and reduce the chance of misunderstanding if the paragraph above is interpreted formally. This is done in the next few paragraphs. The reader is warned that the only reason for the formalism here is precision. No deeper insight results from it immediately.

Let $\langle U, \mathscr{P}, \mathscr{P} \rangle$ be a real environment where $\mathscr{P}$ is the entire class of input properties. Let there also be given a class F of specific modes of combination of sets to obtain new sets (which modes may be operations like union and complementation or may be linear or nonlinear threshold schemes). We now define an ordering 0 $(\mathscr{P}, F)$ on the class $C_{\mathscr{P}}$ of concepts. If the concept C_1 is lower than concept C_2 in this order, then C_1 has a simpler description than C_2.

Given a class of concepts $C \subseteq C_{\mathscr{P}}$, $\mathscr{P}$ will be called *satisfactory* for C if every element of C ranks low in the order 0 $(\mathscr{P}, F)$. If $\mathscr{P}$ is not satisfactory, then a set of concepts C_0 will be said to be concepts "formed in view of C" if $\mathscr{P} \cup \{(c, \bar{c}) \mid c \in C_0\}$ is satisfactory for C.

Evidently, the class C is "formed in view of C" in a very trivial way. A good concept former would be expected to form a class C_0 in some "optimal" way that has not been defined yet.

The restricted class of concepts to be considered for avoiding the difficulty of generalization will be the class that is easy to describe in terms of the language available after concept formation. The major point to be emphasized in this section is that restrictions based on the assumption of simplicity of description have an extremely strong repercussion on what we understand by the "generalizing ability" of a learning algorithm.

Generalizing ability, in the sense discussed before, can at present be identified most closely with the term "confidence level" as used in the field of statistical hypothesis testing. Also, the slight confusion with respect to the acceptable definition of concept formation is reflected remarkably well in the slight confusion that occurs in the use of the phrase "degrees of freedom" in that field (the present author is thankful to Professor Herbert Simon of Carnegie Tech for pointing this out).

This last fact can probably be brought out by an example. Let the experiment consist of exhibiting two-digit decimal representations of the first 99 positive integers, tagging some of the representations with 1 and the others with zero. Let all elements of the set $\{1, 11, 13, 15, 27, 33, 35, 47, 49, 59\}$ be tagged with 1 and let the elements of $\{4, 14, 16, 18, 24, 32, 38, 42, 56, 66\}$ be tagged with 0. If the values of the first and second digits define the only two properties of the environment, one can obtain the contingency table in Table 5.1 for a chi-square test.

The contingency table yields a value of 27 for the chi-square. This has a significance level (with the attendant error arising from the small size of the sample and with a degree of freedom 15) of 0.025, which may not be considered significant. On the other hand, if evenness of a numeral is considered a property of the environment, we could get the contingency table in Table 5.2.

The chi-square this time, for the same hypothesis of uniform distribution, with the degree of freedom 4, is 20. This value (quite accurately this time) is significant at the level of less than 0.001.

Table 5.1

Ending with	Tagged with	
	0	1
1	0	2
2	2	0
3	0	2
4	3	0
5	0	2
6	3	0
7	0	2
8	2	0
9	0	2
0	0	0

Table 5.2

Second digit	Tagged with	
	0	1
even	10	0
odd	0	10

There is little in the theory of sampling itself to indicate which of the two contingency tables should actually be used for testing significance. It appears that to interpret the foregoing phenomenon inside statistics, the latter may have to be enriched by considerations of the available description language. The suggestion made some paragraphs back regarding restricting the generalizable concepts to easily describable concepts was based on the observation that in any contingency table, the cells are always chosen to be the ones most easily describable.

The number of rows in the contingency table is large if the concept being tested involves the union of a large number of simply describable concepts. This will explain the statement in Section 4.1, that the "size" of the connective "or" seems to be larger than that of other usual connectives.

It must be pointed out that even when a concept is described as a union of simply describable concepts, generalization is not impossible. In Table 5.1, for instance, if the entries in each cell were doubled, we could consider the table as a significance indicator for the hypothesis, "All numerals ending in 2, 4, 6, and 8 are tagged with 1." Only more observations would be needed. If it turns out that the structure of the environment and of the language are such that too many observations are not possible in each cell, generalization is impossible without a change in language. We can think, for instance, of the concept of "even integers," described as a piecewise linearly separable concept where the only known feature of an integer is its value. Generalization would be impossible on the basis of observing the two tagged sets mentioned above. On the other hand, if we used the digits in the binary representation of the numeral as features, the concept of even numbers would be linearly separable and, hence, easily generalizable.

A learning and concept-forming algorithm, starting from a fine structure family of properties, could learn concepts by some technique in which the class of learnable concepts is not restricted. If the concepts learned by it are not simply describable (and if enough observations are possible, so the difficulty mentioned above would not occur), then the learned concepts need a large number of tagged objects to establish their significance. Once these are established, concepts may be formed to simplify the description of every concept learned. Attempts are then made to learn later concepts within the restriction imposed by the newly formed concepts. In the environment that follows a restriction dictated by these newly formed concepts, generalization of the learned concepts will be easier: otherwise the class of formed concepts would be modified.

It is the author's belief that the development of this kind of algorithms is essential if pattern recognition is to become a viable branch of artificial intelligence—indeed, if artificial intelligence is ever to become a viable field.

So far the discussions have been carried out with the background of nonnumerical description languages and recognition techniques. In the case of techniques based on the assumption that the objects are vectors of n real numbers, analogous discussions remain valid. It is worthwhile to limit discussions to polynomial discriminant functions. (It may be repeated here that initial restriction of learnable classes to "linearly separable" or "normally distributed" impose conditions on the initial measurements that are extremely ill understood.) That is, let C be such that $x \in C \equiv 0 \leq P(x)$ where

$$P(x) = \alpha_0 + \sum_{i=1}^{n} \alpha_i x_i + \sum_{i,\,j=1}^{n} \alpha_{ij} x_i x_j$$

$$+ \cdots + \sum \sum \sum \cdots \sum \alpha_{ijk\ldots t} x_i x_j x_k \cdots x_t$$

$$+ \cdots + \cdots + \alpha_{12\ldots n} x_1 x_2 \cdots x_n.$$

We assume that if an element is chosen from the concept C, the probability that a specific x is chosen is $f(x, c)$; similarly, the probability of x to be chosen when an element is chosen from $\bar{c}$ is given as $f(x, \bar{c})$. It will be noted that in Baysian techniques of pattern recognition, it is the parameters of f that are estimated. However, since the a's of the above polynomial are functions of these parameters (note that $f(x, c) = 0$ if $P(x) > 0$) it will be assumed that the estimation of the a's is the matter at issue.

Let now k_1 vectors $(y_1, y_2, \ldots, y_{k_1})$ be presented to the learning algorithm tagged with 1 and k_2 vectors $(z_1, z_2, \ldots, z_{k_2})$ are presented tagged with 0. On the basis of these vectors the algorithm estimates coefficients b_0, $\{b_i\}$, $\{b_{ij}\}, \ldots, \{b_{123\ldots n}\}$. (Of course, in any practical case, many of the higher-degree coefficients will be zero.) The b's are functions of the variables $\{y_1, y_2, \ldots, y_{k_1}\}$ and $\{z_1, \ldots, z_{k_2}\}$, which have probability distributions $f(y, c)$ and $f(z, \bar{c})$, respectively. Hence, each b will have a probability distribution and need not be equal to the a's unless k_1 and k_2 are extremely large. However, if the learning procedure is any good, the distribution of each b will be centered around the corresponding a.

In the language of the theory of small samples, each coefficient b is an estimator of the corresponding a. While in the past workers in the field have been generally satisfied if the estimates are unbiased, for discussion of generalization, the efficiency of these estimators must be known. The efficiency will be given by the estimation procedure and the distribution $f(\bar{x}, c)$. In the general case, however, the following discussion is germane.

In any good estimation technique each b will have the corresponding a as mean and will have some variance δ that will decrease with increasing k_1 and k_2. However, the rate of convergence can be seen to be seriously restricted by the number of b's being estimated.

The number of degrees of freedom is not $k_1 + k_2$ but is reduced by the number of parameters being estimated. As a result, the number of observations needed for generalization becomes larger, the larger the number of parameters estimated (i.e., the more complex the discriminant function is). The reduction of the number of parameters is only possible by using carefully chosen measurements for the components of the vector. That the input properties look "naturally numerical" is no indication that the natural choice is reflected in any way on the restriction to the concepts being learned.

An example may make the point clear. Consider the concept $\{4, 5, 8\}$ in the environment indicated in Figure 1.1. Denoting the "natural" property "number of borders" by x and "number of figures" by y, this concept is represented by the set of vectors $\{(2, 1), (2, 2), (3, 2)\}$. The reader may convince himself that this set is not linearly separable. However, if new features z and w are defined as

$$z = 2 \quad \text{if } x = 3, y = 1,$$
$$z = 1 \quad \text{if } x = 2, y = 2,$$
$$z = y \quad \text{otherwise,}$$
$$w = 2 \quad \text{if } x = 3, y = 1,$$
$$w = 3 \quad \text{if } x = 2, y = 2,$$
$$w = x \quad \text{otherwise,}$$

the concept appears as the set of vectors $\{(2, 1), (3, 1), (3, 2)\}$, which is separated by the linear polynomial $w - z - \frac{1}{2}$. A very unnatural numerical measure turns out to be the useful one as far as simplicity of expression is concerned.

An alternative mode of feature extraction may be indicated by pointing out that the "features" z and w may well have been looked upon as functions of x and y that rendered the concept separable. The form of the function $z(x, y)$ is seen to be quite complicated. Hence, if a nonlinear discriminating function has to be constructed by replacing z and w by complex nonlinear functions of x and y in $w - z - \frac{1}{2}$, all semblance of simplicity would be lost. However, if we are faced with a large number of highly complex discriminants for a large number of concepts in an environment of n-dimensional vectors $(x_1, x_2, \ldots, x_n)$ and discover a set of transformations

$$y_i = y_i(x_1, \ldots, x_n) \qquad (1 \leq i \leq n)$$

such that the original discriminants are simple functions of the y_i, we can consider the y's as the significant features of the environment and use them for subsequent learning and generalization.

In the absence of good measurements (good "features" in the general case) concept formation is an essential adjunct to pattern recognition, no matter how sophisticated the modes of combination of the basic predicates may be. As has been said before, past experience has shown that threshold gates are in no way more effective than Boolean gates, if the features are not good. On the other hand, recent work has shown that with good features, quite economical switching circuits (with a very manageable number of gates) suffice for recognition [59].

5.6. LEARNING GAMES BY GENERALIZATION—THE IMPORTANCE OF DESCRIPTION LANGUAGES

It was shown in Section 3.9 that the sets $\{W_i'\}$ acted as adequate approximations to the evaluations of any tic-tac-toe-like game. It might be noticed that all the basic predicates involved in the description of the sets $\{W_i'\}$ are the same as those involved in the description of tic-tac-toe-like games. Hence, the universes and fine structure families of properties needed for describing the rules of the games are adequate for the description of the $\{W_i'\}$. However, if in addition to the basic predicates we also used the derived predicates $\#_s(A) = i$ and $(\exists n)\,((n, A) \in C_s$ and $(n, B) \in C_s)$, then the description of the $\{W_i'\}$ becomes much simpler.

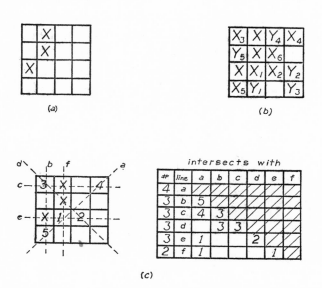

(a)

(b)

(c)

Figure 5.2. A member of J_6 in 4^3 tic-tac-toe and its description.

However, one important point was not made adequately in the previous discussion; that learning descriptions of the $\{W_i'\}$ as combinations of predicates of the form above leads to correct generalization with very little data.

The point is probably best illustrated by an example. Consider any plane (horizontal, vertical, or diagonal) in the cubic board with three cells assigned to X and the rest to $\wedge$, as shown in Figure 5.2a. For convenience, the cells assigned to $\wedge$ have been shown empty. That any configuration in Qubic that contains a plane like this (when it is the player's move) is in W_6' can be easily seen by a perusal of Figure 5.2b. Here each X_i represents the ith move of the player and each Y_i that of the opponent. That this is also a member of J_6 is seen by a perusal of Figure 5.2c and the accompanying intersection matrix (which can be seen to be merely an alternative representation of a weighted graph). The intersection nodes here have been numbered to bring out the reason for J_i and W_i' being the same set.

It will be noted that the intersection matrix of Figure 5.2c also describes other members of J_6. Some of these are shown in Figure 5.3. Also, any position equivalent to one of these under the multifarious symmetries of the Qubic board [60] would have the same matrix. Also, a plane with some extra Y's (for instance, with one between Y_2 and X_4 in Figure 5.2) would

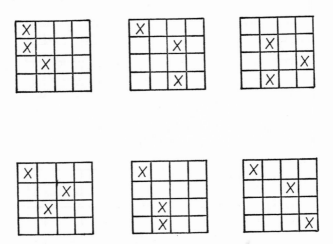

Figure 5.3. Some more members of J_6 with same description as in Figure 5.2.

have identical descriptions. So would a configuration that has the same intersection matrix but with some of the lines in a different plane (and all their symmetrical equivalents). This mode of description (the intersection matrix is merely a convenient representation of the statement forms discussed before) is thus more powerful than storing specific positions and considering the symmetries of the board. This latter method has been a favorite in the field and both Citrenbaum and Koffman have been erroneously criticized for not using this less efficient method, which is applicable only to Qubic. The number of symmetries in games like Bridg-it and go-moku are far fewer but the description shown here remains equally general.

This is also a convenient place to point out that if in Figure 5.2 there were an extra Y between Y_1 and Y_3, the resulting position could have the same connection matrix but would not be a member of W_6. This indicates how some members of $\bigcup W_i'$ are *not* members of $\bigcup W_i$.

Koffman's learning program is designed to learn descriptions of $\{W_i'\}$ when their elements occur in the course of a play of the game. Here generalization is very much facilitated by an analysis of the actual course of a game. The program carries out the analysis as follows.

The first game is played at random by the program till it is defeated (or accidentally wins). The winning move is now removed and the file uncovered by the process is stored in the trivial matrix as a description of W_1'. From then on, no win against the program is possible with a single threat. When the machine is defeated (or accidentally wins) by a "fork," removal of the winning move reveals a position whose description was already available in memory. At this point the previous move is removed, and the line uncovered together with its intersection with the lines satisfying the previous description is stored as a new matrix. Now the program blocks all forks and initiates its own forks when possible. Learning continues in subsequent defeats and accidental wins by deeper forks in a similar fashion. Successive previous moves are removed till no match is found with previous descriptions. The last move removed is then analyzed to reveal the alternative threat that was blocked. The lines of this threat and that of the previous one, together with their intersection pattern, are then stored in a new matrix.

It ought to be pointed out that in the absence of this kind of analysis, descriptions of the $\{W_i'\}$ could be learned as conjunctions of statements from a large number of examples by some algorithm analogous to Pennypacker's. The analysis above, however, leads to a more rapid learning. As a result, Koffman's program needs to play only about 12 games before it defeats its opponent 50% of the time in Qubic and go-moku and wins in Bridg-it every time it plays first.

REFERENCES

1. E. A. Feigenbaum, The Simulation of Verbal Learning Behavior, *Proc. Western Joint Computer Conf.*, *19*(1961), 121.
2. F. M. Tonge, Summary of a Heuristic Line Balancing Procedure, *Management Sci.*, *7*(1960), 21.
3. L. R. Marino, *Winning and Non-Losing Strategies in Games and Control*, Rep. No. SRC 91-A-66-36, Case Inst. Technol., Cleveland, Ohio, 1966.
4. R. E. Bellman and S. E. Dreyfus, *Applied Dynamic Programming*, Princeton Univ. Press, Princeton, New Jersey, 1962.
5. M. D. Mesarovic, Toward a Formal Theory of Problem Solving, in *Computer Augmentation of Human Reasoning*, M. Sass and W. Wilkinson, eds., Spartan Books, Washington, D.C., 1965, p. 37.
6. T. G. Windeknecht, Problem Solving and Finite Automata, A Status Report on Research in Artificial Intelligence and Linguistics, Case Inst. Technol., Cleveland, Ohio, 1964.
7. G. W. Ernst and A. Newell, Some Issues of Representation in a General Problem Solver, *AFIPS Conf. Proc.*, *30*(1967), 583.
8. J. von Neumann and O. Morgenstern, *Theory of Games and Economic Behavior*, Princeton Univ. Press, Princeton, New Jersey, 1947.
9. A. L. Samuel, Some Studies in Machine Learning Using the Game of Checkers, *IBM J. Res. Devel.*, *3*(1959), 210.
10. A. Newell and H. A. Simon, The Logic Theory Machine, *IRE Trans. Information Theory*, *IT-2*(1956), 61.
11. A. Church, *Introduction to Mathematical Logic*, Princeton Univ. Press, Princeton, New Jersey, 1956.
12. S. T. Hu, *Threshold Logic*, Univ. of California Press, Berkeley, 1965.
13. R. L. Ashenhurst, The Decomposition of Switching Functions, in *Proceedings of the International Symposium on the Theory of Switching*, Harvard Univ. Press, Cambridge, Massachusetts, 1959, p. 74.
14. J. S. Bruner, J. J. Goodnow, and G. A. Austin, *A Study of Thinking*, Wiley, New York, 1956.
15. I. H. Sublette, *Recognition of Class Membership by Means of Weak, Statistically Dependent Features*, Radio Corporation of America, Princeton, New Jersey, 1966.
16. W. W. R. Ball, *Mathematical Recreations and Essays*, Macmillan, New York, 1940, p. 303.
17. A. Hormann, Programs for Machine Learning, Part II, *Information and Control*, *7*(1964), 55.
18. P. M. Cohn, *Universal Algebra*, Harper & Row, New York, 1965.

19. A. Newell, J. C. Shaw, and H. Simon, Report on a General Problem Solving Program, *Proc. Int. Conf. Information Processing (UNESCO), Paris, 1959*, p. 256.

20. S. Amarel, *On Machine Representations of Problems and Reasoning About Actions—The Missionaries & Cannibal Problem*, RCA Laboratories, Princeton, New Jersey, 1966.

21. A. Lehman, *A Solution for the Shannon Switching Game*, U.S. Army Math. Res. Center Tech. Summary Rept. 308; July, 1962.

22. R. G. Busacker and T. L. Saaty, *Finite Graphs and Networks*, McGraw-Hill, New York, 1965.

23. C. Berge, *The Theory of Graphs and Its Applications*, Wiley, New York, 1962.

24. J. Hartmanis and R. E. Stearns, *Algebraic Structure Theory of Sequential Machines*, Prentice-Hall, Englewood Cliffs, New Jersey, 1966.

25. F. Rosenblatt, Perceptron Experiments, *Proc. IRE, 48*(1960), 301.

26. S. Ginsburg, *The Mathematical Theory of Context-Free Languages*, McGraw-Hill, New York, 1966.

27. R. B. Banerji, An Information Processing Program for Object Recognition, *Gen. Systems, 5*(1960), 117.

28. R. B. Banerji, Computer Programs for the Generation of New Concepts from Old Ones, *Neuere Ergebnisse der Kybernetik*, K. Steinbuch & S. Wagner, eds., Oldenberg-Verlag, Munich, 1964, p. 336.

29. E. B. Hunt and C. I. Hovland, Programming a Model of Human Concept Formulation, *Proc. Western Joint Computer Conf., 19*(1961), p. 145.

30. E. B. Hunt, J. Marin, and P. J. Stone, *Experiments in Induction*, Academic Press, New York, 1966.

31. E. A. Feigenbaum, The Simulation of Verbal Learning Behavior, *Proc. Western Joint Computer Conf., 19*(1961), p. 121.

32. J. C. Pennypacker, *An Elementary Information Processor for Object Recognition*, Rep. No. SRC 30-I-63-1, Case Inst. Technol., Cleveland, Ohio, 1963.

33. T. G. Windeknecht, *A Theory of Simple Concepts with Applications*, Rep. No. SRC 53-A-64-19, Case Inst. Technol., Cleveland, Ohio, 1964.

34. J. Snediker, *A Generalized Program for Information Retrieval*, Rep. No. SRC 77-A-65-29, Case Inst. Technol., Cleveland, Ohio, 1965.

35. E. C. Milliken, *A Language For Class Description and Its Processor*, Natl. Conf. Assoc. Computing Machinery, Cleveland, Ohio, 1965.

36. E. Mendelson, *Introduction to Mathematical Logic*, Van Nostrand, Princeton, New Jersey, 1964.

37. J. L. Kuhns, An Application of Logical Probability to Problems in Automatic Abstracting and Information Retrieval, First Congr. Information System Sciences, Hot Springs, Virginia, 1962, Session 13, p. 17.

38. G. S. Sebestyen, Pattern Recognition by an Adaptive Process of Sample-Set Construction, *IRE Trans. Information Theory, IT-8*(1962), S-82.

39. W. H. Highleyman, Linear Decision Functions, with Application to Pattern Recognition, *Proc. IRE, 50*(1962), 1501.

40. M. A. Aizerman, Lernvorgänge, bei der Erkennung von Zeichenklassen, *Neuere Ergebnisse der Kybernetik*, K. Steinbuch & S. Wagner, eds., Oldenberg-Verlag, Munich, p. 354.

41. E. B. Hunt, J. Marin, and P. J. Stone, *Experiments in Induction*, Academic Press, New York, 1966.

42. E. Feigenbaum, *An Information Processing Theory of Verbal Learning*, Rep. No. P-1817, October, The RAND Corporation, Santa Monica, California, 1959.

43. R. Narasimhan, Syntactic Descriptions of Pictures and Gestalt Phenomena of Visual Perception, Report dated July 25, 1963, from Digital Computer Laboratory, Univ. of Illinois, Urbana, Illinois.

44. R. A. Kirsch, Computer Interpretation of English Text and Picture Patterns, *Trans. IEEE, EC-13*(1964), 363.

45. B. Raphael, SIR: A Computer Program that Understands, *Fall Joint Computer Conf.*, 1964. p. 577.

46. B. Raphael, *SIR: A Computer Program for Information Retrieval*, Ph.D. dissertation, Massachusetts Institute of Technology, Cambridge, Massachusetts, 1964.

47. J. A. Robinson, A Machine Oriented Logic Based on the Resolution Principle, *J. Assoc. Computing Machinery, 12*(1965), 23.

48. J. A. Robinson, The Mechanization of Theorem Proving, in *Systems and Computer Science*, J. Hart and S. Takasu, eds., Univ. of Toronto Press, 1967, p. 116.

49. S. Sebestyen, *Decision Making Processes in Pattern Recognition*, Macmillan, New York, 1962.

50. G. W. Ernst and R. Sherman, Learning Concepts in Terms of Other Concepts, *Pattern Recognition* (communicated), 1968.

51. D. F. Specht, Generation of Polynomial Discriminant Functions for Pattern Recognition, *IEEE Trans. Electronic Computers, EC-16*(1967), 308.

52. Y. C. Ho and R. L. Kashyap, An Algorithm for Linear Inequalities and Its Applications, *IEEE Trans. Electronic Computers, EC-14*(1965), 683.

53. B. Widrow and F. W. Smith, Pattern Recognizing Control Systems, in *Computer and Information Sciences*, J. Tou and R. Wilcox, eds., Spartan Books, Washington, D.C., 1964, p. 288.

54. A. Novikoff, On Convergence Proofs for Perceptrons, *Proc. Symp. Math. Theory of Automata (Brooklyn Polytechnic Institute)*, 1963. p. 615.

55. L. C. Barbosa and E. Wang, On a Class of Iterative Algorithms for Linear Inequalities with Application to Pattern Classification, *Princeton Conf. Information Sciences and Systems*, 1967. p. 86.

56. L. Uhr and C. Vossler, A Pattern Recognition Program that Generates, Evaluates and Adjusts Its Own Operators, *Western Joint Computer Conf.*, Los Angeles, 1961. p. 555.

57. H. D. Block, N. J. Nilsson, and R. O. Duda, Determination and Direction of Features in Patterns, in *Computer and Information Sciences*, J. Tou and R. Wilcox, eds. Spartan Books, Washington, D.C., 1964. p. 75.

58. C. Newman and L. Uhr, BOGART: A Discovery and Induction Program for Games, *20th Nat. Conf. Assoc. Computing Machinery*, 1965. p. 176.

59. J. G. Simek and C. J. Tunis, Handprinting Input Device for Computer Systems, *IEEE Spectrum, 4*(1967), 72.

60. R. Silver, The Group of Automorphisms of the Game of 3-Dimensional Tic-Tac-Toe, *Amer. Math. Monthly, 74*(1967), 247.

61. A. Newell, H. A. Simon, and J. C. Shaw, Empirical Explorations of the Logic Theory Machine, *Proc. Western Joint Computer Conference* (1957) p. 218.

62. G. Ernst, Sufficient Conditions for the Success of GPS, Report No. SRC-68-17, Case Western Reserve University, Cleveland, Ohio (1968).

63. G. Ernst, Sufficient Conditions for the Success of the General Problem Solver, *J. Assoc. Comp. Mach.* (in press).

64. R. L. Citrenbaum, The Concept of Strategy and its Application to 3-Dimension Tic-Tac-Toe, Rept. No. SRC 72-A-65-26, Case Inst. Technol., Cleveland, Ohio, 1965.
65. E. G. Koffman, *Learning Through Pattern Recognition Applied to a Class of Games* Rept. No. SRC 107-A-67-45 Case Western Reserve Univ., Cleveland, Ohio, 1967.
66. P. Z. Ingerman, *A Syntax Oriented Translator*, Academic Press, New York, 1966.

BIBLIOGRAPHY

S. Amarel, On the Automatic Formation of a Computer Program Which Represents a Theory, in *Self Organizing System*, M. Yovits and S. Cameron, eds., Spartan Books, Washington, D.C., 1962.

S. Amarel, Problem Solving Procedures for Efficient Syntactic Analysis, *20th Natl. Cnf. Assoc. Computing Machinery*, Cleveland, Ohio, 1965.

S. Amarel, An Approach to Heuristic Problem Solving and Theorem Proving in the Propositional Calculus, in *Systems and Computer Science*, J. Hart and S. Takasu, eds., Univ. of Toronto Press, 1967.

R. Bellman, *Mathematical Model Making: A an Adaptive Process*, Rept. No. P-2400, The RAND Corporation, Santa Monica, California, 1961.

R. Bellman, Dynamic Programming, Intelligent Machines and Self Organizing Systems, *Proc. Symp. Math. Theory of Automata (Brooklyn Polytechnic Institute)*, 1963.

R. Bellman and P. Brock, On the Concept of a Problem and Problem Solving, *Amer. Math. Monthly*, 67(1960), 119.

AUTHOR INDEX

Numbers in parentheses indicate the numbers of the references when these are cited in the text without the names of the authors.

Numbers set in *italics* designate the page numbers on which the complete literature citation is given.

SUBJECT INDEX

187